Television's Greatest Year

· 1954 ·

R · D · HELDENFELS

Television's Greatest Year

· 1954 ·

Foreword by
STEVE ALLEN

CONTINUUM · NEW YORK

1994
The Continuum Publishing Company
370 Lexington Avenue
New York, NY 10017

Printed in the United States of America

Library of Congress Cataloging-in-Publication Data

Heldenfels, R. D. (Richard D.)
    Television's greatest year—1954 / R.D. Heldenfels;
  Foreword by Steve Allen
        p.   cm.
    Includes bibliographical references and index.
    ISBN 0-8264-0675-0 (acid-free paper)
    1. Television broadcasting—United States—History. I. Title.
PN1992.3.U5H39   1994   94-28356
                                               CIP

Contents

(Photographs may be found between pages 138 and 139)

Foreword
by Steve Allen

A great deal of my comedy, over the past half-century, has grown out of the fact that I do not perceive words—any words at all—in the way that most sensible people do. Their basic meaning is apparent enough, but I hear additional and sometimes bizarre resonances. The author of this stimulating report on the Golden Age of television, one R. D. Heldenfels—could there be two?—has a last name that at first exposure struck me as double-talk, the kind of words that the gifted nineteen-fifties' funny man Al Kelly used to mutter.

And if a man, in his frame, has the gumption and the zymole to raise his heldenfels—why the very idea is ridiculous!

Having gotten that admittedly irreverent outburst out of my system, I hasten to applaud both Mr. Heldenfels's basic thesis and the engaging, readable style in which he communicates it.

I recall hearing the famous scientist Harold Urey say, to my face, which was much younger and more attractive at the time, that he had literally given up on television. The statement was made in 1961. The reason for Urey's displeasure, of course, was that as a brilliant thinker he had early perceived the educational potential of the dazzling new medium that had brought into our homes pictures that moved. That potential, God help us, has never been more than fitfully realized, which led Urey and many other intellectuals of his time to take a then-to-hell-with-it attitude toward the new medium.

Was Urey right? Of course, but only according to certain high-minded criteria. When it comes to evaluating television according to—well, the factor of ratings—the picture is considerably less shameful.

So, while we must never forget FCC chairman Newton Minow's early description of TV as a vast wasteland, we must still be grateful for such virtues as the field has boasted.

I will no doubt be accused of bias in endorsing Heldenfels's pro-1954 argument, given that that was the year I started hosting the original *Tonight Show* on a national basis (though the program itself had opened some fourteen months earlier on NBC's local New York outlet).

To his great credit, Heldenfels is more interested in quality than in marketplace success. Although he admires some of the hits of 1954, he has looked beyond them to shows that may be less-well known to modern viewers but were nonetheless significant counterweights to the hot-air balloons of video mindlessness that all too often have dominated the medium.

Critics who concentrate on ratings are partly responsible for the general state of affairs. I shall never forget my combined astonishment and revulsion at reading, in the column of a television critic for the *New York Journal American,* that a few days earlier Lawrence Welk had "walked all over Sid Caesar in the ratings." The Caesar shows, at their best, still stand as the highest achievement in the history of television sketch comedy, whereas the Welk show was one of that majority of programs that may fairly be described as bubble gum for the mind.

Even with few channels and technological apparatus that now seems Paleozoic, some of the greatest artists in television—and by artists I mean not only the brilliant comedians and acclaimed dramatists but a newsman of the caliber of Edward R. Murrow, whose like has rarely been seen since—created little miracles every week on what is now sadly known as the *idiot box.*

Today's generation has put so much of its concentration on television yet knows so little of its long history. Just as in my shows I feel it important to tell young people that rock 'n' roll began not with Elvis Presley but with great early black jazzmen playing boogie-woogie and other rhythms, so I hope Heldenfels's book will inform them about a television era now dimly remembered.

I remember writing in 1960 that some of the big names of television from the early fifties had already left the scene. This book is a vivid reminder of their legacy.

THREE
QUESTIONS

* * * * * * * *

Think of this book as a really long barroom conversation where I shout the loudest. The title alone should prompt some debate among television fans, who as a unit and in small discussion groups can build whole Chautauquas around such issues as Kirk vs. Picard, J. R. vs. Alexis, *Hullabaloo* against *Shindig*, Casey or Kildare.

The correct answers, by the way, are Picard, J. R., *Shindig*, and Casey. But that's a debate for another day and a different book. In this case, we're arguing about the greatest year in television history. For reasons that will appear in considerable detail in the following pages, I have picked 1954. And to those of you under fifty I might as well be arguing that the greatest war of all time was the Peloponnesian.

I realize that many of you equate nostalgia with the people in beer commercials who fondly remember *Gilligan's Island* and *I Dream of Jeannie*. I know cable service Nick at Nite treats *The Partridge Family* as classic TV. And frankly, I remember those shows a lot better than whatever I was watching forty years ago in 1954, when I was three years old.

So, while fairness is not a prerequisite in bar fights, I am going to take a stab at it here. The first part of the book is an attempt to put us on a more or less equal footing by offering the general shape of the case for 1954, covering how television had gotten to that point; explaining what it was like to watch TV at that time; and conceding some obvious ways that TV '54 fell short of nineties expectations. From there the book will go into more detail about 1954, both in terms of what had been accomplished by then and what went wrong soon after. Finally, to complete the argument, I will talk about ways television in the nineties could learn from television's past; while it is unlikely that TV will reverse its history to remodel itself to fit the earlier vision, such possibilities are worth considering in light of the debates about TV today.

But first, the three questions.

. . . . .

Why 1954?

L ots of years deserve consideration as TV's best. Nineteen fifty-two, when the Federal Communications Commission opened the door to 2,000 new stations. Nineteen ninety-two, when television provided a political forum for candidates that went beyond what former NBC News President Lawrence Grossman has called "the ghetto of journalism." Nineteen seventy-one, when *All in the Family* ushered in a new era of relevant TV. You can choose a best year based on what viewers saw, or how many were watching, or on how the industry as a whole achieved a dramatic financial or legal advance.

At the same time, just as some of you are framing objections to the choices above, one can make arguments against any year selected. When I told TV and film historian Tom Stempel about my idea for 1954, he soon came up with his five reasons why 1954 did not deserve to be TV's best year. The list:

1. The demise of the classic comedy-variety series *Your Show of Shows,* with stars Sid Caesar and Imogene Coca split into their own series and producer Max Liebman put in charge of what Stempel called "those godawful spectaculars."

2. The premiere of *Disneyland* in the fall of 1954, which ushered in the movie studios' full participation in television.

3. Mr. Peepers married on the sitcom of the same name, a course that the series' makers came to regret.

4. Paddy Chayefsky went to Hollywood to write the movie version of his successful play *Marty* and began a talent drain of playwrights from television.

5. Live dramatic anthologies *Kraft Television Theatre* and *Philco-Goodyear TV Playhouse* dropped out of the top twenty-five in the TV ratings, suggesting a decline in audience interest in live drama.

Then Stempel said, "On the other hand, any year that gives us *Thunder on Sycamore Street, Twelve Angry Men,* and the Army-McCarthy hearings can't be all bad." In fact, I would argue that that makes for a pretty good year—and that two acclaimed dramas and a great political confrontation were not all that 1954 had to offer. For starters, some of Stempel's complaints have a flip side.

The full entry of Hollywood studios into television had dire creative consequences, as we shall see, but it also ensured the survival of struggling network ABC. When *Your Show of Shows* ended, Sid Caesar followed it with a similar show, *Caesar's Hour,* that in terms of quality was comparable to its predecessor. Carl Reiner, the actor, writer, and later director who worked on both shows, has said, "The best work we did was in *Caesar's Hour.* . . . I get tired of reporters raving about some sketch 'you did on *Your Show of Shows* with Sid Caesar' when actually it was on *Caesar's Hour.*"

I made up a list of my own of great television moments from 1954, and *Caesar's Hour* is on it. So is *Disneyland,* not only because it had tremendous impact on television but because late 1954 saw the beginning of the "Davy Crockett" saga on the show; a whole series of political events including Army-McCarthy also fit, as does *Thunder on Sycamore Street.*

Other selections: *Medic,* a classic medical series much admired for its realism; the network premiere of the *Tonight* show with Steve Allen; the arrival of television versions of *Lassie* and *Rin Tin Tin; Father Knows Best,* one of the finest family comedies on television; the news interview series *Face the Nation;* Leonard Bernstein's first TV appearances as a commentator, on *Omnibus;* a major break for a young comic named Johnny Carson when he filled in for Red Skelton on that great clown's show; and *Annie Oakley,* the first TV western starring a woman.

Taking just the comics working in television in 1954, you can assemble an all-star starting nine of Steve Allen, Lucille Ball, Milton Berle, George Burns and Gracie Allen, Sid Caesar, Jackie Gleason, Ernie

Kovacs, and Red Skelton, then need a bench big enough to hold Red Buttons, Eve Arden, Imogene Coca, George Gobel, Dean Martin and Jerry Lewis, Bud Abbott and Lou Costello, and such up-and-comers as Soupy Sales. In other fields, I can cite the great live dramas already mentioned, or the most important police drama in television history (*Dragnet*). And I'd still just be wallowing in a sort of easy nostalgia that barely begins to get at why 1954 is so important in TV history.

If people today have any general perception of TV in the early fifties, it rests on three elements: the filmed situation comedies such as *I Love Lucy,* which continue in rerun to this day; a handful of TV dramas that showed the quality of serious work from the period; and the folkloric saga of Senator Joseph McCarthy, whose downfall included two television confrontations, one with broadcaster Edward R. Murrow and another with a TV-savvy attorney named Joseph Welch. That's a strong tripod, to be sure, and one with far-reaching impact; sociologist Todd Gitlin has said that "McCarthy's comeuppance is the most-remembered televised event among the early New Left generation." But even in praising such moments, we at times forget that these were parts of a more complex fabric of television, one not all that far removed from the nineties viewing experience.

Suppose we talked about a television year that included a Texas billionaire using television to push his political beliefs, a comedian playing himself on a TV series, another show presenting the backstage antics of a self-absorbed TV star, the President using television, live telecasts of Senate proceedings, four commercial networks vying for viewers, and a burst of attention for late-night TV. Suppose further that a critic of the day complained that "virtually everything about the medium carried with it 'here-we-go-again' overtones."

Even as such talk could be about 1993, it is just as easily applicable to 1954. H. L. Hunt put his money into a propaganda campaign long before Ross Perot did likewise. George Burns and Gracie Allen, not to mention Jack Benny, had sitcoms that echo in *Seinfeld* today; Benny as well as Milton Berle broke ground covered by *The Larry Sanders Show.* President Dwight Eisenhower had Robert Montgomery, an actor and director, advising him on his TV appearances. The Army-McCarthy hearings filled hours of daytime TV on two networks. ABC, CBS, NBC, and the now departed Du Mont battled for viewers. Steve Allen set the stage for the eventual battle between Jay Leno and David

Letterman. And the critic, George Rosen, was weary of TV while many of today's jaded critics were still watching *Howdy Doody*.

As Eisenhower's relationship with Montgomery shows, you do not even have to look at what's on the screen to make the case for 1954. TV dinners had started taking up space in freezers across the nation. In the halls of Congress, politicians and protestors attempted for the second time to curb what they saw as a disturbingly violent trend in television, especially for children; the TV industry offered assurances that it could control the content of its programs without government regulation. That set the tone for debates over TV's content well into the nineties but with a crucial difference—in 1954 television functioned in a way that made responsible behavior far more demonstrable.

Debates such as the one over violence and situations such as the intermingling of television and politics showed the basic point about the medium in 1954. Television as we think of it today, as a national force, as a binder of the nation, had finally come into existence. TV reached into more than half the homes in America, its impact evident far beyond the urban centers where it had grown to the heartland of America itself. And it presented programs that were often better than those we see today.

That is undoubtedly a tough argument for the modern viewer to accept. especially when the fuzzy images and few channels of the past are stacked against the hundreds of channels of today and tomorrow, the color pictures, the satellites beaming scenes from around the world. Over the course of this book there will be a juggling of two perspectives, that of the nineties, to consider the quality of older broadcasts by modern standards, and the fifties, to show how people of the period reacted to what they saw. And there will be times that people remembering TV of the fifties will find it wanting, especially in technological terms; sports broadcasts in the years before videotape replays, computer graphics, and roaming cameras do not measure up against the modern programs.

But television is not defined by technology any more than diversity is determined by the number of available channels. In the same way that I do not believe that a color telecast is automatically better than one in black and white, I do not accept the notion that a five-hundred-channel universe is better than a four-channel one. What has happened in television in recent years is comparable to changes in the magazine business, with the emphasis less on broad-based publications than on increasingly specialized ones. No one would seriously suggest that a single narrowly focused magazine, or even a fistful of them, is fundamentally the superior of *Life* in its heyday. Nor is a home receiving dozens of specialty issues any better off than a home getting one very good general-interest magazine a week. Why then do we think that having hundreds of TV channels is truly better than having a few that attempt to meet a variety of viewer desires and needs?

Television was a home to few channels but diversely programmed ones in 1954. And it was at a historical crossroads, making choices that would determine whether it became a genuine service to the nation, a simple collector of advertising tolls or a delicate balance of the two roles. The decision-making process had been going on for a long time by 1954, when audience growth made louder the siren call of financial gain. Indeed, TV had already wrestled with issues that perplex viewers and programmers to this day—the commercial and service implications of news, TV's effect on politics, how to deal with TV violence, what TV did to live sports, the benefit and burden of pursuing a mass audience instead of a specialized one (the latter being what television had begun with).

Unlike movies or theater, where one leaves daily life for a few hours of escape into fantasy, television has for more than forty years been part of daily life—"the electronic hearth" in one observer's words. That creates a problem in judging the medium in historical terms. Because it has been there throughout most viewers' lives, they often see television's birth as simultaneous with their own and its growth as paralleling theirs. The young people who love seventies sitcom *The Brady Bunch*—inspiring numerous spin-offs, two books and a live stage performance of old episodes—did not come to it as adults; they watched daytime reruns as children. To them, the Brady kids were their playmates—if impossibly untroubled ones—and the reserve of affection is no less rose-colored than it would be in remembering a long lost, real-life childhood pal.

Only over the last fifteen years have the videocassette recorder and the reissue of older shows by companies such as Rhino, Video Resources, Madacy, and MPI made it possible to show young people in a systematic way the variety of television past. As a result the fifties tend to be treated as part of television's youth because most of the people watching it and thinking about it now were young in the fifties, if they had been born at all. But history shows that television in the fifties was young only as Peter Pan was, with outward appearance belying the passage of years. In 1951 the *New York Times* published a seven-part series on the impact of television on America, including education, sports, politics, and culture. Still, well into the sixties people spoke of the newness of television.

In a 1967 *Playboy* interview, Johnny Carson, five years into his reign as the third host of the *Tonight* show, argued that "this is still a very young industry." Carson then recalled his first television experience, on a University of Nebraska hookup that broadcast from the college theater's basement to a screen in the auditorium above. That was in 1949, and Carson was right that not many people saw what was going on in the telecast. But those who saw surely responded when they did, and those who made the telecast were learning how to make the medium work for them.

As Carson gave TV a try in Nebraska, Peggy Wood was starring in the dramatic series *Mama,* playing live in a system that included only fifty-one television stations and less than a million homes with TV. In her 1963 memoir Wood said this of the early days:

> I was told by those who had preceded me by a few minutes, "This is a new medium." . . . I lost no time in replying it was *they* who were in a new medium; I was already an old hand at it, having performed many times on television in London during 1938 and 1939.

In the true early years of television, from the late twenties into the fifties, producers, directors, writers, and actors were figuring out forms and techniques that survive to this day. In England, where the British Broadcasting Corporation was widely studied by American television pioneers, the medium had made great strides by World War II. As one BBC history says:

> There was a wide and ambitious range including variety shows, cartoons, talks, plays, opera, newsreels and fashion parades. . . . The greatest triumph was the televising of the Coronation procession of George VI in May 1937 and estimates of the viewing audience varied between 10,000 and 50,000.

Nor was the U.S. television industry idle. In January 1928 the General Electric Company presented the first demonstration of home reception of TV broadcasts. In May of that year it had the first regular schedule of telecasts, in August the first remote broadcast (of New York Governor Alfred E. Smith being told he was the Democratic nominee for president), in September the first televised drama, *The Queen's Messenger*. The technology of the period was crude, indeed would give way to a more sophisticated means of making television in the 1930s, but the training in production and performance for the small screen was valuable nonetheless.

While World War II slowed television's expansion, experimentation continued. In 1944, WRGB—G.E.'s television station in Schenectady, New York—was broadcasting three nights a week. During one eighteen-month period around that time it put on 499 telecasts; an audience survey "showed that light operas, news commentaries and full-length plays are favored in that order." A WRGB brochure from the time added:

> Although the sports' group, as a whole, was not among the first three in popularity, audience reaction to the boxing and wrestling matches, which are regularly broadcast during fall and winter, was so favorable that as a separate group it would have ranked a high first over all other types of programs.

But for all the adventurousness of television in its early years, it was talked about far more than it was actually seen. Consider Milton Berle's *Texaco Star Theatre,* one of the early sensations in network television. In the 1950–51 season, the show was seen on average in about 62 percent of all homes with television. However, only about a fourth of all the homes in the U.S. had TV, so only about 15 percent of all American homes tuned to Berle. These days, with virtually all homes having television, a 15 rating is respectable, in some weeks good enough to put a show in the top ten in prime time, but hardly extraordinary. (The writer Arthur Frank Wertheim has argued that the decline of Berle's popularity was not a loss of audience—his viewers stayed constant—but that audience's proportional decline as greater numbers of viewers came to television as a whole.)

Not until 1952, when the Federal Communications Commission

ended its four-year freeze on TV station licenses, did viewer access to TV grow in a big way; at the end of the freeze there were only 108 television stations serving 63 television markets. The early attention television received was less a function of its audience size than of its audience's location—in large cities such as Los Angeles, Chicago, and especially New York, from which national news organizations and columnists could spread the word to the rest of the nation. Steve Allen, for one, had favorable writeups in *Time* and *Newsweek* in 1953 based largely on the successful late-night show he was doing for NBC's station in New York City; other cities had to wait until the following year to see Allen's program, when the NBC network began carrying what it called *Tonight*.

When the *Times* pondered the significance of TV in 1951, it did so in a city with seven stations. That paper's critic, Jack Gould, was accordingly among a group doing remarkable and prescient writing about television in the fifties. He, John Crosby of the *Herald Tribune*, Harriet Van Horne of the *World Telegram*, George Rosen at *Variety*, and others were well schooled in TV by the fifties and expressed many ideas that have been unknowingly echoed by those of us following them into TV criticism.

To read those critics in the fifties is to encounter a well-developed medium, one of great range, complexity—and controversy. The battles over television in the fifties tend to be forgotten now, lost in a more general and misplaced nostalgia fueled by sunny portrayals in TV, film, and oldies radio. One recent album of fifties songs called it "the happiest decade in history," the television series *Happy Days* was set in a generally carefree fifties and the movie *My Favorite Year* took place in 1954.

The minorities who struggled for equal rights certainly did not think of the fifties as happy days. Neither did the GIs fighting in the Korean War, or people being subjected to secret radiation experiments, or the entertainers who could not find work because they had been blacklisted. The recession of the early fifties took its toll as well; close to four million people were out of work in early 1954.

Television, for that matter, was far from perfect. Much of what went on the air was controlled by shows' sponsors, leading to numerous tales of arbitrary censorship in the name of commerce. The sitcoms and dramas of the era were not all classics; one critic complained at the end of the 1954–55 season that the ratio of forgettable TV plays to admirable productions was about six to one. Television was no better than the rest of the nation in its treatment of black characters and women. And it was woefully unhealthy, with cigarette smoke visible almost everywhere, including in seemingly constant advertisements.

At the same time, censorship had its merits, as anyone concerned about the content of television in the nineties must admit; television operated within a moral, even a religious, framework that provided content safeguards far less in evidence in the eighties and nineties. Cultural programming was frequently seen on commercial network television, as were thoughtful shows for children; the confinement of such shows to public broadcasting and cable had barely begun. The portrayals of woman and minorities, while often unfortunate, were not as unremittingly bleak as hindsight sometimes suggests. Local stations produced an array of programs that not only provided entertainment for local viewers, but created a link between communities and their stations (and viewer participation in TV) that is hard to imagine in an era when local TV generally means only news, public affairs, and talk.

National news, supposedly so primitive in bygone days, had established basic formats and techniques in the late forties and early fifties. Don Hewitt, much celebrated as creator and guardian of *60 Minutes*, knew more about making TV news in the early fifties than many producers do now. *60 Minutes* is firmly rooted in qualities both of reporting and showmanship that television had in the fifties, and it sticks with them even as others mistakenly look to the bells and whistles of advanced technology as the key to success.

Technological advances, after all, improve the speed with which a story can be told, but not the story itself. Anyone impressed (or appalled) by the way TV organizations fight for scoops now should consider the network battle in 1953 to be the first with footage of Queen Elizabeth II's coronation (see chapter 8). Anyone who thinks of TV news in the fifties as a bastion of seriousness should consider J. Fred Muggs, a chimpanzee who appeared on the *Today* show and became, even NBC's official history of *Today* acknowledged, "the most famous anthropoid in America."

Finally, television was better in 1954 because it was smaller than it is today. Fewer people worked in it, fewer channels were on the air, fewer people watched it. When the television audience grew, as I have said, the potential and actual revenues became greater and activities that risked hurting those revenues decreased. The experimentation and daring that marked television even into the fifties fell victim to a system where it seemed one did not need great invention or innovation to attract huge audiences.

In television, as in most businesses, daring comes from two sources: pioneers with everything to gain and people in danger who had nothing to lose. Television had both in the fifties. Giants of broadcasting such as William Paley at CBS and David Sarnoff at NBC still oversaw their networks. Du Mont, a gutsy little network run by one of TV's most successful inventors, was far less successful, but in its short life was often steps ahead of its bigger counterparts in program innovation. ABC, also struggling in those days, tried things the networks did not because it was, in top executive Leonard Goldenson's view, "acutely desperate for programming."

Rather than exulting in its youth in 1954, television felt all the pressures of adulthood. Too often today networks' bows to youth resemble a senior citizen tricked out with a bad toupee and modish fashion; the supposedly new TV toys are really filigree on a sturdy old medium. Pay-per-view was being tried out in the fifties. Home shopping, all the rage in the nineties, dates back to the forties. Every time I hear the word *interactivity* applied to the computerized TV universe of the future, I think of live call-in shows on radio and TV, which were interactive courtesy of the telephone. As a general rule, when a TV publicist says something is new, it means he is too young to remember the last time it was tried.

Still, was television really all that good in the early fifties? I think so, and I've watched a pretty good bit of it. As was mentioned, home video has made more of it available. The Museum of Television & Radio in New York City is also a good resource for looking at past TV, both good and bad (with the first episode of the sitcom *December Bride* in the latter category). I have also watched some shows with my sons, now ten and five and well aware of nineties TV and the complexities of Super Nintendo. It says a lot about fifties television that they giggle at Sid Caesar, get wide-eyed at *Superman,* or, as my younger son did, want the things they see in old TV commercials.

That said, if 1954 is to be considered a peak year in television, then a downhill slope thereafter has to be visible. I think it is. As much as I love many programs of recent years, as often as I channel-hop through cable choices, I well understand why Bruce Springsteen summed up a dead-end love affair as "fifty-seven channels and nothin' on." For that I blame what happened in television in the midfifties.

By the late fifties Du Mont was gone, CBS and NBC were reaping great rewards, and even little ABC was playing a conservative, revenue-oriented game. Real adventurousness in television did not resume until the seventies, when old-fashioned and cautious TV (much of it holdovers from the fifties) was no longer bringing new viewers to set, and the eighties, when competition from cable began to force the networks to rethink their old strategies.

Disenchantment with television appeared as early as 1950, when critic Gilbert Seldes said

> There are prophets who say we have already passed the golden era of television, that everything first rate will go down within a year or two and we will have nothing but the crudest forms of entertainment.

Reginald Rose, who in 1954 wrote the acclaimed *Twelve Angry Men* and the even better *Thunder on Sycamore Street,* wrote his first television play in 1951 "in sheer desperation as a protest against the nightly agonies television had to offer." But Seldes was premature in his complaint, Rose among those who did bring greater quality to television later in the fifties. It is likely that in 1954 television still had a chance to sacrifice some profit to save its soul.

But it did not. One of the lessons television learned from the McCarthy saga was that controversy and public responsibility come at a high cost, both in public good will and financial terms. In 1955, Edward R. Murrow would lose his sponsor because of yet another controversy; he then lost his prime-time pulpit in part because a more successful, and less confrontational, kind of program became a success. But that form, the big-money quiz show offering even hundreds of thousands of dollars in prizes, would by the late fifties be at the center of TV's worst scandal.

Disneyland, as has been mentioned, helped ABC and the Disney organization but its success caused a crucial shift in television power away from the stage-based New York City community and toward the movie-oriented Hollywood power structure. The appearance of public broadcasting in the early fifties provided commercial broadcasters with a convenient excuse for abandoning worthwhile programs they deemed unpalatable for the mass audience. But public TV (then called educational TV) was so poorly and erratically funded that from its beginning it had to figure out not only how to perform a public service but how to bring in enough viewers to justify corporate support; that put it in a bind much like that facing commercial TV. Moreover, in the long haul commercial TV's retreat from some programs created opportunities for PBS and later narrowly focused cable channels to nibble at the network audience.

In 1955, the boom in adult Westerns began, overwhelming network's prime-time schedules. In 1956, one of the great visionaries in television, Pat Weaver, left NBC. In 1958, Murrow gave his classic warning that TV might become "merely wires and lights in a box." In 1961, Federal Communications Commission chairman Newton Minow said anyone watching a day of television would see "a vast wasteland."

While there is much talk these days that the information superhighway will create a brave new world of television, history suggests no such thing. Cable, after all, slid into the network tracks, beginning with a vision of diversity that was realized only to a limited degree as networklike channels such as USA and TNT have come to the fore. Newer channels, looking to fill the envisioned five-hundred-channel universe (or the more visible one-hundred-channel one), include competing game-show channels and other forms of escapism.

So when we look back at 1954, we are also looking at the future; the decisions made in the early fifties may have been unavoidable short of government intervention (and that could have created a nightmare of new problems), but considering them may provide a clue to making television better in the next century. Already we have signs that television is trying to reinvent its past, in the occasional live commercial, the *Today* show moving into a studio meant to invoke its earliest setting, David Letterman's repeated bows to Steve Allen, Roseanne Arnold appearing on the cover of *TV Guide* made up as Lucille Ball.

Still, I did not set out to write a history of television, even of this one year, any more than I wanted just to rehash warmed-over anecdotes about TV's good old days. Instead, this is a rumination on what television was at a crucial moment that too many of us have either forgotten or misunderstood. For those of us who write about television on a daily basis, it is all too easy to lose track of history, especially things that took place before we took television seriously. For instance, in the summer of 1993 a reporter referred to TV as "an untried arena for the musical" because his knowledge of TV began after the heyday of musicals on TV, including the "spectaculars" beginning in 1954. When I started this book I thought I had a pretty clear understanding of how TV in 1954 resembled TV in the nineties, only to be confronted by still more parallels.

Television in 1954 included great programs, the awareness of the path to additional greatness, and a sense of what the cost of that effort would be. What was good about television, then and now, is not a matter of abundant channels, but of what is done with the channels that are available. And that brings us to the second question: what it meant to watch television in 1954.

What's On?

> After a few recent shows, dogs in this section
> have been dragging television sets out into
> the yard and burying them.
>
> Fred Allen, 1950

The program landscape of television in 1954 would appear at once familiar and jarringly different to a viewer arriving from forty years in the future. A modern viewer would immediately recognize certain kinds of genre programs, among them soap operas, situation comedies, news, sports, game shows (then more commonly known as quiz shows), Westerns, certain kinds of children's programs; some shows bore brand names still in use—*Today, Tonight, Meet the Press, Mr. Wizard, The Guiding Light.*

Nor did television in the early fifties take a back seat to the modern day in its star power, and in the tempestuousness of some of those stars. Roseanne Arnold gets a lot of attention for her exacting standards and flamboyant ways but has many tempestuous predecessors. Milton Berle, one of the earliest national television sensations, is quite frank in his memoirs that he "pushed and shoved and bullied" to get his comedy-variety show the way he wanted it.

> I ran like a maniac all week, directing when we had a director, getting into the dance blocking when we had a dance director, setting shots for the camera men, giving readings to actors, demanding costume changes, light changes—hell, I got into everything.

Dean Martin and Jerry Lewis rode high on TV thanks to appearances on *The Colgate Comedy Hour* but Lewis, as show-business biographer Arthur Marx has said, "starting to throw his creative weight around in areas that were clearly outside his domain," for instance insisting that his entertainer father be allowed to do his Al Jolson imitation on the air.

When two highly paid *Colgate* writers—Norman Lear, later famous as a producer, and Ed Simmons—began getting more publicity than Lewis thought seemly, he tried to fire them. After their contract proved ironclad, Lewis, as Marx wrote, "paid them their full $10,400 per script, but each time they turned one in, he dropped their creation into his wastebasket and used the other writers' material."

Where Lewis and Berle had some evident talent with an audience, they took a back seat in the ego department to the far less obviously able Arthur Godfrey. A radio star since the thirties who had moved to television in the forties, Godfrey dominated the medium—and his staff—like no star before or since. He had no obvious talent—to call his singing indifferent is to grant it high praise—but he had a knack for talking to people, most notably as he poked fun at the supposedly all-powerful sponsors of his radio and TV shows, and a warmth in his voice to which people responded. Steve Allen has said:

> No one ever said, "I must watch the Arthur Godfrey show because he's the most talented man I've ever heard of." The question never came up. He was just great fun to listen to. He was warm and interesting and believable.

For several years in the fifties Godfrey hosted two of the most popular shows in prime time—the only noticeable difference being that one showcased his established performer "friends," the other up-and-comers touted by talent scouts—as well as a hit daytime show. TV historian Robert Metz has said Godfrey was at one time responsible for 12 percent of the network's total revenues. Bob Hope once joked that "NBC is a subsidiary of RCA, like CBS is a subsidiary of Arthur Godfrey."

The power that came with that success was not used gently. The Museum of Television & Radio has film of a 1948 TV rehearsal shot as Godfrey did his radio show; the star's voice is all honey and charm as he joshes with the audience, ribs his coworkers and complains about the TV lights. The look on other performers' faces, though, is a mix of uncertainty and fear as they try to gauge the boss's mood, and weigh such acts as his thumbing his nose at the camera.

Roseanne Arnold may have fired writers and others from time to time, but Godfrey canned a singer, Julius LaRosa, on the air during his morning show in 1953. LaRosa's apparent error: getting too cocky for Godfrey's taste. The firing was such big news that, according to *Time* magazine, a Chicago columnist was fired for missing it—even though it was the columnist's day off.

For most entertainers that would be a tough act to follow. Godfrey topped himself in early '54 when he buzzed the control tower of a New Jersey airport in his private plane (Godfrey claimed he was forced into the move by a tough crosswind). His extremes of public charm and private toughness were so intriguing, he can be seen in not one but two fictional characters of the fifties—the egomaniacal radio and TV star Herb Fuller in Al Morgan's novel *The Great Man* and the even more off-the-meter Lonesome Rhodes in the movie *A Face in the Crowd.*

While such incidents resound today in the breathless tabloid reporting of star antics, Godfrey and his friends, and foes, nonetheless functioned in a different TV environment than exists today. And some of the genre shows of the period had distinct differences from their successors. But before we talk any more about what was on the air, we should look at the world in which the viewer went digging for video treasures.

Since at least the sixties, when television went into more than 90 percent of American homes, it has been safe to assume that almost all people watch television sometimes. No such assumption could be made in 1954.

Katie Kelly, later a nationally known television critic, recalled in her 1980 book *My Prime Time* what college life was like in 1954:

> If you were in school you were there for one of a number of things: studying, partying, finding a husband. Watching television was not one of those things. Remember, it was our generation that invented toga parties, barfing on Kappa Sig's front lawn, and the fine art of tee-peeing the trees.

More than 26 million homes had television at the end of 1953 and that was pretty dramatic; in 1950, fewer than 4 million homes were TV-equipped. But almost 45 million homes (98 percent of the country) had radios; almost twice as many radios as televisions were manufactured in fifty-three, although much of the difference consisted of radios in automobiles.

Still, radio filled a lot more hours than TV did and was the dominant broadcast medium into the early fifties. Fred Rogers, later a renowned children's TV host but at the time a floor manager for NBC, recalled, "Those were the days when television was taking a big second chair to radio." Indeed, radio was the target of barbs that would later fly at television, including charges of excessive commercialism and of harming children; in the late forties one parents organization complained that radio shows like *The Lone Ranger* and *Superman* "are tending to dull the minds of children." The often-discussed information overload of the TV and computer ages had its parallel in the mid-forties, when a commentator considering just radio and newspapers concluded:

> In the old days the difficulty of communicating even news of importance automatically screened out the drivel that serves no higher purpose than a peep show. Furthermore, the reader had time for thought and discussion. . . .
>
> As a result of the speed and abundance of news, the modern is confused. His time and mental capacity are limited. He is painfully aware that an attempt to assimilate anything beyond the smallest fraction of the day's news would result an acute attack of mental indigestion.

But television steadily seized ground formerly reserved for other media; Gilbert Seldes wrote in his 1950 book *The Great Audience,* "When television began to broadcast newsclips within ten hours of the event, the slow-moving newsreel, released once every three or four days, was doomed." By the early fifties, as radio stars moved steadily into television (and television ad revenues outstripped radio's), the shift of power between the two broadcast forms became evident; even some stars whose hearts were in radio took their turn before the TV camera.

As for what the audience for those stars was encountering, let's head back to New Year's Day, 1954, in Schenectady, New York. (I've picked that city not only because it used to be my home but because it is one of the birthplaces of television. It also reflects many of the conditions at work in TV at the time.) You are now part of a family that has set aside the newspaper stories of U.S. troop withdrawals from the Korean conflict, Suez Canal negotiations between Egypt and Great Britain, and that day's Rose Bowl confrontation between Michigan State and UCLA. The Christmas records, including a new one by Dean Martin, have been put away, tucked next to the mambo albums in the hi-fi cabinet. Mom has turned off the radio. Dad has stubbed out his Camel (the cigarette of William Holden, John Wayne, and Alan Ladd). The occasion: The family is about to make its first journey into home television.

Naturally, everyone will travel together. Only about 3 percent of American homes have more than one TV. And the picture is in black-and-white. Although color programming has begun on a limited basis, no local station will be able to transmit it until summer; even then, the only color shows will come from the networks, with locally produced color shows still many months away.

Besides, the local dealers still do not have any color TVs and any one that you find will be expensive. The lowest estimates are $800, the highest $1,000 and more. Considering that a factory worker's gross salary is about $70 a week, a color TV is just a dream. And even in dreams you hope you'll be better off than a guy TV personality Dave Garroway joked about on his variety show:

> Saved all his money and finally got enough for a color TV set. Then a terrible thing happened. He found out he was color blind. The Green Hornet was black. Red Barber's hair was black. He got so mad, he saw gray.

In addition to living with a black-and-white image, viewing is going to be potluck, consisting of whatever happens to be on at the time you are watching. A home videotape recording system will not be available until 1965. TV production itself is either filmed, live, or on kinescope, a crude recording process of limited usefulness; although a videotape system was demonstrated in 1953, a workable one is still two years away. So forget those videotaped "instant replays" when you watch sports.

Cable is also exceedingly rare and basically a community antenna bringing TV stations to areas where geography interferes with the over-the-air signal. Absent cable, the family is at the mercy of whatever antenna they hooked up and the resulting potential for fuzz in the picture. But thanks to patience and a careful study of *Popular Mechanics,* they at least managed to set the TV up on their own. As the magazine will note in its *Do-It-Yourself Encyclopedia:*

> Television installation and service were for a long time considered as things to be attempted only by the skilled technician. . . . [Now] there is no reason why any television owner cannot perform many, if not most, service and replacement needs on his set.

That technical confidence is tempered somewhat by the awareness that this black-and-white, tube-filled, wobbly-antennaed contraption did not come cheap. This is the era of big, boxy televisions that dominate a room, not because they offered stereo sound and mammoth screens for a "home theater"; rather, this television is a major furnishing, as much a part of the room's decor as a striped wing chair or a blond oak lowboy.

Some ads for TV sets mention their design style: French provincial, modern, eighteenth century. Others combine the TVs with phonographs and radios. Many bear high-toned names; Magnavox alone has the Metropolitan, Envoy, Holiday, Cosmopolitan, and International Modern, not to mention the Wedgewood and Belvedere. Andrea, a manufacturer touting its "fringe-master tuner," sells the Riviera and the Lido.

Just by sitting in front of that television set, a family entered a relationship that was significantly different from the one between viewer and viewing in the nineties. While modern viewers occasionally sit as a family in front of the set, the proliferation of multiset homes, especially with small TVs, moves the viewing experience to the kitchen and bedroom, at once fragmenting the viewing and forcing the TV program to compete directly with other activities. The bond between TV and its audience is accordingly weaker now, the challenge much greater for the programmer. It's a long way from how TV playwright Tad Mosel expected his shows to be watched, during "reflective evenings in an easy chair."

Kirk Browning, who started in TV in the late forties and was still directing productions in the nineties, once said:

> I have often thought, God, it would be absolutely wonderful if all the people in charge of the technology had decided they were only going to make the screens bigger and bigger and bigger until they finally got so big, every house would have to have one room with one huge wall that could be a television wall. And that's the only way you could see television.

Ben Gross, long the radio-TV editor of the *Daily News* in New York City, assumed in 1954 that the future of television would be big.

> The small screens of today will be nonexistent. Pictures will be received on the glass walls of houses, with a mere turn of the dial producing an image ranging from a few to a hundred feet in size.

Gross—who was far closer to the mark when he envisioned something very similar to computerized TV shopping—expected TV to turn into something the loss of which Browning now mourns. As Browning said in early 1994:

> When you have a technology that will give you a set in the bathroom, a set in the bedroom, a set in the kitchen, and you can go and flip and dial and put on the mute . . . there is not the environment in which you are going to sit down and pay attention to good material. It's television-zak, it's background stuff.

Modern TV has to be louder, flashier, and fancier to lure a viewer busy chopping carrots to a five-inch image under the kitchen cabinet. In the fifties, such was not the case. Even when the most frantic comedian was on the air, television moved at a more leisurely pace. With many programs live and the technology still limited, shows did not engage in the sort of jumpy cutting of the MTV age. The half-hour and hour-long programs of the day had more time to tell a story than their modern counterparts because commercials took only about six minutes out of a program hour, about half what they consume today.

And since a single commercial usually ran a minute, there were fewer spots in a break; the National Association of Broadcasters' Television Code also recommended against running more than two spots per break. Although complaints about ad bombardment were loud in the early fifties, it was nothing compared to the shelling today.

The very act of watching TV in the fifties involved a commitment. An old newspaper cartoon showed various people, all stopped midway in their dressing or undressing, drawn into the living room by the hijinks on their TV; that sort of gathering does not happen when the TV is two steps from the closet. Similarly, the commitment to a single program was far stronger without a remote to allow a change of channel from across the room; it's wonderful what we viewers will tolerate when the alternative requires rising from a well-dug groove in the couch.

So the search for the perfect television took time and thought. You have considered RCA and Du Mont, General Electric and Olympia, Philco and Capehart, CBS-Columbia and Silvertone. Sears had a 17-inch Silvertone with mahogany veneer for $198.88, a 21-incher for $60 more. But Philco pushed a 21-incher for its "lowest price ever," $200.

To the modern consumer that should probably be "only" $200, but these are old-time dollars. A five-figure income is a dream for most Americans. Moreover, in the erratic economy of the early fifties, unemployment doubled between October 1953 and October 1954.

A three-bedroom home is selling for under $12,000, a 1948 Chevrolet is going for $495, ground beef is 39 cents a pound. The Bendix washing machine the family almost bought was "only" $169.95. What tipped the scales: the washing machine did not have Arthur Godfrey.

Once the family decided the washer could wait a while, its dream TV became a fully equipped G.E. console set, with mahogany finish and half-doors to close over the TV screen; able to get VHF (Channels 2–13) and UHF (Channel 14 and beyond); and a big 21-inch picture, all for $439.95. And, as a bonus, you've started getting this magazine, *TV Guide*, not even a year old yet but promising insight into the wonderful world of TV.

So the moment has arrived. The family is gathered round. It's 7 A.M. and the test pattern gives way at last to something to watch.

Well, one thing to watch.

In January 1954 viewers in Schenectady can choose from a total of two TV stations, and then only if their set is equipped for both UHF and VHF reception. Nor is this all that unusual since the Federal Communications Commission froze the issue of station licenses from 1948 to 1952. Even after the FCC lifted the freeze, it did so by granting a lot of UHF licenses in communities where VHF had been the rule before.

The total number of stations, only 108 serving 63 television markets at the end of the freeze, will have tripled by the end of 1954, but the old-line stations will have had the advantage of time, experience, and long-standing ties with the four commercial networks. In your city, the VHF station—G.E.-owned WRGB—has affiliation agreements with ABC, CBS, NBC, and Du Mont, picking what it wants from the available programs; the lone UHF competitor (which will be joined by two others before the year's end) has to settle for shows that the VHF station does not want. For that reason—and because of its tight financial situation this uphill competitive battle has caused—the UHF station, WROW, does not even sign on until 1:30 P.M. on New Year's Day, and that early only because it has a football bowl game to carry; come Monday it will be back to its usual sign-on time of 5 P.M.

Not that things are all that great at the big stations. *Time* magazine has recently suggested "TV broadcasting may be nearing the saturation point" because an FCC survey of eighty-three older stations concluded that only sixteen are making money. And that's before stations around the nation had to face the additional outlays to make color telecasts possible (see chapter 15).

But at least WRGB has a day full of programs, starting with NBC's *Today* show in the morning, then going into CBS's soap operas, plus shows from the other networks as well as local productions. Nor are local shows confined to news; television is a local thing across the board.

The existing networks did not fill the kinds of hours they do now. Prime time—which started at 7 P.M. on ABC and Du Mont, 7:30 on CBS and NBC—was a rich field overall but still had gaps; Du Mont's schedule was a checkerboard of programs and empty spaces for stations to fill. The existing network newscasts, only fifteen minutes long, were also in prime time rather than the early evening hours. *Today* was the lone network early-morning show, although CBS would make its first try at a morning program in March 1954 (then give it up three years later after numerous, unsuccessful changes).

NBC had ventured into late-night several years ago with *Broadway*

Open House but its late-night standard, *Tonight,* did not begin its network run until September 1954. When *Television* magazine tried to assess *Tonight*'s chances for success, it studied how local late-night shows were doing in some markets, among them Soupy Sales's *Soupy's On* in Detroit, *Pantomime Parade* in Cincinnati, *Polka Revue* in Cleveland, and "hillbilly singer" Ernie Lee's show in Dayton.

When *TV Guide* announced its awards for the 1953–54 season, three pages were devoted to the network winners and four to outstanding local personalities in the twenty-four cities where *TV Guide* circulated. The local winners included a children's show host in Milwaukee, a comedienne from Dallas, a singer from Fort Lauderdale, an educational filmmaker in New York and a couple hosting a show for teenagers in Denver. Bandleader Lawrence Welk was a winner for his musical show in Los Angeles, Soupy Sales for his Detroit shows.

In addition, network shows were identified less with their broadcasters than with their sponsors, who could put their names in the shows' titles (*Camel News Caravan, Kraft Television Theatre*), display their products on the sets, and weave their commercials into the program itself. A Rhino videotape celebrating the worst in television history includes the fifties quiz show *Penny to a Million* whose cigarette-company sponsor was mentioned several times in a series of questions about tobacco.

And finally, given the relative rarity of stations, and the even rarer examples of successful ones, local stations had more power in choosing and scheduling programs, including those of their own making that might more readily appeal to local viewers. Over time, as networks locked stations into lucrative but exclusive agreements, as the networks began to fill time slots they had previously ignored, and as it proved cheaper for stations to buy shows than to produce them, the situation would change. One TV veteran later said:

> You could do the best local entertainment program you could, with good performers and beautiful sets. And half an hour later, Dean Martin could go on and stand in front of a curtain and get five times the audience.

But for the moment, local programming was a major distinction between 1954 TV and what viewers are getting 40 years later. To talk about other differences let's look at some genres:

Sitcoms: This would be most familiar to modern viewers, since shows like *Ozzie & Harriet, Make Room for Daddy* (later called *The Danny Thomas Show*), *Jack Benny,* and *Burns & Allen* survive in various formats and venues to this day; the most popular show of the period was *I Love Lucy,* in 1994 enjoying renewed attention through reruns on Nick at Nite. Groucho Marx's long-running show *You Bet Your Life* (in its heart a situation comedy with Groucho playing a rascally but lovable quiz-show host) was also on view. Other shows, much admired in their day, are less well remembered; *Mr. Peepers,* a comedy starring Wally Cox as a teacher, still has ardent fans but is little seen because, done live, it survives only in untelegenic kinescopes.

Drama: There were dramatic series, most notably the landmark police show *Dragnet* and its imitators. *Mama,* stories about a hard-working and loving Norwegian family, had been around since the late forties. But the dramatic strength of the period lay in the live anthologies such as *Studio One, Philco-Goodyear Playhouse,* and *U.S. Steel Hour,* as well as lesser lights such as the live-and-film anthology *Schlitz Playhouse.* The anthologies filled a very similar role to the modern television movie (which did not yet exist in 1954)—bringing diversity to the schedule and showcasing well-known actors—but the sensibility was not from the movies but the New York stage.

Whether dealing with grand historical moments or small personal stories, anthologies also provided an opening in television for actors, directors, and most significantly writers such as Rod Serling, Horton Foote, Reginald Rose, and Paddy Chayefsky, who became marquee names on the small screen. And because new plays were needed each week, other writers had opportunities to get work and gain fame that would be far harder to come by in the more rigid world of dramatic series to come.

News: Two major weeknight newscasts on CBS and NBC were already on the air; although just fifteen minutes long, their basic format was that of the modern newscast. *See It Now,* a weekly half-hour hosted by Edward R. Murrow, examined stories with the range and detail that would later be seen in network news magazines. Plus there were commentary shows with various newspaper columnists, the early-morning *Today* show, and Sunday public affairs series such as *Meet the Press*. (This is covered in more detail in chapter 8.)

Daytime: The soap opera was making the transition from radio to television, but the talk show was not the force it is today. Instead of talk, one had variety shows, such as those hosted by Arthur Godfrey and Bob Crosby, which mingled music, games, and a bit of chatter, all aimed at the supposedly homebound hausfrau. Later in 1954 NBC launched *Home,* an all-purpose information show for women, as well.

Daytime TV was also considered a province for children at home. As anyone who ever unrolled a red strip of black-dotted pistol caps knows, the little ones feasted on Westerns with stars such as Roy Rogers and Gene Autry. They also enjoyed puppet shows (cartoons had not yet taken over children's TV), ventriloquist Paul Winchell, the early space opera *Captain Video, The Adventures of Superman* and such thoughtful fare as *Ding Dong School,* which on recent examination seemed a prototype for *Mr. Rogers' Neighborhood.*

Grandmotherly educator Frances Horwich hosted the show, talking to the camera as if it were the child at home, offering little lessons and activities and exposing children to culture (for instance when a cellist came to visit). Nor can we forget Don Herbert, better known as Mr. Wizard, whose practical approach to science included the maxim, "Never use an Ehlenmeyer flask when a milk bottle will do"; in 1954 Herbert's show won a coveted Peabody award.

Sports: Athletic feats, notably prime-time boxing and wrestling, had been crucial to the early success of television; by 1954 boxing had a lot of clout but wrestling was coming to the end of its first run of success. Tennis, hockey, basketball, football, and the most important game of all, baseball, had places on the schedule. But they had not swallowed up the weekend television schedule to the extent they would in later years. Major sports leaders feared that television, even as it brought in an audience that might not be able to see a live game, would prove fatal to those places with flourishing local venues (see chapter 12). And as critic Ron Powers has written, some elitist network executives saw sports as something that dirtied their hands.

Cultural programs: One advantage to the sports vacuum on Sundays was that it opened up program hours to public affairs and cultural shows. Sunday was the home to televised operas and symphony concerts as well as the classic series *Omnibus,* a mingling of all sorts of intellectual fare and hosted by the urbane Alistair Cooke, later linked to PBS as host of *Masterpiece Theatre.* But opera also had a small place in prime time, and both jazz and Broadway music—more commonly heard in these days before rock'n'roll entered the mainstream—were often featured around the dial. (In a wonderful bit on *Caesar's Hour,* jazz was ultimately defined as "a beautiful woman whose older brother is a policeman.")

Religion: Sunday shows with religious themes appeared on the networks and local stations; prime time also had its religious stars, especially Catholic Bishop Fulton J. Sheen (see chapter 5).

Variety: A term that encompasses shows with a heavy comedic bent, others with a musical twist, shows with immensely talented hosts and another whose host could barely speak (Ed Sullivan), the variety show offered some of the most spectacular moments in TV in the forties and fifties; for that matter the "spectaculars" (later known as specials) that began to appear in 1954 were often variety shows held together by the barest of plots.

In any case the shows mingled comedy, music, and other forms of entertainment in various formulas: *Colgate Comedy Hour* boasted hosts such as Eddie Cantor, Martin and Lewis, and Abbott and Costello but still found room for song; one Cantor-hosted show featured the cast (that night including Eddie Fisher and Frank Sinatra) singing Harold Arlen tunes with the composer himself at the piano. Ed Sullivan—well, you never knew what to expect from the newspaper columnist turned impresario (and neither, judging from the recollections of people who worked on the show, did the staff of what was then called *Toast of the Town*). Jackie Gleason was demonstrating his mastery of sketch comedy on his series, including in a series of "Honeymooners" sketches that would lead to a separate show in 1955; Sid Caesar was doing the impossible with a grand ensemble of writers and actors on *Your Show of Shows* and *Caesar's Hour;* Milton Berle was still at it; master clown Red Skelton had a weekly half-hour.

For all that TV had to offer in 1954, the modern viewer would still feel some disorientation, when the newscasts ended after their brief turns, when variety shows (now so rarely seen) popped up with such regularity, when the black and white images were unrelieved by more than a smattering of color. And in three major areas many nineties viewers would find this glimpse of television past not merely startling but appalling. Which brings us to the last question.

What's Wrong
with This Picture?

Now there are women drivers, even in space.
TV Guide, 1954

From the nineties' perspective, television in 1954 mistreated two major audiences—women and minorities—and failed all viewers with its seemingly endless endorsement of smoking. Of the three, the worst is not the stereotypical portrayals but the health hazard, which perpetuated an image of smoking as glamorous and exciting as evidence of its risks began to mount. And the presentations of women and minorities, while far from desirable, were by no means as bad as some observers in more recent years have suggested.

Writing in *Channels* magazine in 1981, Mel Watkins summed up the black perspective on television by quoting a man in a Harlem bar: "In the fifties you didn't see no part of no blacks on TV." In the weekly series of the fifties, Watkins saw only three occupations for African Americans: "singing and dancing, working as a servant or . . . just grinning." At that, images were so rare Watkins said, "I can recall waiting anxiously in front of the television set any time a black performer was scheduled to appear."

Television was indeed slow to present people of color to the viewers of America. That hardly made TV unique, given that only in 1954 did the great age of the civil rights struggle begin, with the Supreme Court decision desegregating public schools. But television's approach to racial issues seemed timid, with programmers often blaming their concerns on Southern audiences and stations, even though fewer Southern homes had televisions on a proportional basis than did other, supposedly more enlightened parts of the nation; in the midfifties, 91 percent of the homes in the Northeast had televisions, but just under half of those in the South.

In 1949 CBS tried a variety show with an all-black cast including singer Harry Belafonte and comic Timmie Rogers; variously titled *Uptown Jubilee, Harlem Jubilee,* and *Sugar Hill Times,* it proved short-lived. So did two early fifties series hosted by singers Hazel Scott—"an above-it-all black goddess," in historian Donald Bogle's admiring view—and Billy Daniels. In January 1954 ABC announced plans for a series with Sammy Davis, Jr., but it was stymied before it ever got on the air. ABC Chairman Leonard Goldenson said in his memoir *Beating the Odds:*

> We built a pilot around Sammy's family, all entertainers. But no advertiser dared to back a "colored" star at that time. We couldn't sell it, so "The Sammy Davis Jr. Show" never went on the air.

An even more telling example of video prejudice that year struck Reginald Rose when he finished his TV play *Thunder on Sycamore Street.* An effective story about mob rule and discrimination, the play originally focused on how a white neighborhood reacted to a black man's moving in. Rose wrote not long after:

> This was unpalatable to the networks since many of their stations are situated in Southern states and it was felt that viewers might be appalled at the sight of a Negro as the beleaguered hero of a television drama.

Forty years later, Rose said it even more directly: "They could not handle the guy being black. They were too afraid of offending." Rose accordingly changed the character from black to a white ex-convict, unquestionably reducing any controversy (and attention) for the play but not really hurting it dramatically; as a TV production it is superior to Rose's better known play about a deliberating jury, *Twelve Angry Men.* TV historian Erik Barnouw has said *Thunder* became "an extraordinary social Rorschach test." Rose discovered after the play aired that viewers thought the ex-convict

> was meant to symbolize a Negro, a Jew, a Catholic, a Puerto Rican, an ex-Communist or fellow traveler, a Japanese or Chinese, a Russian, an anarchist or an avowed atheist. Not one single person I spoke to felt that he was actually meant to be an ex-convict.

For black viewers looking for a reflection of themselves, *Thunder* provided only symbolic help. But that is not to say the small screen was lily-white. Consider some of the images of black people to be found on TV in 1954: integrated vocal group the Mariners, who had been singing on Arthur Godfrey's shows since 1948; a well-spoken football player at Oberlin College, presented matter of factly in an *Omnibus* feature; Representative Adam Clayton Powell talking about school integration on *Chronoscope;* James Edwards and other actors in *The Reign of Amelika Jo,* a *Fireside Theatre* play believed to be the first network drama with an entirely black and Asian cast; Rosetta Le Noire and Josh White, Jr., in *The Challenge,* a play about an African missionary, shown on the religious series *Lamp unto My Feet.*

News series *See It Now* repeatedly showed black people in America. When it went to Korea, the pictures it brought back sometimes had black GIs in them. Its examination of school desegregation showed how people both black and white were reacting in two Southern towns. The show also did a two-part report on conditions in South Africa. And the nation watched on *See It Now* and other telecasts as Annie Lee Moss, a black woman working in an Army code room, was bullied by Senator Joseph McCarthy and his crew.

I realize that I am mixing images from real life with those from entertainment shows. In the Mixmaster of a viewer's mind, all those images blend together to form a more general impression. For that reason alone, one cannot put aside images from sports as well, such as of the heroic Willie Mays of the then-New York Giants. At the end of the Giants' pennant-winning season (they went on the win the World Series as well), Mays was in constant TV demand, starting with two competing, live, Sunday night shows, Ed Sullivan's *Toast of the Town* and *Colgate Comedy Hour.* Sports journalist Charles Einstein said:

Mays got back from Philadelphia after the season's finale there in time to appear on TV at the beginning of Sullivan, hustle over to NBC, and appear again at the end of Colgate. At 7:30 the next morning he was on the "Today" show. At 12:15 that night he was on the "Tonight" show.

Such a hero's welcome—while seeming small in an era when any such star would have had to work his way through network sports, ESPN, CNN, MSG, and SportsChannel just for starters—is nonetheless significant in the context of a smaller TV universe, and in Mays's being black. It made a difference that people saw black athletes, because the world of the fifties was much more isolated than today, when global linkage by television is taken for granted.

In that *Omnibus* segment just mentioned, a young woman from Miami says she went to college in Ohio because "I wanted to see what snow was like . . . and what Northern people were like." And do not forget that Mays's triumph comes just seven years after major league baseball had formally integrated; even then, the last team to integrate, the Boston Red Sox, did not do so until 1959. One prominent baseball historian has said, "There were probably more Polish players in the fifties than blacks."

Granted the modern viewer would be made uneasy by some scenes from '54, such as Ethiopian soldiers performing their victory chant on *See It Now*. And you can easily imagine the public outcry if a scientist today echoed Margaret Mead's reference to children she knew in New Guinea as "little savages." Not to mention that the remark—heard on the educational series *Adventure*—came during a discussion of childlike and primitive islanders who, upon encountering Western culture, "wanted to be like us."

At the same time, the much reviled sitcoms of the era have with the passage of time gained renewed respect from thoughtful viewers. Mel Watkins is among the many writers to acknowledge that the early fifties' *Amos 'n' Andy*—often attacked for its presentation of black characters as devious, lazy, and malaprop-infected—was also hilarious.

I grew up watching the adventures of cabdriver Amos Jones, his friend Andy Brown and the real center of the show, George "Kingfish" Stevens. But singer-actress Diahann Carroll has a different memory.

> At home, it was very important that we not watch *Amos 'n'*
> *Andy.* It was very important to my mother that we not see
> something that was so racist. It was years later that I realized
> they were brilliant. They were really funny.

Carroll's comment is in *Color Adjustment,* a tough documentary
about blacks in television comedy, by Marlon Riggs. The filmmaker
himself had similar ambivalence about the show: "What I remember
was laughing, like anybody. They were funny. . . . I was totally unaware of how that shaped my consciousness and the consciousness of
the nation."

But the consciousness of the nation was more likely what it brought
to a show like *Amos 'n' Andy,* not what it drew from the viewing. A
clownish central character surrounded by a mix of normal and comic
characters was not the sole province of *Amos 'n' Andy.* Think of Jackie
Gleason in *The Honeymooners* or Lucille Ball in any of her series.

Consider, too, the case that Bogle has made for shows with black
characters as servants—the maids on *Beulah* or *Make Room For*
Daddy, or the manservant played by Eddie "Rochester" Anderson on
Jack Benny's shows. Bogle argues that the trouble with such shows
lies in the white characters, whom he calls "patently fake, hollow,
artificial through and through, inhabited by plastoids rather than human beings." The black characters "always strike us as real people,"
he said.

> Although we might despise the fact that blacks were depicted
> only as comic servants on the sitcoms, we should not ignore
> the fact that the actors themselves helped make many of these
> series watchable.

As has often been said about the early sitcoms, the trouble was not
what was on the screen but what was missing—positive images to
balance the negative ones. And in that respect, black viewers had a lot
of company.

Television in its early years had a noticeable ethnic richness, span-
ning the Cuban Ricky Ricardo, the Norwegian Hansens of *Mama,* the
Jewish family, the Goldbergs, on the show of the same name, the
Lebanese Danny Williams on *Make Room for Daddy,* the Italians
of *Life With Luigi* and *Bonino.* But some of those shows are not
remembered fondly.

Luigi, with J. Carroll Naish as a simple-minded immigrant, and *Bonino,* where singer Ezio Pinza played an opera star raising eight children, topped a critics' survey of the worst sitcoms of the fifties. TV critic Rick Du Brow praised *Luigi* as a radio show (many of the ethnic shows came from radio) but called the 1952 TV version a mistake.

> The world was changing, away from ethnic humor, and there was great sensitivity about it. Italian groups would protest about Italian stereotypes, Jewish groups about Jewish stereotypes. . . . Network executives got scared and they took [*Luigi*] off the air.

But other ethnic characters presented a quite positive image. Desi Arnaz—successful, articulate, and almost always the straight man to his wacky Anglo wife Lucille Ball—was undeniably an inspiration to Cuban Americans. For the tormented musicians in Oscar Hijuelo's 1989 novel *The Mambo Kings Play Songs of Love,* the acme of their career is an appearance on *I Love Lucy,* which makes them celebrities not only to their Cuban friends but the Irish and Germans in their neighborhood.

Fifties Western *The Cisco Kid,* starring Duncan Renaldo as the dashing hero and Leo Carrillo as his humorous sidekick Pancho, has a somewhat mixed reputation with Latinos. Luis Valdez, who directed a 1994 TV movie version of the adventure story, has said that the series characters were like *Amos 'n' Andy* to Latino audiences. On the other hand, Cheech Marin, who played Pancho in the 1994 movie, said of the old show, "Here was a Mexican who put the white guys in jail every week. . . . We didn't see that a lot on TV."

Carrillo's Pancho, a "Mexican buffoon" in Valdez's view, can discomfit viewers leery of stereotypes. But keep in mind that the tandem of hero and comic relief was common in Western movies and TV shows, including Roy Rogers's, Gene Autry's and *Wild Bill Hickok.* Renaldo, who as a producer of *Cisco* had like Arnaz important off-camera power, saw to it that his character was inoffensive. That care, combined with the canny decision to make the show's episodes in color, assured the series a long video life; even Valdez, for all his reservations, said that Renaldo's Cisco "was a hero to me."

Danny Thomas once looked at the origins of his sitcom and said, "It was the day of the White Protestant American United States, and a guy like me wasn't exactly family fare." He had the chronology backwards. Whatever the prejudices besetting America as a whole, television in the early fifties had a noticeable degree of ethnic diversity. Television critic David Zurawik has attributed this to an urban audience that was comfortable seeing (if not living with) other people in a multiethnic society. Los Angeles–based *Dragnet*, for example, looked at Latino characters, among them a Latino police detective (unfortunately played by Harry Bartell, a frequent *Dragnet* actor, in dark makeup).

As TV became available to the country as a whole, as advertisers sought revenues from everyone, diversity was squeezed out of TV in favor of characters whose backgrounds had been tossed into the melting pot and blended into a blandly appealing soup. In the early sixties writer Stan Opotowsky said of one major TV advertiser, "The company will permit offense to no one—not Negroes, not bigots, not even butterfly lovers or butterfly haters—in its shows."

As the civil rights movement bloomed, black actors finally found more doors open in TV. The doors might have opened earlier had not the controversies of the fifties blanded out television. By then a black character was trouble on two fronts: to racist white viewers annoyed at the sight, and to black viewers monitoring their TV counterparts for hints of stereotyping. The irony of the situation became evident in 1956 when singer and actor Nat "King" Cole got his own variety show on NBC. A mainstream popular singer, Cole was also, as Donald Bogle wrote, "a model gentleman: smooth, polished, soft-spoken, debonair, easy-going, urbane." If any black entertainer could have succeeded on television, Cole should have. But in those uneasy days of bus boycotts and other battles, he had trouble getting sponsors. It took another nine years, to 1965, for a network series to have a black star as *Amos 'n' Andy* had. Bill Cosby in *I Spy*, which premiered a month after President Johnson signed the Voting Rights Act, finally began a more open TV era.

The change in the portrayal of women on television in the fifties had a pattern and perplexity akin to what had happened with ethnic characters. Because of the comedies that endured in rerun over the ensuing decades, the fifties and early sixties are often cited as the June Cleaver-Donna Reed-Harriet Nelson era, in which women stayed home, elegant even as they vacuumed the rug, and the men went off to work.

And for some women that was life as God intended. On an early fifties episode of *The Bob Crosby Show*—a daytime variety series hosted by Bing's brother—Crosby asked a woman about her marriage.

"You like it? Very happy?" he said.
"Happy not to be able to work," she replied.

For others, though, such a peaceful life was what sociologist Stephanie Coontz bluntly labeled "the way we never were." Women did not all sit home. One pundit looking at 1954 said, "It seems reasonably certain . . . that more (women) will work at two jobs—homemaking and bringing home the bacon for the family larder." Some 19 million women, half of them married, held jobs, forming 30 percent of the total work force.

However, as society moved farther away from World War II, journalist Brett Harvey has argued, it made "a dramatic retreat from the trends of the previous decades." Women who had pursued higher education and jobs in the prewar years were now "surrounded by powerful inducements to early marriage," Harvey said, and TV and other media were doing a lot of the inducing. Television, for one, had *Bride and Groom,* a daytime series of wedding ceremonies.

The assumption that a woman's place was in front of the Philco lay behind lawyer Joseph Welch's assessment of his work at the televised Army-McCarthy hearings. The live daytime telecasts, Welch contended, were seen not by men but by their wives, who created marital discord when the hearings habit kept them from putting Hubby's dinner on the table. "I sense that I may have won the female vote at the cost of losing the male vote," Welch said.

These were the days when women were girls, and a girl's greatest quality was beauty. When Frieda Hennock, a highly successful forty-three-year-old lawyer, became the first woman on the Federal Communications Commission in 1948, the FCC chairman said, "We've had rectitude, fortitude and solemnitude, but never before pulchritude." (Hennock, as shall be seen, brought considerably more to the FCC.) The Miss America pageant, first telecast on ABC in 1954, promoted its scholarship competition with ads asking, "If you like beautiful girls (and who doesn't?) . . . don't miss the Miss America contest." Host John Daly, the ad promised, "will provide the commentary . . . as if *that* were necessary."

At least television made room for working women on its sitcoms: Ann Sothern on *Private Secretary*, Celeste Holm as a reporter on *Honestly, Celeste!* teacher Eve Arden on *Our Miss Brooks*, secretary Elena Verdugo on *Meet Millie*, newspaper reporter Mary Shipp on *My Friend Irma* (although Marie Wilson starred as Irma Peterson, "possibly the kookiest secretary in the entire world," as Tim Brooks and Earle Marsh put it). One could find June Havoc playing a lawyer on *Willy* and Gail Davis as the most independent woman in TV Westerns, *Annie Oakley*. The Space Academy on *Tom Corbett, Space Cadet* had its first female graduates (hence the snotty note at the beginning of this chapter) and a woman appearing regularly as an atomic physicist. In *Dear Phoebe*, where a man wrote a newspaper advice column, his girlfriend was a sportswriter.

Robin Morgan, later a nationally known writer and feminist but in 1954 a young TV actress, eventually saw the merits of the mischievous Dagmar, whom she played on *Mama*.

> Dagmar did routinely thrash the neighborhood bully whenever he tried to cramp her assertive style. Not coincidentally, the Hansen family was matriarchal less in structure than in affirming that its primary source of wisdom and strength was the title character.

But television's occasional nod to women, particularly working ones, took place in the fantasy world of situation comedy. The most popular woman on television was still daffy Lucy. The women journalists of *Dear Phoebe* and *Honestly, Celeste!* got far more air time than TV's lone real reporter in skirts, NBC's Pauline Frederick. *Time* magazine pondered *My Friend Irma*, *Meet Millie*, *Our Miss Brooks*, and *Private Secretary*, then concluded "in refreshing contrast to real life, the girls are seldom asked to do much work." Ann Sothern, for that matter, got letters from real-life secretaries complaining she did not use the typewriter properly.

Then again, would you want to sit on a bus driven by Ralph Kramden? The unreality of television went well beyond women's roles. Media critic Edwin Diamond has pointed out that the "dese-and-dose" workingmen of *The Honeymooners* and its contemporary *The Life of Riley* (a comedy about an aircraft worker and his family) "were not the typical workers of the postwar era; they were figures from the thirties and early forties." At least conceding that working women on TV had "vague ties to reality," *Time* said:

> Two of the girls have glasses and sometimes wear them; none of them lives in the marble-bath mansions that Hollywood ordinarily assigns to its movie working girls, and Eve Arden's rooming house is pictured as a place where the plumbing seldom works and the phone bill is often unpaid.

Kramden was not intended to be realistic, nor was Kingfish Stevens, nor Annie Oakley. But viewers and the press paid attention to those characters, picking up messages both deliberate and unintended. Robin Morgan, having created a strong impression as Dagmar, saw the name take on a completely different connotation when it was attached to a bosomy late-night star of the fifties; Morgan said at the time "the name has lost a lot of warmth and sentiment it had before."

Gail Davis as Annie Oakley was a trailblazer, and a potential role model since Westerns in the early fifties were considered children's shows. *TV Guide* acknowledged in a profile of Davis that Oakley "is the first western heroine to be featured on TV . . . able to take care of most desperadoes without any help from the male sex." (Dale Evans, after all, could always count on Roy Rogers.) Still one can see the limits on where Oakley could lead her little charges. She wore fancy outfits with long skirts, even when she had to ride a horse; when she visited her sometime beau, deputy sheriff Lofty Craig, you know who made the coffee. Plus Lofty was there to handle the fistfights when he wasn't pining after Annie so quietly that *TV Guide* noted "the scripts give her little opportunity for romance."

Even cowgirls got that news: TV's women, working or not, better have a man or want one. Eve Arden's Connie Brooks was strong-willed about everything except her fellow teacher, Mr. Boynton; the producers of the show felt compelled to explain that Miss Brooks was not man-crazy, just Boynton-crazy. Daytime TV often preached the gospel of the ornamental woman. When NBC premiered *Home,* "the electronic magazine for women," in March 1954 its approach to "everything that interests women" began and ended with experts on "food, fashion, beauty, child care, family affairs, leisure activities, decorating, [and] gardening" ensconced in a set containing a "kitchen, workshop, garden, [and] fashion salon."

Reviewing the show in the *New York Times,* Jack Gould said, "Fundamental pioneering in the realm of women's daytime programming has not been especially evident thus far." A jaded viewer from the nineties might just be glad to find a daytime show that was not about women who sleep with neo-Nazis. And I would still argue that, whatever its shortcomings in the realm of women, television in the early fifties was a sight better than the images that lay ahead. I will concede Harriet Nelson (although *Ozzie and Harriet* experts will remind you that she had been a working woman, singing in husband Ozzie's band) and maybe Margaret Anderson on *Father Knows Best;* but the domestic fantasia about which so many people carp belongs more accurately in the late fifties—*Leave It to Beaver* premiered in 1957, Donna Reed in 1958. Annie Oakley had ridden into reruns in 1956.

Having made some concessions to television on women and minorities, we come to the place where no apologies will suffice: smoking. Just watching fifties TV is enough to cause a dry cough. Smoke rises through the air on interview shows. Stars smoke their sponsors' products in shows and commercials. Ed Murrow, the news icon of the era, is rarely without a cigarette on camera. And it was not as if they had not been warned.

Reports of the dangers of smoking had already circulated in the early fifties. In June 1954 the American Cancer Society had released a report on cigarettes and health. While it stopped short of saying cigarettes caused heart attacks and cancer, it did decide "regular cigaret smoking causes an increase in death rates."

The news was tough enough that in early '54 the Tobacco Industry Research Committee—an organization backed by the major cigarette companies—took out reassuring full-page advertisements in newspapers around the country, announcing plans to finance new research. It said in part:

> Recent reports on experiments with mice have given wide publicity to a theory that cigarette smoking is in some way linked with lung cancer in human beings. . . .
>
> We believe the products we make are not injurious to health.
>
> We always have and always will cooperate closely with those whose task it is to safeguard the public health.

> For more than 300 years tobacco has given solace, relaxation and enjoyment to mankind. At one time or another during those years critics have held it responsible for practically every disease of the human body. One by one these charges have been abandoned for lack of evidence.

That combination of a promise of responsibility and evasion of that same responsibility continues to mark the tobacco industry's reaction to complaints about its products. At congressional hearings in early 1994, tobacco company executives still could not admit a definite link between smoking and cancer. In the interim, the TV landscape had become cleaner; cigarette advertising on TV was banned by law in 1971. But in the fifties television was still benefiting from the smoky windfall. R. J. Reynolds alone spent more than $13 million a year on network TV advertising, more than it put into newspapers, magazine, and radio combined; it ranked third among network TV advertisers in 1953, behind only Procter & Gamble and Colgate-Palmolive.

Under the circumstances it is hardly surprising that TV for the most part preferred to await for more damning research into tobacco's effects; Max Wylie, an articulate defender of the TV industry in the early fifties, took that tack in his book *Clear Channels*. *See It Now*, already on shaky ground, did itself no good in becoming the first program to look closely at the cigarette-cancer link. Yet however effectively reported that telecast was, it was no match in propaganda terms for the glamorous Murrow standing, say, in a frozen Korean field, a smoke close by. "The cigarette in his own hand now seemed as much a part of him as the hand itself," wrote biographer Joseph E. Persico.

Murrow had at least publicly examined the issue. What defense could *Penny to a Million* make? Or "The Lucky Strike Program," better known as Jack Benny's show, which in one episode had Humphrey Bogart repeating the cigarette's jingle as part of a comedy sketch? (Bogart, and Murrow as well, would be felled by cancer.) When *Life* magazine reported on the dangers of cigarettes, its back cover was taken up by an ad for Lucky Strike, "toasted" to taste better.

So in considering the merits of television in 1954 I do not deny its drawbacks. An attempt to make an argument for any other year will also come to places where an opponent can declare, "Yeah, but. . . ."

The viewers of television in 1954 at times felt their viewing was too violent, too bland, too predictable, or too commercial; again, one can find such complaints about television in any year. The very framework of television in 1954 still provided a basis for better overall programming. So let's look at how that framework fit together.

HOW TELEVISION
WAS BETTER

• • • • • • • • • • •

The success of early television had to do with how it was made
and where it was made. Localness gave it a connection to communities that would fade in the coming years. The medium's center,
New York City, enabled it to have a cultural and ethnic foundation that
sagged as the audience stretched beyond large cities, and as production
control began to move to the moviemakers in Hollywood.

Television also worked within a system of content controls, both
explicit and implicit. Either way those who had to function under the
controls at times found them grating; at the same time, though, viewers
could take comfort that a set of strictly enforced standards prevented
television from stretching limits to the extent that makes contemporary
cries of protest so pervasive.

Finally, the people making television in the early fifties saw it not
as just another way of delivering movies or radio shows; they understood it was a unique medium for which new techniques had to blend
with the old reliables. While TV pioneers such as George Burns, Desi
Arnaz, and Jack Webb are better remembered for what viewers saw
them do, behind the scenes they tried out things that became standard
in the vocabulary of television. There was nothing dum-da-dum-dum
about how *Dragnet* made use of TV.

4

The New York Attitude

NEW YORK (CITY), the chief city of New
York State, commercial and financial
metropolis of the Western Hemisphere,
largest city in population in the United
States, and second largest (after London) in
the world.

Early 1950s encyclopedia entry

L ocalness in television, discussed in chapter 2, was not merely a
fact of video life. It was one of the medium's fundamental
strengths. Stations as well as networks took the lead in producing
all sorts of programs, creating a vast proving ground for the TV arts
and artists. Comedy writer Everett Greenbaum, whose many credits
include the classic *Andy Griffith Show,* acted on TV in Buffalo early
in his career. Rod Serling got his start writing television plays for a
station in Cincinnati. Lawrence Laurent, in the early fifties television
critic for the *Washington Post,* says the first documentary he saw about
water pollution was done by a local station.

The local production produced a bond between viewers and stations
that no longer exists in a substantive way. In late 1993 media critic
Ben Bagdikian said:

> Different voices have less of a chance of getting on television
> now than they did in '54. My impression is that there was
> greater chance for civic groups to get access to stations in
> their communities than today.

Community groups had more access because they had more programs in which to take part. Baby boomers who fondly remember sitting in the audience on local children's shows (many, like one called *Breadtime Stories,* sponsored by area bakers) have made a special, lifelong connection with their station. An aspiring dramatist who can try to write for a local program has a more realistic shot at testing his skills than one who must first journey to New York and join a crowded competitive field. Theater groups with access to performance shows prepare, and respond fondly to, a presentation that goes beyond a clip during the midday news.

A sizable amount of local non-news programming in the long run could have eased the burdens now placed on local newscasts. A station producing entertainment shows, which in turn need hosts and performers, has a reserve of personalities associated with the station; they can then take on assignments as parade marshals, dinner hosts, public speakers, and all-round emissaries for the station. Precious air time devoted to the display of baby pictures by the proud anchor parent, newsmen playing in charity Monopoly tournaments, midnewscast pleas to find homes for lost pets—all that stuff meant to connect a station's personalities with the audience could instead be done by a quiz-show host or variety star.

A local home show would provide a place for cooking and consumer tips now stuck into midday news shows. Local newscasts would accordingly have room for more fires and murders. Unfortunately, broadcasters for the most part went for the quick fix, using the political clout accompanying their vast audience to "whittle away at the public-interest requirements of the FCC," as Bagdikian put it. The viewing community, the stations and newscasts all suffered terrible long-term damage. A financial cost came due as well in the late eighties when local stations struggled to reestablish strong ties with an audience that made no distinction between network and cable shows; by then most stations had only their news operations and public-service announcements through which to reaffirm community ties.

While local television was a major component of TV in the fifties—and national programs originated in Los Angeles, Chicago, and Washington—TV had an unmistakable center of power and creativity in New York City. These days television resembles a set of feudal states: executives, soap operas, and David Letterman in New York; more executives and major studios in Hollywood (where *Seinfeld,* a series set in New York City, is taped); Ted Turner's imperial seat in Atlanta; other productions from studios in Florida; Vancouver, a low-cost home of action shows. With a camcorder and a satellite transmitter, just about anywhere can serve as a production facility. In the early fifties the most powerful people in television, both at the networks and the advertising agencies that provided them sustenance, worked in New York.

Although Hollywood was growing as a production center—and by the early seventies TV critic Robert Lewis Shayon would write of two TV power centers, New York and Hollywood—the movie industry's resistance to television was just coming to a formal end in 1954. Whether you were Pat Weaver, the son of a California roofing contractor on his way to becoming one of TV's great visionaries, or Steve Allen, starring on a network radio show in California before entering TV legend, the road to Oz headed East.

The preeminence of New York was evident in the resentment television producers elsewhere felt about TV's capital. When critic Robert Lewis Shayon examined Chicago's TV productions in 1950, he reported a litany of snarling comparisons to New York. One producer, calling the shows in New York "money-built," said Chicagoans "have to put our accent on quality, originality, ingenuity, cleverness, taste, low-cost production."

Television aside, though, New York was the most important, most glamorous, most adventurous place Americans had ever known. New York was the dominant city in the dominant sport of the era; the Cleveland Indians should have felt honored to lose the 1954 World Series to the New York Giants, since they were the only team not from New York to get into the series between 1951 and 1956. New York had glorious night life; Danny Thomas and Desi Arnaz, playing nightclub performers on TV, set their respective shows in New York.

Newspaper columnist Bob Considine described the life of his well-to-do children in New York in the late forties; while it included Central Park as a playground and a swimming hole only in faraway Westchester, there were also "the endless wonders of a great city," Considine said.

They know every inch of the tremendous stuffed whale in the American Museum of National History and are on speaking terms with a panda. . . . Their idea of a cozy neighborhood movie is the Radio City Music Hall. They've met Toots Shor and Joe DiMaggio in person, and secured the autograph of Gene Autry on the steam-heated lone pray-ree of Madison Square Garden. They live near the Metropolitan Museum of Art—by which, at the moment, they are mightily unimpressed—have breakfasted at the Stork Club after Mass at St. Patrick's Cathedral, and are charter members of the Howdy Doody Club.

Makes you want to sell the farm and catch the next train to the big city, doesn't it? And while we're there, let's not forget that it's the media capital of the nation, the home of top newspapers and many of the great columnists of the era. Harriet Van Horne, one of the major television critics of the fifties, determined as a young reporter in Greenwich, Connecticut, that she would "crash the big-city newspaper game." She did, at New York's *World-Telegram*. And in doing so, she joined the fray that was coverage of TV and radio.

In his novel *The Great Man,* Al Morgan described what the newspapers did when radio and TV star Herb Fuller died:

> The *Times* gave it two right-hand columns on page one. . . .
> The *Herald Tribune* put it in a three-column spread on the
> bottom of page one. The *Daily News* had a black headline
> and two pictures. The *Mirror* had the same two pictures and
> on page four they had the first of an eight-part bio of Fuller.

And more besides. But no one could confuse New York's fascination with broadcasting with sycophancy. Van Horne, Jack Gould, John Crosby, and other critics formed a demanding and sharp-tongued brigade. Many of them had cut their teeth on radio and knew the possibilities and perils that awaited TV. Their standards and expectations were high, just as they were in other big cities. The *Washington Post*'s Lawrence Laurent remembers his boss telling him in the early fifties "it was going to take 10 years to improve the [TV] taste of the community." He went on to speculate:

> Now, can you imagine how arrogant some callow television
> critic like me would have to be, thinking he was going to

improve the taste of the community? But I honestly believed it. And it accounts for much of what I wrote, too.

Laurent's rueful punchline: "I looked up 10 years later and *Beverly Hillbillies* was at the top of the ratings." Still, the critics pressed their case. Gould scourged what he saw as excessive commercialism, devoting one memorable column to a list of product plugs heard during telecasts of the New York Easter parade. He also watched closely how TV covered itself; when the New York welfare department went after the CBS game show *Strike It Rich* (see chapter 10), Gould pointed out that it took thirty-six hours for the network to include the story in a newscast. "There is nothing quite like aging a news bulletin to bring out its increased flavor," he wrote.

Crosby is fondly remembered for his wit, strong enough to merit inclusion in Bennett Cerf's *Encyclopedia of Modern American Humor;* in complaining about the problem of finding something new to say about longtime performers, he wrote, "Radio entertainers never retire and there are grounds for suspicion that they never die." But he too had a sharp eye and ear, wondering if man-in-the-street questions hurled at Governor Thomas E. Dewey during a campaign telecast were rigged—as they turned out to be.

And Van Horne was no less tough than her male colleagues, practicing a singular elegant brand of butchery. "Are we a nation of morons?" she asked in one column.

> Do we all have mean little souls, beguiled by bloodshed, bored by beauty? To judge by the entertainment set before us these evenings, the television industry gives a strong affirmative reply.

The columnists were not without flaws. Gould once claimed a Reginald Rose–written production was inaccurate. Rose accordingly wrote to Gould that the details of his drama were correct. Gould wrote back: "Dear Reginald Rose, you may be right." "And that," Rose said, "was the last good review I got from Jack Gould."

John Crosby, meanwhile, got the comeuppance any critic should be wise enough to avoid when he agreed to host a TV series, *The Seven Lively Arts,* in the late fifties. John Houseman, who produced the Sunday afternoon series, acknowledged that Crosby as TV host was "ethically dubious" (particularly for a critic who by other accounts shunned publicists and the like, "refusing to be influenced by anything but what he heard on the air waves"); the problem, though, was that the bespectacled Crosby chose not to wear his glasses (or an uncomfortable set of contact lenses) on the air, then forgot his carefully memorized lines. The pause before the production recovered "added up to eighteen and a half seconds," Houseman wrote. "It seemed like six months. And it made TV history."

But make no mistake: Crosby was a gifted writer and critic. And the carefully thought out criticism from the columnists already mentioned pales next to the invective hurled by Jack O'Brian of the *Herald American*. An avid Red baiter, O'Brian repeatedly tore into CBS newscaster Don Hollenbeck after the latter said he agreed with Edward R. Murrow's televised criticism of Senator Joseph McCarthy. The attacks by O'Brian (who also called Murrow "Egghead R. Murrow") added to a host of personal problems that led to Hollenbeck's suicide. Nor did O'Brian stop at the grave, claiming then that "Hollenbeck was typical of CBS newsmen. He hewed to its incipient pink line without deviation."

Vitriol aside, the enduring contributions of the New York critics were a hard-to-beat literary standard, and regular reflections on how television could be better. Crosby admitted that being positive was sometimes difficult; his rave review of the television opera *Amahl and the Night Visitors* "took hours. My admiration for this work was so boundless that it struck me dumb." But praise had impact. TV director Kirk Browning still remembers the excitement when the *Times* put its review of *Amahl* on the front page. Paddy Chayefsky, long after he had achieved success, exulted that Jack Gould "gave his entire column" to a review of Chayefsky's play *Marty*. (Gould's review, while positive, actually shared column space with a second, brief item.)

The press coverage therefore added to the sense of how New York fit Steve Allen's description as "the hub of television." While Allen said he could have done the *Tonight* show anywhere since his personality was always the same, New York offered a range of guests.

> You had all the nightclub people who were available, you had all the Broadway people who were available. You had a lot of jazz people who were available, you had a lot of pop singers who worked out of New York.

The hottest stars could find themselves in the middle of battles between shows, and not just because they competed for talent. When Arthur Godfrey fired singer Julius LaRosa, Ed Sullivan—who worked for the same network as Godfrey—signed LaRosa for a series of appearances on *Toast of the Town,* thus benefiting from the very publicity that was killing his rival Godfrey. But then Sullivan, an old-time newspaper columnist, just indulged in what an associate called "newshawk opportunism." In bringing a newspaperman's sensibility to television, Sullivan hit one of the keynotes of people working in television in the early fifties; instead of having spent whole careers in TV, they had worked in other fields, studied other media, and developed frames of reference that extended far beyond the four corners of a television screen.

For example, when Everett Greenbaum talked about the making of the sitcom *Mr. Peepers,* he made comparisons not to other sitcoms (which he generally did not like) but to the films of French writer-director Marcel Pagnol. Even more interesting, Pagnol took his inspiration from the stage—film historian Ephraim Katz said Pagnol's films were "essentially photographed theater"—much as the fifties television dramatists did. Although the writers of the classic dramas battled restraints of time, technology, and commercial interruption—creating a production uniquely different from stagecraft—Erik Barnouw has written that "from the start, artists from the theater were active in the anthology series."

That happened for two reasons. First, although established stage and movie talent often looked down on television, the younger medium offered the promise of serious work for an important audience. The television audience of the forties and early fifties basically broke into two groups: the masses that sought out Milton Berle and flocked to saloons to see boxing; and well-heeled viewers who could afford a television in the home and whose taste was thought to be elevated.

Delbert Mann, a TV and later movie director who had done the honors on Chayefsky's *Marty,* called the latter viewers

> an audience that is theater literate, that is book literate, that is perhaps a little higher on the economic ladder, who are more sophisticated in most every way.

They were, in other words, New Yorkers. Hollywood did not compare. A Western critic looking back at a fifties theater season lamented, "We can't escape the fact that our year is often dressed in hand-me-downs from earlier Broadway seasons."

More fundamentally, television kept the stagestruck from starving. TV playwright and eventual Pulitzer Prize winner (for *All the Way Home*) Tad Mosel said of his TV work, "I simply wanted to make a living and have enough time to write for the stage." A 1954 magazine article alluded to the acclaimed Chayefsky "having his plays announced as 'under option' more than any other unproduced (stage) playwright."

TV needed writers. Mann recalled how *Philco-Goodyear Playhouse,* for which he worked, began in the late forties with adaptations of stage plays but good ones "proved to be few and far between," he lamented.

> Then they shifted to novels as a source of material. They proved to be slim pickings because most of the good ones were picked off by Hollywood.

David Shaw, a TV dramatist for *Philco* and its major rival *Studio One,* said his first TV jobs were "writing adaptations of bad books." And a comedy he wrote for *Gulf Playhouse* in the fifties underscored the trials of getting established talent into television. The show has Jessie Royce Landis as a stage actress so determined to revive her career, "she'd even consider a television show." Using a live TV drama as a springboard, she still calls it "degrading myself" until the telephoned congratulations roll in after the show. "I had no idea how many people looked at television," she coos, and her career is back on track—to another Broadway show.

"Sort of by default," Mann said, "we came into the period of depending on original material, which undoubtedly was the source of people's golden memories of what is now called the Golden Age of Television." By 1954, the biggest stars of the Golden Age dramas were not so much the actors moving from show to show, or the producers and directors making things work, but the writers who got their names on the screen on a regular basis. The announcement in 1954 of a series called *Playwrights '54* got considerable press attention, including a *Life* feature on the "bright galaxy of playwrights"—Shaw, Chayefsky,

Mosel, Richard Nash, Robert Alan Aurthur, and "most famous and experienced of the group," Horton Foote, in more recent years acclaimed for writing the films *Tender Mercies* and *The Trip to Bountiful* (which was a TV play in the fifties).

Success was relative, of course, with the writers not making a lot of money (and *Playwrights '54* falling apart when NBC refused to come up with a hoped-for $25,000 to finance it). Reginald Rose remembers "the first dozen plays I wrote and sold, I did at night and on weekends because I was working at an ad agency as copywriter and I simply couldn't afford to quit." He did only after his agent got him the first contract given an anthology writer, guaranteeing him payment for at least six plays (from a promised twelve outlines) a year.

That, along with the ambition and ego of the writers (as well as their producers and directors), made for intense competition. Shaw offered an example.

> Paddy [Chayefsky] was the first one who wrote a movie, called *The Goddess*. And Bob [Aurthur] went to a screening. I saw him and I said, "How was it, Bob?" And he said, "It was so good, I had a headache for three days."

Philco producer Fred Coe "would make fun of me because I also used to work for *Studio One*," Shaw said. "He'd see me coming and start humming the *Studio One* theme. But it was all in good fun."

Actors as well satisfied their need for money and attention with television work. Paul Newman and James Dean both worked in TV in the early fifties. Eva Marie Saint, a stage and movie actress who returns often to television, was "televiewers' favorite actress" according to one fifties critic; Saint herself also remembers less glorious times playing a cheerleader in a sneaker commercial. Older actors, their stage or movie careers stalled, turned to TV, too. Pat O'Brien, after movie roles dating back to the twenties, gave numerous TV performances in the early fifties.

Having actors and other participants in TV come from other frames of reference (stage, radio, movies) gave television a freshness that would be hard to duplicate in the more insular industry to come. By the nineties TV found itself reaching beyond its walls for new ideas and voices—to Oliver Stone for *Wild Palms* or David Lynch for *Twin*

Peaks, to stand-up comedians with road-polished styles and characters (Tim Allen, Jerry Seinfeld, Brett Butler).

As vital as the New York theatrical foundation was to television, the merits of TV drama as a whole can be overstated. "Many of these early New York TV plays were formula dramas," TV critic Martin Williams has said.

> In play after play we are confronted with character A charac-
> ter who has a problem, usually has an unconscious problem.
> Perhaps the author thought of the problem as a flaw—dra-
> matic if not tragic—but sometimes it seems little more than
> a bad habit.

Scanning the array of fifties dramas, two hundred of them in a week, *Time* critic Robert McLaughlin said, "The majority of these shows— whether live or filmed, whether made in Hollywood or Manhattan— are dreadful." And whatever was good had a short life; the end of the era of New York drama is marked variously by historians but was definitely over by the sixties. Mid-decade New York theater critic Howard Taubman complained the possibility of television as a home for fine drama had gone unrealized.

> Drama on the airways became hopelessly stereotyped. Writ-
> ers with a shred of talent were pulverized into mediocrity,
> required to grind out mechanized situation comedy, soggy
> mysteries, private-eye serials and westerns. It is true that tele-
> vision gave . . . the hungry children of theater a chance to
> eat, but its lavish salaries and fees exacted a costly toll, for
> the medium rubbed out individuality, standardized impulses
> to freshness and disarmed and crushed the creative spirit.

Another argument, made by historian Frank Sturcken, is that the promotion of dramas as quality entertainment was a fatal blow in a medium bent on selling escapism (a variation on the theory that a child will never eat broccoli once he's told it is good for him). Sturcken argues that another strength, the liveness and spontaneity of TV dis- cussed in more detail in chapter 5, should have been emphasized in- stead. Martin Williams, on the other hand, described a basic flaw in the fundament of television drama in a 1967 essay.

The outlooks and attitudes of these young TV playwrights, the style and purport of their dramas, were by and large those of the New York stage of the time. The TV critics of the time were largely committed to those same attitudes and those same modes of drama, and the majority of set owners at the time were northeast and urban. The plays could not, I think, long interest and hold a mass audience of the kind TV has today.

So the very thing that many people thought made drama good, its New York-ness, may have worked against it as television reached outside the big cities. I don't entirely buy that theory, for reasons I'll get to in a bit. Still, one can find evidence not only in TV drama but in comedy that a New York state of mind did not always translate into success.

Some comedians have musical counterparts. Eddie Murphy at his peak took on all the attributes of a rock star, and still takes occasional tries at a singing career. In the fifties, three of the more inventive laughmakers—Sid Caesar, Steve Allen, and Ernie Kovacs—were comedic jazzmen. They riffed on the medium, they bebopped around and through the already firm conventions governing much of television. You never knew where the camera would end up with those guys, what adventure awaited in the next scene.

Where jazz played fine in the cities, it did less well out in places where Patti Page, not Dizzy Gillespie, was the norm. Still Allen flourished as TV expanded, Kovacs had an erratic career, and Caesar's TV ratings slid downhill even though, in the view of many, the quality of his work was undiminished. The explanation for their different outcomes lay largely in that evanescent television quality of likability. Kovacs's approach to television as a wonderful toy included a certain personal detachment from a medium where personality proved supreme; I also suspect his looks, recalling a mortgage-toting Snidely Whiplash come for Little Nell, worked against him. Allen, in contrast, could innovate as Kovacs did but with a personal style that warmed the audience. Allen's roots in radio—and the example of Arthur Godfrey—showed that audiences would be open to all sorts of outrageous behavior once they liked and trusted the transgressor.

Allen, for that matter, came to New York from California, where other comics trained in radio and the movies—among them George

Burns, Jack Benny, and Lucille Ball—brought to television an aware-ness of how to play to a mass audience, and the importance of a gentle brand of humor to career longevity. Groucho Marx as well, though a verbal anarchist onstage and in movies, projected a far kindlier manner on TV, the hard edges of his persona smoothed, the restless physicality contained by a desk.

Caesar, though, like New York comics such as Milton Berle, Jackie Gleason, and Martin and Lewis, engaged in aggressive physical—and personal—slapstick where no one was safe from either the slap or the stick. It was hardball comedy, derived from a theatrical tradition in which—as avid comedy student Allen has said—the straight man used "assorted slaps in the face, yanks on the necktie or jacket, and shoves." That's not to say California comedy was passive, not while Lucy was around. The guiding premise of her show was "What does Lucy want this week?"—and the pursuit of same. But that pursuit took a course where the outcome was not the physical pain people inflicted in New York comedy, but either a battle that was woman-against-machine or a personal confrontation whose culmination was more embarrassment than abrasion.

Part of this, of course, has to do with the differences between sketch comedy and situation comedy; you can break Sid Caesar's arm in one sketch if he plays a different character two minutes later, a luxury a sitcom did not have. And the fans of Caesar's brand of comedy, such as Ted Sennett, have argued that the battling couple the Hickenloopers, from Caesar's *Your Show of Shows,* are truer to life and funnier than the Ricardos or the Kramdens.

But television audiences, especially in the genteel suburbs of Eisen-hower America, do not always want truth; ample doses of that are administered every day. Those viewers want something unlike their lives. They want something that promises consistency of style and reassurance in tone. They want desperately to like people if they are going to spend time with them; irascible alcoholic detective Andy Si-powicz on *NYPD Blue* became a cult hero because the show's writers, and actor Dennis Franz, made people like the guy. Dabney Coleman has trouble keeping series about nasty people on the air because his acting prowess will not let a little warmth slip into a character who, based on the available evidence, has none. *All in the Family,* as close to a throwback to fifties New York comedy as the seventies produced, was careful to lighten Archie Bunker's nasty side with a reserve of sentimentality and other, warmer characters.

The unapologetically New York comics such as Caesar and Berle, whatever their ultimate reputations, accordingly hit a tough patch as television grew. But two other elements, neither controllable by the people making shows, both alluded to in Martin Williams's comment about TV drama, added to the difficulties of a New York TV culture.

One was the critics. When *Your Show of Shows* neared its end in 1954, Jack Gould wrote that the show "simply had run its course." He pointed out:

> Millions of persons now know "Your Show of Shows" backward and forward. Within its framework there is hardly anything that Mr. Caesar and Miss Coca can do that seems fresh and bright. It is not a case of a viewer not liking the show; he has just seen it before, not once but many times.

For a New York television critic the perception was indisputable. For someone with access to one of the 3 million TV sets in the United States when the series started, that may also have been the case. But for the millions of viewers who had bought their sets in the ensuing years—for the people, say, in Miami who had not seen the series live before 1954—*Your Show of Shows* was far fresher and newer. For them, had NBC decided to continue *Your Show of Shows* rather than divide its brain trust like Gaul, the series might have had a longer life than critical eyes imagined.

Now, the critics of the day had no choice but to write from their experience. Modern critics face a comparable quandary when they embrace and nurture a new series—for instance *Seinfeld*—long before the larger audience discovers it. The critic, having seen every episode from the beginning, approaches later shows from a different viewpoint than fans who come in later. In the early fifties, though, shows that depended on the kindness not only of audiences but network executives and sponsors were faced with the quandary of being treated as old hat by critics read daily by the very people who decided the shows' fate—before the rest of the country had seen them at all. And regional critics, busy reviewing the new shows coming down the pike, might not pause to consider a show that had been around for four years.

The other, and even more serious, drawback to New York centrism is the very elitist attitude that fueled drama and cultural programs in the early years. The same wisdom that tells New Yorkers they are sharp and sophisticated tells them that no one outside New York could possibly be the same. They look at the declining ratings for cultural shows as television moved outside the big cities as vindication. They do not see the self-fulfilling prophecy at work.

Fred Rogers tells the story of how *The Children's Corner,* a children's series developed for fledgling educational television station WQED in Pittsburgh, got a chance at commercial network broadcasting. When Paul Winchell went on vacation, *Children's Corner* was asked to fill the slot temporarily. Despite the grueling schedule of five live shows in Pittsburgh during the week, then traveling to New York for a sixth on commercial TV on Saturday mornings, Rogers and host Josie Carey agreed. The show did wonderfully, thousands of letters poured in, but when renewal time came, a New York executive said, "My daughter loves your program. And what that says to me is that it can't be a program for the masses."

Take it from someone who has spent a lot of years talking to viewers: They are not slobbering fools looking for the most mindless program available. They will at times opt for certain brands of entertainment over others, but they also like to take nourishment from their viewing. Frank Sturcken supports his don't-call-it-quality argument with a comparison of ratings for a production of *Romeo and Juliet* and the likes of Arthur Godfrey and *I Love Lucy* opposite. He further quotes Gould's contention that no one should expect Shakespeare to do well against that competition. But there's a next step to be taken: if you really want people to watch Shakespeare, you don't put it against Lucy. And if you want people to see good television, you don't assume like that New York executive that the war is lost before it's begun.

Elitism notwithstanding, some of the people approaching television saw great possibilities not merely to entertain or enlighten but to do so in ways uniquely suited to the new medium. We've touched on some of that already. But the idea of making television *as* television merits more detail.

5

·····

Making TV Unique

TV is the thing this year.
Dinah Washington song, 1953

In the nineties, movies and television—especially when the latter includes pay-cable channels—at times seem interchangeable. Some telecasts embrace the letter-box format that replicates how classic films looked on the big screen. Major television movies in the U.S. end up resold as theatrical releases overseas, or competing for shelf space at Blockbuster Video. "Direct to video" movies have become common. And the big-screen business regularly mines TV for ideas such as *Star Trek, The Fugitive, The Addams Family, Beverly Hillbillies,* and *The Flintstones.*

Some similar crossovers had occurred in the early fifties. *Marty,* a TV drama in 1953, was expanded and recast for movie production in 1954, the same year that a movie version of *Dragnet* hit theaters. The Hollywood studios' public resistance of television was over by 1955, although the sense of relative status—that movies were somehow more important than television—continues in some circles to this day. And on TV's side, the people working in the medium had a strong sense of their own uniqueness—that neither radio nor movies nor theater did exactly what TV did.

The programs that best understood the notion of television *as* television, where old rules did not apply, are among the most enduring and influential. Desi Arnaz oversaw development of a multiple-camera system for filmed programs that is still in use today. George Burns understood that radio comedy, his former specialty, would not work on TV and made adjustments such as breaking the fourth wall between viewer and performer; George Gobel and Garry Shandling are among the comics who took advantage of Burns's breakthrough. And, as has been discussed, Arthur Godfrey saw the overriding importance of likability for television performers, creating a need for what one magazine called "the charm boys."

Another influential idea in television, which dates to its beginnings, is that viewers respond best to live programs—to seeing things as they happen. Shortly after the first demonstration of television transmission to homes in 1928, an editorial writer speculated:

> Instead of depending upon Mr. McNamee's vivid description of a football game, radio listeners may now actually see a game a thousand miles away. The spellbinders in the Democratic national convention holding a session for two weeks may now be witnessed waving their arms at the milling audience. The convention itself may be seen without leaving the comfortable chair in your library.

In sum, the most dramatic possibility in television lay in its immediacy. Richard Hubbell, an early veteran of television production, reached a similar conclusion in his 1945 book *Television Programming and Production.*

> Film can be transmitted over television, just as easily as a "live" program. But, although motion pictures can provide a permanent record for television, they cannot transmit television in its true sense—cannot retain its speed of communication, its immediacy.

Television carried live programs from the beginning, and what came to be known as "event programming" sustained the medium. In 1948, for instance, a New York hotel sold out its TV-equipped rooms on the night of a televised heavyweight boxing match, and received reservations for those rooms on World Series days three months before the actual games. In 1950, critic Gilbert Seldes called sports "ideal material for television . . . giving it a chance to do what no other medium can do; in sports, television transmits instantaneously and completely an actual event the outcome of which cannot be foretold."

When television ventures away from film and videotape into live programming, it is as if Seldes's dictum was tattooed on every producer's forehead. Sports, award shows, natural disasters—in none of these cases can the outcome be foretold. PBS's *Live from Lincoln Center* continues to eschew videotape because, says director Kirk Browning, "My producer feels there is a psychological factor that makes all the difference in the world in how the audience perceives it." *Saturday Night Live* also offers viewers a measure of risk taking, at least on the East Coast; several times excesses that went out to sleepy viewers in the East were deleted from the videotape shown in the West.

Even with some videotaped events, such as CBS's prime-time presentation of the 1994 Winter Olympics, telecasts have been structured as if the competition was live. Although viewers could have known the winners and losers for hours, the telecasts followed a dramatic arc that climaxed with the unveiling of those same results in the last half-hour of a night's coverage.

By 1954, about a third of sponsored network shows were done on film, including major hits such as *I Love Lucy* and *Dragnet*. But live TV was still seen as a strength in many circles. As with the fifties process of watching TV—sitting in front of a single, large set—live programming created a special bond between the viewer and the program. Comics like Martin and Lewis were draws on television because viewers did not know what the twosome might do next. *Today* and *Tonight* seemed more immediate because they were live. Ed Sullivan's show was virtually seat-of-the-pants production on camera and off. TV director Kenneth Whelan (author of the wonderfully titled memoir *How the Golden Age of Television Turned My Hair to Silver*) said that Sullivan himself would still be making changes in the show minutes before air time. Sullivan producer Marlo Lewis wrote that because of Sullivan's search for the hottest material, "Ed was constantly booking acts with little regard for the rehearsal and necessary technical preparations. . . . Other shows took four to six weeks to get ready. We never had that luxury."

That created a sense of anticipation in the audience, including reviewers. They had to watch live shows, finish columns as the programs ended, hand them to couriers (if the columnist was lucky enough to work at home) or copy boys, then see their thoughts in print the next day. As Reginald Rose said, "Live television shows were reviewed just the way they reviewed theater."

But live TV was also very difficult to do, with no chance to eliminate mistakes. Producer Hal Roach, Jr., a booster of filmed productions, said at the time, "Who wants to see a stagehand in the wrong place, or hear an actor muff his lines? That's what spontaneity means."

"When we look back on those shows, we are kind of in a dream world about them," said director Delbert Mann.

> When you go back and look at the kinescopes, the physical quality of the production was shabby. Just awful. The lighting and the mistakes that were made—the cameras in shots, and the boom shadows and actors forgetting lines and Lord knows what.

Even so, like many Golden Age survivors, Mann saw a specialness in live TV that prompted audiences to forgive the errors. "The audience was kind of participating in it because it was live, the same way you do with a football game today, when you don't know when the next event is going to be."

The goofs became a shared experience as memorable as the quality of productions. Did you see the horse relieve itself while Frankie Laine sang "I Believe"? Did you see Westinghouse spokeswoman Betty Furness struggled with a stuck refrigerator door? "I have a hundred stories," said writer Del Reisman.

> Dick Powell's celebrated show, live, where a guy was shot dead, and got up and walked away while the camera was on him. . . . Philip Reed, a Hollywood leading man, had never been in live television before and was fascinated by the mechanics of it. He was watching a monitor, and the actors realized he wasn't there.

Whelan gave horse players "one terrible Saturday morning in 1954" when he was pressed into service on a live telecast of a race. As they neared the finish, the six horses had bunched into two groups of three. Seeing one camera had a tight shot of three horses, Whelan put it on the air until they crossed the finish line. Unfortunately for Whelan, it was a shot of the three horses that lost the race.

In his book *Which Reminds Me* actor Tony Randall recalls how David Niven tried to relax everyone before a telecast of *Playhouse 90;* Niven introduced the show in his shirt and tie but—since the camera showed him only from the waist up—without his trousers. After completing the introduction, Niven hurried to his dressing room only to find he had locked himself out. After that, Niven told Randall "if [Randall] ever saw [Niven] on live TV it would be safe for [Randall] to assume [Niven] was in terrible trouble financially."

While such stories abound, and can still amuse, they're the TV equivalent of Yogi Berra's malaprops; just as strange expressions have obscured Berra's standing as a great catcher, blooper stories overlook the tremendous ingenuity going into the making of television—often under tremendous pressure. One actors' guide from the early fifties warns that TV's requirements "are more stringent than in most fields," and went on to explain:

> It combines movement of the stage, camera work of the screen and the intimate technique of delivery used in radio. What's more, all this is called for without the length of rehearsal time of theater, the interrupted sequences of film work or the static concentration of radio.... For an actor this means fast study, few rehearsals, infinite hours of sitting around, the strain of camera-day, the restriction of movement, the annoyance of bright lighting and the feeling of being "on the spot" every moment of air time.

Naturally, stage training helped deal with the pressures of television. But television still was not the stage, as writers who had been working in TV since the forties were well aware. "You can't on television have two people sitting at a desk and talking forever," said David Shaw. "You've got to move it around."

The intimate dramas of the period, sometimes called the "kitchen sink" dramas because of their domestic settings and intimate stories, were at least partly a result of the technical limitations of TV. The small screen (and even the 21-inch screen of the midfifties looked small to people used to theatrical movies) taught producers, as Hubbell wrote, "The most effective shots of early television have all been close-ups."

But television used the available technology to the fullest possible extent. Images from two cameras were superimposed for dramatic effect. The musical special *Follies of Suzy* had picture-in-picture scenes—the inset a man at his typewriter, the larger screen filled with the performance of his script.

Such techniques spread. In 1952 Robert Wade wrote *Design for TV,* a book just for TV artists and art directors. And Wade acknowledged:

> There are many good books about television. Hundreds for the engineer, scores for the producer and director, dozens for the production supervisor and special effects expert, and not a few for the layman.

Collections such as the Best Television Plays of the Year series, begun in 1950, included not only scripts but schematics of sets and photographs from productions. A local station could accordingly see how *Studio One* managed in 1949 to do a play about the German battleship *Bismarck,* from the opening words in a radio report by Douglas Edwards to a voice sobbing "Oh God! God! God!" as the ship sank. In television, as director Thomas Hutchinson said in 1946, the only answer to the question "Will this be good on television?" was "Try it and see."

One vivid (and in this case, filmed) example of TV's ingenuity came on *Omnibus* when Leonard Bernstein gave a talk on how Beethoven wrote his Fifth Symphony. To demonstrate the orchestral selection process—the introduction and removal of various instruments from the piece—the studio floor was turned into a music sheet, with the staffs for different instruments (flute, oboe, clarinet, and so on) named on the floor. Musicians in each section would then walk onto the music when they were included in a section, step back when they were not. To be sure, the presentation was helped by Bernstein's irreverent monologue ("We already know the opening bars of the symphony, almost too well, I should say"). But the creative team on *Omnibus* found a way, without benefit of computers or color graphics, of illustrating Bernstein's ideas in a memorable fashion.

Even the massive undertaking of a live, televised opera was not beyond the imagination of TV's makers. Kirk Browning, who began working on NBC's opera telecasts in 1948 and started directing them in 1950, said many years later that early televised operas "were pretty much done with a box set like you have in a theater . . . and the cameras just looking in." *NBC Television Opera Theatre*, in deliberate contrast, was conceived and developed specifically as a TV production.

"Realizing there was no opera tradition in the United States . . . we did versions of opera that were as close to music theater as you could get," Browning said. Productions were sung in English, starting with Kurt Weill's folk opera *Down in the Valley*, "a very clever way to begin because it was an American subject, American folklore, and it was Kurt Weill, not someone who is going to put you off." And instead of seeking top-shelf opera stars—who in Browning's view would not have wanted to spend the time needed to learn an English translation for TV—productions drew on people from the musical theater. A March 1954 production of Vittorio Giannini's *Taming of the Shrew* included John Raitt, then well known as star of the musical *The Pajama Game*.

The logistical problems of mounting an opera were difficult but not insurmountable, Browning said.

> We isolated the orchestra in a satellite studio. This sounds simple but in fact when you separate the orchestra it means two things. The orchestra doesn't hear the singers because they can't have the leak of the singers piped in (to the audio mix). So they're totally dependent on the conductor. But the conductor doesn't see the singers. He is looking at my television output on a monitor, wearing a headset. . . . In turn the singers are hearing the orchestra piped in through a little mike at a level so low that it won't leak into their mikes. So you have this extremely hostile environment in which no one is really joined up in the happiest fashion with the rest of the elements. But this is what we began to do, and in all the years we did it we never had a breakdown.

Opera Theatre was also fortunate in that its producer was Samuel Chotzinoff, formerly a music critic and piano accompanist to violinist Jascha Heifetz (whose sister Chotzinoff married), and a major contributor to cultural broadcasting. In 1936 Chotzinoff persuaded conductor Arturo Toscanini to come out of retirement in Italy and conduct the NBC Symphony. Fifteen years later Chotzinoff commissioned Gian-Carlo Menotti's *Amahl and the Night Visitors,* the landmark television opera. Most important, though, "Shotzi" was a close friend of David Sarnoff, chairman of the board of RCA, NBC's owner.

"I can't tell you what a posh situation I had," Browning said with a laugh. "Anything I asked for, I got. If I wanted ten cameras and two studios and a set built on four levels, I got it." Such lavishness put to shame another production, the Du Mont network's series *Opera Cameos,* where musical selections were performed with what looked like the same curtain and vase in every scene.

Whatever the network politics involved, *Opera Theatre* shows how the people making live TV in the early fifties overcame serious technical challenges in inventive ways. But it was not only in moments of high seriousness that innovation came to television. Comics coming out of radio were quick to figure out that TV presented different challenges and possibilities. When Ernie Kovacs began hosting a morning TV show in 1950, "it was inevitable that he would start to exploit the visual and aural possibilities," says Kovacs biographer Diana Rico.

> He began straying from the expected by drawing cartoons or twitching his features in sync with the records (or, sometimes, out of sync with them), then by ad-libbing to goofy props that crew members tossed to him from offstage.

Kovacs's visual approach to television still draws raves from other comics and continues sales of a home-video collection of his work. "I think he played with the medium . . . more than anybody on television at the time," Chevy Chase said. "That had a great effect on me."

Steve Allen, also a Kovacs fan, brought his own brand of inventiveness to a series of television shows including his historic, original version of the *Tonight* show. One of the most popular *Tonight* bits, called "Crazy Shots," began as an alternative to the standard images of Allen playing the piano.

> Dwight [Hemion, the director] took pictures so incongruous they were automatically funny. One was a very tight close-up of my left eye, another a shot of my right ear. . . . A stage-left camera moved up close behind me and wandered

aimlessly around the plaid pattern of the sports jacket I was wearing.

Over time the routines became even more absurd, to Allen's delight. No wonder he has praised not only Kovacs but Jim Hawthorne, a Los Angeles TV personality of the late forties, because "both men specialized in fresh, inventive sight gags and camera tricks rather than simply doing radio comedy on TV." When Allen prepared to leave *Tonight* in 1957, Kovacs was one of the people he recommended to succeed him.

Making the transition from other performing venues to TV was tough for many comedians. "We all have a great problem—Benny, Hope, all of us," radio legend Fred Allen told critic John Crosby in 1949. "We don't know how to duplicate our success in radio," he went on.

> We found out how to cope with radio and after seventeen years, you know pretty well what effect you're achieving. But those things won't work in television. Jack Benny's sound effects, Fibber's closet—they won't be funny on television. We don't know what will be funny or even whether our looks are acceptable.

Life magazine echoed Allen's concern in a 1950 examination of older comics (among them Allen himself, Jimmy Durante, Eddie Cantor, Bobby Clark, and Ed Wynn) who were being showcased on two new NBC variety series. "Some comics, like Clark, have dipped too often into old gag bags," the magazine said; "some, like Fred Allen, were uneasy with the new medium. Wynn, who graced *Life*'s cover and who had done TV before, "profits most. . . . With his cockeyed suits, mad millinery and incredible inventions, Wynn must be seen to be fully appreciated."

Fred Allen's troubles with television are especially disturbing, given the high regard in which his astringent humor and his cast of radio characters was held. "It's a little ironical, and certainly doesn't speak well for the television racket, when its only first-class mind is now looking for a sponsor," Groucho Marx wrote to Allen in 1954. "Satiric and fearless and cerebral," as one colleague described Allen, he struggled in TV—and even against more mass-appeal entertainment on radio—in part because he was not likable.

"He didn't want you to love him," Henry Morgan, a comic who like Allen had his share of battles with broadcast brass, said on *Camera Three* after Allen's death in 1956. "He didn't much care what you thought about him personally."

That attitude could prove fatal in a medium built on personal charm. But others take issue with that view of Allen, suggesting the problem was not his style as much as it was finding a format. Consider the mess that was *Judge for Yourself,* which Allen hosted. A combination quiz show and talent showcase, it required Allen to share the stage with performers, three professional judges, and three judges chosen from the studio audience. Groucho's tough assessment:

> The chief trouble with it is the fact that there isn't enough of Fred Allen. . . . If you are going to have a Fred Allen show, you had better have Fred Allen.

Judge for Yourself made some changes before ending its brief TV life and Pat Weaver, the head of programming at NBC, lamented that Allen "was never allowed to settle in one format in which he could feel at home." He has said more than once that Allen might have found his niche as host of the *Tonight* show; Weaver said the only hosts he considered for the show were the two Allens, Fred and Steve. Fred, Weaver said in his memoirs, "was too big for the job." Allen's uncertain health was also a problem, especially in stamina-straining television; when it came time to replace Steve Allen, Fred Allen had passed away.

Sadly, because he did not create a body of television work to be repeated every time a network needs a sweeps retrospective, Allen has not endured in public memory the way contemporaries who made the transition to TV did. But neither was he alone in his struggle to change media. *Fibber McGee and Molly,* the radio show with the famously overstuffed closet, did not even become a television series until 1959, after its long radio run was over; it lasted only a season. *Duffy's Tavern,* which made a stab at TV in 1954 after a decade on radio, did not last either.

And some of those who made the transition did so reluctantly. Jack Benny made clear his heart belonged to radio, where he came to audiences "gently—quietly, through their ears. I suggested subtle images to them, picture jokes." Television to Benny presented "magnification combined with intimacy" that would make any comic seem stale after a while. Which makes the case of Benny's friend George Burns all the more interesting.

While he felt some reluctance about moving from radio to television, Burns also realized that the TV required a different kind of act than the one Burns and Allen had used onstage and in radio and movies. Burns had laid virtually all the credit for his success to his wife Gracie; his memoir of her begins with the heart-rending, "For forty years my act consisted of one joke. And then she died." But a close reading of Burns reveals that the guy standing next to Gracie was a thoughtful tactician alertly fine-tuning their act; producer George Schlatter remembers well how, working on one of his first television shows in the fifties, a guest named George Burns repeatedly gave him *sotto voce* suggestions to improve the program.

In the forties, when their radio ratings began to slip, Burns searched for an explanation. He concluded that the act—which assumed both Burns and Allen were single—was no longer convincing to an audience that knew the couple was both married and in their forties. Burns simply went on the air, announced that they were now married on the show as well, and saw the ratings rebound.

When it came to television, Burns later wrote, he decided they should not play characters as they had in movies but simply be a televised George Burns and Gracie Allen, two married performers at home. Burns then added the wrinkle that set the show apart—stepping out of the action to address the audience, then rejoining the story. Other comics had done that onstage and in the movies, and Burns himself said he stole the idea from Thornton Wilder's *Our Town*. Still, Burns added,

> nothing like it had ever been done on television before. Of course, television was so new that if an actor burped, everyone agreed it was an innovative concept and nothing like it had ever been done on television before.

Burns likes to underplay his importance, but let's give him some credit. From the first installment of their series in 1950, Burns and Allen understood they were doing TV, not radio. They acted. Burns, cigar in hand, played to the camera like a master. Whether done live or, after 1952, on film, the show seems at once more assured and more casual than the sketch-oriented and stagebound Jack Benny program. Burns and Allen performed in a way that was not only arresting to the TV audience, it was based in a funny, affectionate, and utterly believable relationship, much like the one Lucille Ball and Desi Arnaz brought to TV in 1951.

Ball certainly had all the skills television required. Well remembered as a visual comedienne, she also had the verbal knack of putting all sorts of topspin on a line. And she had Desi Arnaz, like Burns someone who looked closely at ways to make TV work, even if it meant going to film at a time when, as we have seen, television was thought to be most effective done live.

A CBS executive said in 1954 that the network had wanted *I Love Lucy* done live, and the sponsor insisted on a filmed show. The question arose, though, because Ball was pregnant and did not want to move from Los Angeles to New York in order to do the show live for the dominant audience in the East. CBS on the other hand did not want Ball to perform live out West and on kinescope for the rest of the country, as the relatively crude recording process would be off-putting to viewers. And Arnaz flatly said in his memoirs he did not want to do the show live because of the possible mistakes.

> In a revue or a variety show, those kinds of mistakes some-
> times even add to the fun. But we were not doing those types
> of shows, we were doing situation comedy, which, to be
> funny and real, also has to be believable.

To Arnaz, that meant using film. He accordingly engaged Academy Award-winning cinematographer Karl Freund, who developed (and even more importantly, figured out how to light) a three-camera system for filming shows. With three cameras—one for an entire scene, a second for a medium shot including two or three people, a third for closeups—the show could be done like a play for the studio audience. There was no need to pause to relight the scene or ask actors to do retakes.

It does not sound so revolutionary now, when sitcoms do it regularly, but when *I Love Lucy* pioneered the practice, the camera system was a new way of making television different from other media. The show was not a movie, although it was shot on film; the studio audience had a play-going experience but one that was not a play because they had to see around cameras and over cables. And it certainly was not radio, where the wonderful looks on Lucy's puss would have been unavailable.

The enormous success of *Lucy* and, three months later, *Dragnet,* suggested that the idea of live-ness as television's strength may have been mistaken. Arnaz contended in his memoir *A Book* that "a family sitting at home, watching a show, couldn't care less about how that show was mechanically done, live or on film. They would only be interested in watching a good show."

Leonard Goldenson, whose successful effort to pull ABC out of a financial sinkhole included the filmed series *Disneyland* in 1954, phrased the film versus live argument in much the same way. He claimed NBC's Sarnoff told him "this is a medium of spontaneity. The public is never going to watch film." And Goldenson replied, "I don't think the public would care whether it's on film or live. All they want to do is be entertained and informed."

But, even in going to film, television's innovators did not opt simply to make movies. *Dragnet,* which also moved from radio to TV, had a visual style that is sometimes forgotten because it had so many strong audio flourishes: the theme music, creator Jack Webb's narration, the public repeating of "Just the facts, ma'am," a simplification of the series's "All we want are the facts, ma'am." Webb, a *Time* magazine cover boy in 1954, was a notorious workaholic who—like Arnaz and Burns—took nothing for granted. *Time* reported on Webb's chronic soaking up of information—about lighting, directing, editing—while a young movie actor. "Before he ever dreamed of television triumph," the magazine said, "he prepared for it."

In the show itself he went after a look that approximated reality— no makeup, minimal rehearsal—but with a strong visual element such as its use of tight closeups of faces and objects. This is a pure television technique, writers Gary Coville and Patrick Lucanio have argued, ne- cessitated by Webb's realization that his show would be seen on small TV screens. And just as the closeup was an effective TV device in the early years of television, so it became a hallmark for *Dragnet; Time* included two pages of closeup faces in its Webb profile.

Like Arnaz, Webb also broke ground in television production. Tight with a buck, Webb began using TelePrompTers off camera so actors could read their lines rather than waste time memorizing them. It did not make for expressive acting—Leonard Nimoy, who appeared briefly on one *Dragnet* episode, called it a mechanical experience, acting opposite not people but the prompters. Still, buoyed by a distinctive look and strong writing (*Dragnet* mainstay Jim Moser went on to create the groundbreaking medical anthology series *Medic*), the show was a hit with critics and audiences.

The retreat from live programming did not become a stampede until 1955 when Warner Brothers followed Walt Disney into full television series production. The year 1954 is therefore noteworthy because, as one producer put it at the time, "there's room in this business for everyone . . . live and film and tape." But it is also of note that television audiences were indicating their preferences for certain kinds of television, and kinds of relationships, which would encourage endless imitation.

The likability issue in characters has already been discussed, and it drew a line from Arthur Godfrey to the likes of Art Linkletter, Bob Crosby, and Bill Cullen. Partnerships formed another pattern, from Western shows to comedies to police shows; Webb's Joe Friday, listening to the comic prattle of various partners, is not far removed either from cowboy stars and their sidekicks, or from George and Gracie, and Lucy and Desi. As television looked for ways to duplicate past success, it often ironed out innovation. Steve Allen has said this of his *Tonight* successors:

> When I was there, some nights the *Tonight* show wasn't a talk show at all. For example we would just book Richard Rodgers as the guest and spend 90 minutes around the piano. . . . When we did a talk show Jack [Paar] evidently saw that it was an easy thing to do, and a good thing to do . . . so he put on terrific shows, just on a narrower canvas. And Johnny [Carson] just continued the form that Jack Paar had done before him.

Although Allen called Carson "a marvelous host," he saw no great experimentation in the show by the time Carson came in 1962. On the other hand, as has already been argued here, many viewers prefer not to be experimented upon so Carson's course was undoubtedly one factor in his late-night longevity.

Innovation and experimentation in television in the early fifties often had to work its way through webs of directives, mandates, unwritten laws, and formal codes. People who chafed under such restrictions will tell you how difficult they were. But, as we shall see, a framework that allowed innovation while creating an atmosphere of restraint was one with merits many viewers would call for today.

6

TV Controlled Itself

*If a sponsor is responsible, reasonable and
solvent, the writer can turn out good prose.*
Ben Hecht, 1953

The roadblocks to creative television in the fifties were considerable in comparison to the nineties. Technology was far more limited. Time limits were also fixed, with ninety minutes a long time for a show and most shows an hour or less. The composer Benjamin Britten, for one, was less than pleased when his opera *Billy Budd* was cut by one-fourth for telecast.

TV plays such as *Marty* and *Twelve Angry Men* were able to expand their storytelling capability from less than an hour on the small screen to about ninety minutes when they became movies. While one could make a strong argument that *Marty* is a more effective TV production, *Twelve Angry Men* unquestionably benefited from the expansion; on TV, writer Reginald Rose said, the show "really concentrated on about half the jurors. The others were nonentities."

In addition to such structural problems, television faced the fundamental issue of what was appropriate and what not—and who had the right to decide which was which. Government, through the Federal Communications Commission and congressional hearings in 1952 and 1954, could bring considerable pressure to bear. Special-interest groups also had their say; repeated complaints about *Amos 'n' Andy* had hastened its demise while early children's series *Mr. I Magination* was spared cancellation by an outpouring of viewer support. But the forces most potent in controlling television's content were internal: network censors, a broadcasters' code of conduct, and sponsors.

The sponsor, or the advertising agency representing its sponsor client, is often cited as an arbitrary and unreasonable source of censorship in early television. A *TV Guide* report on "TV taboos" in early 1954 mentions how a reference to a "member of Parliament" was changed to "a member of the House of Commons" rather than give a plug to Parliament, a cigarette competing with the show's sponsor. A meat company had a children's-show character changed from a horse—which might be associated with its products—to an elephant. Kraft forbade a character named Borden on one of its shows. Westinghouse rejected a script that involved a leaky refrigerator.

Film and TV historian Tom Stempel has said that any case for picking a year in the fifties as TV's greatest is hurt by the restrictions on content; he leans more toward something like 1986–87 when *Cheers, Hill Street Blues,* and *L.A. Law* were not only creative but able to take advantage of fewer content restrictions. Everett Greenbaum, a distinguished comedy writer in the fifties and sixties, looks fondly on *Roseanne, The John Larroquette Show,* and *Seinfeld* and notes "they have much more freedom than we had."

But any liberalizing of censorship has another side, summed up by writer David Shaw. "You couldn't say 'pregnant' on television," Shaw complained in early 1994, but he added, "Now all they say is 'penis.' Condom and penis. It's something." Indeed. Something many viewers find hard to take, forcing broadcasters to make regular public assurances that program content is under some measure of control.

Although some viewers in the fifties were deeply concerned about what they saw on the air, the television system offered three clear pieces of evidence that it was controlling content. One was at the point of production, where the sponsor, network, and producers themselves exercised control. The second was the Television Code, a standing list of video don'ts established by the National Association of Radio and Television Broadcasters; the code was directed at local stations, making them responsible for content and doing so on a community level that enhanced the relationship between stations and their viewers. The third was the visible collaboration between organized religion and television, which meant that responsible clerics found television acceptable, and that broadcasters accepted religious work among their responsibilities. Taken together, these elements reassured viewers in a way that the far less codified system of television in the early nineties could not. Nor did they necessarily stifle creative programming.

Consider the much maligned sponsors. Granted they had enormous power over the network television schedule and the content of the programs. When the first sponsor of Ed Sullivan's show dropped out after six weeks, Sullivan producer Marlo Lewis said "it was as though a sand bag had landed on my head"; fortunately another sponsor signed on. Kraft literally controlled Wednesday nights at 9 on NBC from 1948 to 1963, filling it variously with an acclaimed dramatic anthology, musical and variety programs (including Perry Como's), and a mystery anthology, all with Kraft in their title.

Sponsors would often integrate their pitches into shows. One episode of *Burns and Allen,* for example, had announcer Harry Von Zell tout Carnation milk at a women's club meeting Gracie was hosting; by 1954 that sort of practice was being discouraged by the Television Code but persisted in some shows.

Sponsors were also an effective pressure point for the zealots driving suspected Communists out of TV and radio; Syracuse grocery-store owner Lawrence Johnson was notorious for pressuring companies supporting what he called "Stalin's little creatures." *The Goldbergs,* successful with audiences, could not find a sponsor after one of its actors, Philip Loeb, was targeted by the witch-hunters. The show paid Loeb to leave; unable to find other work, he committed suicide.

But for all the stories told about the bad side of the sponsor system, good work also arose from it. Some shows were fortunate to have strong-willed producers who resisted advertiser pressures: Fred Coe at *Philco-Goodyear Playhouse,* Worthington Miner at *Studio One,* Max Liebman at *Your Show of Shows.*

Writers were also ingenious. Golden Age playwright Tad Mosel said in 1961 that "if a line is really crucial to a play, I write in something far worse, and then bargain with them until we get back to what I originally had in mind." As has already been discussed, *Thunder on Sycamore Street* had to make an important change—turning a black character being driven from a neighborhood into a white ex-convict—which may have increased the play's resonance for viewers.

Reginald Rose, who wrote *Thunder,* grated under sponsor rules but also found benefit in them. "With one sponsor, the whole feeling about ratings was different," he said. "When Westinghouse was sponsoring *Studio One,* I don't think they were as concerned about the ratings from week to week." Unlike the current system, where a terribly low-rated show is pulled after one or two telecasts, a single sponsor willing to wait for good numbers—or to settle for lower numbers because the show increased the sponsor's prestige—could keep a show going; the network in turn continued to make money from the advertising revenues.

And sponsors did support good causes. TV historian Erik Barnouw has described how Du Pont and Alcoa sponsored shows not so much to sell products as to improve battered public images. (Companies such as Mobil have derived similar benefit from their support of public television, where sponsorship goes under the more genteel name of "underwriting.") Barnouw praises Alcoa's "remarkable steadfastness" in sticking with *See It Now* through its heated confrontation with Senator Joseph McCarthy.

Sponsors also took activist roles in programming where the networks did not. In sports, Gillette (with *Cavalcade of Sports*) and Falstaff (which backed a national package of baseball broadcasts) were crucial players. Procter and Gamble was instrumental in bringing the soap opera to TV in 1950.

"It seemed like a foolhardy flight past the sound barrier . . . the notion of luring a housewife from dishes and diapers to watch a program intended to help her do those chores," corporate chronicler Alfred Lief has written of P&G's venture. Serials had been tried before—Du Mont put on a prime-time soap *Faraway Hill* in 1946, and a daytime and night-time effort, *A Woman to Remember,* in the late forties. And even P&G's first initial effort, *The First Hundred Years,* made mockery of its title by running eighteen months. But the next venture, *Search for Tomorrow,* clicked in 1951 and ran thirty-five years. By 1954 there were fifteen soaps on the air.

An especially instructive example of what an enlightened sponsor could do was *Voice of Firestone,* a series of classical music broadcasts that enjoyed a long radio run and went on TV in 1949. The show was a pet project for the Firestone family (a member of which wrote the show's theme), which saw to it the show was well made. Performances on *Voice* featuring Dorothy Kirsten, Robert Merrill, Anna Moffo, Joan Sutherland, Richard Tucker, and others are still available to classical enthusiasts on home video.

The Firestones wanted, and got, the 8:30 P.M. Monday slot on NBC for their first five years on the air. But in 1954 NBC dropped the show, which was getting clobbered in the ratings by *Arthur Godfrey's Talent Scouts;* that in turn appeared to hurt the rest of NBC's Monday lineup. Undeterred, Firestone took its show to the weaker—and therefore more cooperative—ABC.

"For three or four years we loved it," ABC's Leonard Goldenson says in his memoirs. "But as we came along with newer programs, we had to pay more attention to ratings and audience flow." In 1957 *Voice,* in spite of a small but ardent following and its status as a cultural bright spot, lost its weekly sinecure. That came about not because of a sponsor, which supported the show wholeheartedly, but the network.

To be sure, enlightened sponsors and fearless producers were rare in television in the fifties—and the nineties. And for those without such patrons on their side, at least it was clear what constituted acceptable conduct. Rod Serling, a TV playwright in the early fifties and later famous for *The Twilight Zone,* wrote in 1953:

> Because TV is a mass medium you have to be governed by mass media taboos. . . . Sound strapped? I suppose it does at the outset. But experience brings acceptance and understanding.

And Serling biographer Gordon F. Sander has pointed out that writers found ways to get their messages through the system. Nor was Serling alone. *Twelve Angry Men* did not need jurors screaming vulgarities to get its point across.

When Serling wrote about TV's restrictions, he said they included, "Easy on sex. Easy on violence. Nix on religion." Exceptions could be found to each rule. Early television often used risqué humor, with the volatile mix of live TV and desperate comedians giving censors a huge headache. The *Saturday Evening Post* in 1952 said a comic before a laughless TV audience "reaches back into his barnstorming past and exhumes a joke . . . which, like some tomatoes, is a touch too ripe." What violence there was on television—and modern observers rightly contend it was not comparable to later TV slaughter—was potent enough to disturb some contemporary viewers. As for religion—well, the year before Serling's words saw print, Paddy Chayefsky made his

TV breakthrough with an acclaimed play about a Jewish cantor struggling with his loss of faith.

While Serling told aspiring writers to stay away from religion, the Reverend Billy Graham was doing a fifteen-minute prime-time show on ABC. Oral Roberts had his own show. Bishop Fulton J. Sheen's series *Life Is Worth Living* was ending its second year on Du Mont. Sunday mornings included half a dozen network shows with religious themes, as well as syndicated shows. Edwin Broderick, director of radio and TV for the Roman Catholic Archdiocese of New York, had finished a book called *Your Place in TV: A Handy Guide for Young People;* in the introduction, Francis Cardinal Spellman recommended television "as a career in which they may well serve their fellow man and the interests of their country."

Television has long had an ambivalent relationship with religion, but in the early fifties the relationship at least contained a sense that both medium and missionaries were partners. Networks had religion departments. Sheen proved religion could be an asset to TV when he drew an audience against the formidable Milton Berle—and did so with clear TV skill.

"Jackie Gleason used to come into the booth [during Sheen's program], where I sat all the time, and he marveled," said Broderick. "He said, 'What a sense of timing that guy has.'" (Gleason biographer William A. Henry III said Gleason also incorrectly hoped Sheen would help the comedian out of his unhappy, Catholic marriage.) *Life Is Worth Living* was a simple show—brief talks with blackboard illustrations, the latter erased off-camera by a stagehand who became known as Sheen's angel. But Sheen could do it without a script and, Broderick recalled, could end precisely on time with just a cue that thirty seconds were left.

Billy Graham had also demonstrated his TV appeal in appearances since 1951. Graham's official biography says "Contemporary experts . . . thought Graham the TV personality of their dreams." NBC in 1953 offered Graham a series that could have earned him a million dollars a year. Although Graham could have used a religious theme within the show, overall it was a secular project; he turned it down.

That left him to the tender mercies of ABC, where Goldenson decided in early '54 that "a network isn't the proper place for regularly scheduled religion" and canceled Graham's series. Graham continued in television by buying time on the air. Capital Cities, which absorbed ABC in the eighties, had a standing policy against program time to religious groups but—as Capital Cities historian Walt Hawver wrote—"some stations bent that policy" to sell time to Graham.

In his book *Beating the Odds*, Goldenson does not elaborate on his sweeping conclusion about religion and network TV. He says he told Graham that his series's low ratings were hurting the flow of the network's entertainment shows (the same argument he would make against *Voice of Firestone* a few years later). But by the time Graham's show was canceled, it was at 10:30 Sunday nights, the last stop on ABC's schedule, where flow would not have been an issue; in fact, ABC did not program the slot, giving the time to its local stations for several years after Graham's cancellation.

Moreover, Goldenson did not mind having Graham on the network for specials, which in one case ran longer than some series; ABC sold Graham a weekly Saturday night slot in the summer of 1957 for a Madison Square Garden crusade that proved to be Graham's TV breakthrough; other crusades ran on ABC in 1958 and 1959. And ABC picked up Bishop Sheen's show, which had been running on Du Mont, about a year and a half after it dropped Graham.

Not even concerns about politics in religious programs makes sense. Graham, in Goldenson's view, mixed "anti-Communist politics and fundamentalist Christianity." But Sheen also attacked communism, beginning one talk:

> Any good citizen, if asked by Congress if he were a member of Murder, Inc., would immediately deny it. Why is it, then, that some of our citizens insist on their constitutional rights when asked if they are Communists?

Rather, one has to conclude that Goldenson, like other network executives, simply felt uncomfortable about televised religion. Others shared that feeling. Bishop Sheen got on Du Mont partly by default—the network had no other way of programming against the mighty Berle.

Broderick, who brought Sheen and TV together, called such time periods "obituary space" where, because no one was watching, programmers were happy to put religious shows. "We got any number of offers for 6 A.M. on Sunday morning," Broderick said. "Even the priests weren't up at that time."

No audience, no possible offense. Sheen, for that matter, had a long TV run because—his anti-Communism notwithstanding—his homilies "never offended anyone," Broderick said. Sheen even avoided direct proselytizing.

> Some priests I knew used to say, "When is he going to talk about the Church? When is he going to make a landing? He's flying around the airport all the time." So I spoke to him one day and he said, "I'm really trying to cultivate the situation and plant a seed. We have 52,000 branch offices all over the United States if people are interested in the Catholic Church.

Sheen's situation shows how even the avoidance of controversy can draw criticism. Implicit in Serling's admonition is the idea that *any* discussion of religion guarantees anger from some corner—from true believers within a faith, who feel their message is inadequately conveyed; or from members of another faith, who either disagree with the message being propagated or want comparable air time for their own message. When Pat Robertson's *700 Club* attacks the major media—and both show and host often do—the effectiveness of the attack depends on whether viewers feel they have been disenfranchised by the mass media. Just as viewers lost an important link to their stations as local programming diminished, so networks appeared to disenfranchise the religious community as they wiped religious shows off their schedules—as when CBS dropped long-running religious shows in 1979 to make room for the more potentially profitable *CBS Sunday Morning*. Stations still offer the window dressing of religious involvement by carrying programs that buy time, but there is no true partnership in such an arrangement. A TV evangelist buying time still treats stations as a quasi opponent because he must beg money from the faithful to buy air time.

A more logical arrangement was Cap Cities'—refuse to sell religious time on its stations but reach out to churches in the community, and give them free Sunday-morning time for programs and services. Pat Robertson actually praised a network program, *Christy,* and urged people not only to watch but to write positive letters to advertisers; the show benefited not only from having a strong Christian message but from being produced by one of Robertson's companies—making

Robertson, at least for that one show, a partner with nominal adversaries.

The religion-TV alliances of the early fifties benefited both sides, giving religious groups a way to spread their message and television organizations a way to demonstrate their sensitivity and responsibility. Broderick recalls three thousand people from TV, radio, and advertising gathering for communion breakfasts sponsored by the diocese.

"We'd have a good speaker and try to get people who worked in the industry to feel that it was a great industry, and to work together for the good," he said. Because of that, Broderick recalls having "a great relationship" with participants, including executives who occasionally sent him scripts for comment. Broderick in turn spoke out for television as a positive force and for viewer as well as network responsibility. A common theme in talks Broderick gave—and in a popular pamphlet he wrote for the diocese—was "whoever controls the dial on your TV runs your house." When people called Broderick to complain about a program they had seen, his first question was, "Well, why were you looking at it?"

Exclusion of religious groups from television has fourfold consequences. It creates animosity with organizations who under other conditions have worked with TV. It removes a way for television to present a positive public image. It eliminates a cautionary element from the making of television—a programmer whose schedule includes religious programs may think carefully about what is scheduled around such shows. And it loses a measure of control over the religious broadcasters themselves; the pay-as-you-go arrangement enjoyed by Jimmy Swaggart and Jim Bakker meant there was no mainstream network official on hand to keep a rein on them.

Now, those who are satisfied with television as it exists will ask why the medium needs more internal control. Why especially should religious organizations have more say than other groups? The practical answer, already discussed, is that you make friends out of enemies.

The philosophical answer is, television already lets some censors into its tent. In his 1992 tract *Hollywood vs. America*, Michael Medved argues that the entertainment industry has responded to appeals from environmental activists, antidrug organizations, and advocates of condom use. So why not let other advocates participate?

"An industry that has committed considerable resources to saving the rain forests might be persuaded of the comparable importance of saving the institution of marriage," Medved said. One way to accomplish that is to let religious groups—"the one group that is now most seriously underrepresented among the entertainment establishment," according to Medved—into the discussion and production process. There would undoubtedly be disagreements, just as Broderick did not like some of the things he saw in scripts. But debate would occur in a far different environment than *us vs. them.*

Religious associations notwithstanding, television is regularly called upon by viewers to show that it is doing God's work. Another way of showing that was a secular system, the Television Code. An extension of a set of standards first applied to radio broadcasters, the code was designed not only to give programmers guidelines but to persuade government that legislated standards were unnecessary.

The code went into effect in 1952 and was cited by broadcasters in their defense during congressional hearings that year (see chapter 10). It was sweeping and specific. Among the rules: "Profanity, obscenity, smut, and vulgarity are forbidden" (and regular lists of unacceptable words would be issued); "Reverence is to mark any mention of God, His attributes and powers"; "Drunkenness and narcotic addiction are never presented as desirable or prevalent"; "The costuming of all performers shall be within the bounds of propriety and shall avoid such exposure and such emphasis on anatomical detail as would embarrass or offend home viewers."

While there is ample evidence that the code was a straw man from the beginning (see chapter 10), it at least gave viewers one more way of demanding broadcasters be responsible—by adhering to their own code. Unfortunately the code ceased to exist in 1982 after a federal judge struck down a portion restricting TV advertising, and the National Association of Broadcasters concluded the code *in toto* was unenforceable. In 1993 and 1994, though, we have seen a movement back toward a uniform code, again because some forces in government are more than willing to impose their own standards.

Still, some viewers—and writers and directors and producers—would argue that any extensive system of checks on program content is unduly limiting. But the plain fact is that television content faces layers of control regardless. At least with a codified system, programmers and viewers know what the rules are and can argue specific taboos (or the lack of same).

The more scattershot practices now used lead to rules changes on a series-by-series or episode-by-episode basis, and often leads to controversy of content after, not before, a program has been made. As the single-sponsor system faded in the fifties, leading to a magazine-style approach of multiple advertisers in a single show, television took off the yoke of one control and put on the chains of satisfying many advertisers at once.

That was the hard truth confronting *thirtysomething* when it made Richard Kramer's script "Strangers." Because the show included a scene of two men in bed after making love, it was hit with advertiser defections that took $1.5 million out of ABC's till. The network declined to rerun the episode and face additional losses. Had *thirtysomething* been sponsored by a latter-day Falstaff or Alcoa, sponsorship would not have been an issue.

Of course, a less enlightened sponsor might never have agreed to the episode in the first place. The Television Code forbade "illicit sex relations." And one can easily imagine what Bishop Sheen would have said about "Strangers." Either way, the fifties system or the nineties system, debates over content happen. With clear standards, the argument is better defined.

TELEVISION'S
FINEST HOURS

• • • • • • • • •

T he peak in the early development of television is undoubtedly the prolonged drama involving anti-Communist standard-bearer Senator Joseph McCarthy.

TV legend tends to focus on the role of broadcaster Edward R. Murrow—a home-video collection of Murrow telecasts contends his work was "the beginning of the end" for McCarthy and McCarthyism. But Murrow's work was one part of a series of events in which television demonstrated its power as a political force, its potential for changing history and, on the troubling side, areas in which TV could both manipulate the political process and be manipulated by it.

Television had plenty to regret in 1954, including its willing blacklisting of actors and others suspected of leftist leanings. But it could take fierce pride in the way it came under fire from all sides in the McCarthy events, for the ferocity of criticism and the intensity of debate showed that no one took TV lightly. Issues that plague both viewers and telecasters to this day—such as how to balance profit and public service—came into play during the Army–McCarthy hearings.

But before turning to the McCarthy drama, context is needed. The events of 1954 did not mark a sudden, unanticipated collision of television and politics. The politicians of the fifties had been coming to terms with TV for several years. And television news had been traveling a hard path to respectability before McCarthy. At various points in the next two chapters, the progress of politics and news will interlock and overlap. McCarthy then brought them simultaneously to convergence and confrontation.

7

Politicians and TV

I don't like or trust radio or TV.
Dwight D. Eisenhower, ca. 1951

Television rarely gets respect for what it does. Grudging admiration is more the rule of the day. When Theodore H. White wrote the first of his *Making of the President* books in 1960, he acknowledged television's "primitive power" in giving the 1952 model Richard Nixon a national platform from which to plead his case for staying on the Republican ticket. However, White's concession to TV ended there.

> From 1952 to 1960 television could be used only as an expensive partisan instrument; its time had to be bought and paid for by political parties for their own candidates. The audiences such partisan broadcasts assembled, like the audiences at political rallies, were audiences of the convinced—of convinced Republicans for Republican candidates, of convinced Democrats for Democratic candidates.

Not only is White's point a gross oversimplification—since television was often used, including in Nixon's 1952 "Checkers" speech, to reach the unconvinced—he admits that himself elsewhere in his book. John F. Kennedy's discussion of religion and politics in a paid broadcast in West Virginia was, White said, "exquisite use of TV." And rival Hubert Humphrey's crude, underfinanced attempt at a televised call-in show demonstrated that "TV is no medium for a poor man."

Politicians knew that by 1954, when campaign spending was $13.7 million, 25 percent more than four years earlier. *U.S. News & World Report* declared, "TV gets credit, or blame, for causing the increase in expense." White should have known that no politician spent that kind of money just to buck up his supporters, especially any campaigner who has been watching how television affected his business.

The first politician to appear on television was probably New York Governor Al Smith, who did so in 1928. Viewers in New York and Philadelphia saw live coverage of the 1940 Republican convention. Thomas Hutchinson said people at the convention occasionally turned to TV receivers in the hall to see speakers elsewhere in the same hall; "the television audience knew more about what went on than many people who were there in person." In fact, in his 1946 book *Here Is Television,* Hutchinson was already laying down the law to future campaigners.

> There is nothing so dull on television as a speaker reading a speech. That is radio. His only chance is to "put across" his personality so definitely and favorably that we want to *watch* him talk. Just as radio changed campaign methods, television may usher in a completely new order. While it will help some candidates it may prove a serious handicap to others. . . . This does not mean that all our future statesmen must be Adonises but they must have a personality that puts them in a favorable light with a majority of voters. . . . They must not only sound but *look* convincing.

Television provided politicians another big convention showcase in 1948, including, John Crosby reported,

> five Hawaiian ladies in front of the camera, singing for dear life, while [a reporter] scurried about trying desperately to get somebody—anybody—to interview.

The 1948 coverage also provided an early example of politicians' tailoring their actions to the camera. When Southern delegates in protest exited the Democratic convention, Gilbert Seldes wrote,

> before the TV camera they tore off their badges and flung them on a table, and a close-up of the mounting pile drama-

tized their emotion. It was not, however, a spontaneous gesture; after the interviews were over the delegates returned and put their badges on again.

More maneuvering, even chicanery, lay ahead. The 170,000 homes with television in 1948 had grown to 15 million by 1952, when the coaxial cable made simultaneous coast-to-coast telecasts possible. Some estimates put the viewership for the 1952 national conventions at 55 million. Former NBC News President Reuven Frank has written, "Television was a novelty in 1948; in 1952, it was a fact." At the Republican convention in 1952 the Robert Taft campaign hired dubbed "Belles for Bob," adorned them with Taft signs and buttons, and sent them after TV cameras. As Frank told it:

> Taft's managers said openly that their aim was to "overwhelm" the TV picture on all three networks. The incongruity of the models' flashing teeth and aggressive busts representing bald, bespectacled, austere, intellectual Bob Taft was overridden by hunger for television exposure. . . . Old hands were learning, new ones growing up conditioned to know, that no decision is judged solely on its merits. First you asked how it will look on television.

So rapid was the change in televised conventions, pioneering CBS newsman Sig Mickelson has written that "the coup de grace to the national political convention as a legitimate news event" was delivered in 1956, when the Democrats presented a film they expected to be televised—and CBS refused. Mickelson said:

> The convention thereafter would be a showplace for party functionaries, a stage for a quadrennial extravaganza extolling party virtues, a revival meeting . . . but hardly a site for selecting candidates for the presidency.

Those candidates, meanwhile, were not simply concocting "Belles for Bob." For example, Ben Gross, an early television critic, saw in Harry Truman much of what Hutchinson had decreed for politicians. Shortcomings—an average speaking voice, a lack of eloquence—were evident on radio, Gross said, but overcome when Truman appeared on

TV—"the vivid image of the 'little fellow,' the average man." And Prescott Bush, the father of future president George Bush, took to TV in his 1950 Connecticut senate campaign, in one appearance singing "Shine on Harvest Moon" as part of a quartet of Yale men.

Thomas Dewey, unsuccessful Republican candidate for president in 1944 and 1948, used television to improve his image during his 1950 campaign for governor of New York. He had the advantage of a television boom town in New York City, where the major networks were based and seven TV stations operated at a time when major cities like New Orleans, Houston, Phoenix, and Milwaukee had one apiece. He also needed every advantage he could muster for a campaign that Dewey biographer Richard Norton Smith considered "for those who like their politics bare-knuckled."

Blazing a trail for Bill Clinton and Ross Perot, Dewey assembled an ad hoc network of stations around New York and in one memorable broadcast took questions from the TV audience. Smith said:

> Sitting on a desk, his jacket sloughed off under the hot lights, chuckling when asked about his mustache and cigarette holder, reeling off facts and figures . . . Dewey came across as mellow and conversational. He took an instant shine to the new medium, booking several more appearances before Election Day, including a final eighteen hour marathon.

Ben Gross was among those impressed by Dewey's TV performance. "This was a new form of vote-seeking, abandoning as it did, for the first time in broadcasting, the formal oration for the methods of the seminar," Gross wrote. John Crosby called Dewey "the first candidate to understand . . . how to use television properly."

The TV appearances, Crosby wrote at the time, humanized the candidate. "Dewey will never exactly compete with Arthur Godfrey in charm, but it certainly gave voters the most intimate glimpse of Dewey they'd ever had." Crosby further decided, a bit prematurely, that the traditional campaign speech "is a dead form of oratory on television." But he rightly realized that television was tightening political rhetoric, since even Dewey's marathon was broken into fifteen-minute segments.

> Before radio came in campaign speeches ran as long as four hours. Radio drastically reduced these orations. It looks as if

television will reduce them even more. And when a candidate is cut down to fifteen minutes he had better marshal his facts in the most concise form.

Dewey made no secret of his enthusiasm for a medium that had done him so much good. "Politically, television is an X ray," Dewey told the *New York Times*. "If a man doesn't know the business of government, he cannot long stand in its piercing lights and stark realism." That statement was a bit misleading; Crosby, even as he believed "television throws a merciless light on phoniness," suspected exactly that in Dewey's call-in programs.

"Many of the questions hurled at Dewey seemed rigged," Crosby said. "All of them were certainly screened; the embarrassing ones were probably eliminated." And advertising man David Ogilvy, familiar with the Dewey method, years later upheld Crosby's complaint. When people on the street asked questions of Dewey in the studio, Ogilvy said:

> The day before, [Dewey's] staff had carefully *selected* the passers-by. They had *told* them what they were interested in, and rehearsed their questions.

Another major lesson in how to use television came in 1951, when crusading Tennessee Senator Estes Kefauver headed a series of hearings on organized crime. First televised in New Orleans, the hearings became a sensation when they were broadcast from New York City. They gave faces to criminal names people had long read in the paper (and in one historic session gave hands, because a mobster refused to allow his face on camera). They provided a grand real-life drama. As Eric Sevareid put it:

> This reporter has been mesmerized by the television screen, watching the play of wit, of cunning, of righteous wrath and outraged innocence. . . . It is like seeing, through a microscope, the red and white corpuscles maneuvering around a point of infection.

Kefauver enjoyed tremendous popularity because of the hearings—magazine articles, a best-selling book, TV and film appearances, even a special Emmy award for outstanding public service on television. He broke out of the political pack to become a celebrity—or, when he appeared on *What's My Line?* a mystery celebrity.

The popular quiz show of the day featured a panel of celebrities asking people yes-or-no questions to determine their occupation. A standard feature was also the "mystery celebrity" (more commonly known as the mystery guest) whose identity the blindfolded panel would have to guess. When Kefauver appeared on the show after the hearings, panelist Arlene Francis's first question was, "Are you in the entertainment business?" The audience's roar of laughter almost drowned out Kefauver's "No, ma'am."

"Are you in the public eye?" Kefauver was then asked.

"Slightly," he replied.

But the hearings also prompted some worries about the power of television. As Jack Gould summarized in the *New York Times* in 1951:

> One thought receiving wide expression was that the politician of tomorrow must become an "actor" and that a premium might be placed on personality rather than competence.

President Truman said televised hearings "tend to make Roman holidays of them." Governor Dewey, who had first made his name as a prosecutor, worried that pursuing wrongdoers "under the piercing glare of kleig lights . . . smacks too much of the Russian method to fit in with our institutions." While that question persisted, the more immediate lesson to politicians was that television helped make Kefauver a star. Indeed, when he accepted his Emmy, it was by telephone from New Hampshire where he was running (unsuccessfully, it turned out) for president.

By the early fifties it was painfully clear that candidates needed to figure out television. Those who did not, such as Taft and Adlai Stevenson, were doomed. Those who did, most notably Dwight Eisenhower, had a far better chance at success. Media historian Craig Allen is among those who have seen in Eisenhower's accomplishments the first television president. In fact, his use of the medium began before he took the White House, in his 1952 campaign.

Opinion at first divided on how Eisenhower would fare on television. As he told CBS's David Schoenbrun, he did not trust broadcast media because "I don't like the idea of something where you have to depend on the integrity of the men who run it and not the basic integrity of the institution itself." (Then again, in what institution does integrity not depend on the people running it?) Still, Jack Gould was among those who thought Eisenhower had a way with TV. Gould called the general "a natural" when he reviewed Eisenhower's press conference after he resigned from the Army.

> Purely from the standpoint of his appeal on the screen, which in itself might have important political implications, General Eisenhower admittedly has at least a temporary advantage over such veteran television campaigners as Senators Robert A. Taft and Estes W. Kefauver.

But others, including those in Eisenhower's own camp, were not so optimistic. Eisenhower was not good at the prepared speeches, then a staple of campaigning, on the stump and on TV. His advisers concluded that the best way to market Eisenhower was in spots, commercial-sized advertisements. And so the world changed.

As Edwin Diamond and Stephen Bates wrote in their classic analysis of political advertising, *The Spot,* Ike's campaign "first raised the major, disturbing—and continuing—questions about politics, advertising, and television." They asked:

> Should presidential campaigns be run by marketing principles and ad-men, or by political tactics and party professionals? Do thirty-second or sixty-second spots ignore issues and content in favor of image and emotion? Does the best man win, or the most telegenic performer? Can money buy enough media to buy elections? Every four years since 1952 these questions have reappeared, and each campaign has provided enough contradictory answers to keep at least some of them alive and unresolved.

Since 1952! Think about that. Presidents have been sold like soap since before many voters were born. One can understand why the hidebound campaigners around Eisenhower's opponent Adlai Stevenson reacted as they did—asking if Republicans equated the White House with a box of corn flakes—because they were not prepared to sell themselves. But the high-minded rhetoricians of the nineties who declare that television tactics are unseemly have not noticed that the boat sailed a long time ago. And it left Taft and Stevenson at the dock.

Where Eisenhower, however grudgingly, did what TV required, his main Republican opposition, Taft—so aptly described by Reuven Frank—did not. James T. Patterson, author of Taft biography *Mr. Republican,* detailed Taft's difficulties with the personality game.

> Hostile columnists noted that he often refused to smile for photographers or to kiss babies. When people crowded around for autographs, he sometimes blurted, "no, no." Autographs took three times as long as a handshake, he told them; if you want my signature, send a letter and ask for it. . . . He still found it hard to chatter, tell stories, unbend with reporters, even accept the plaudits of a crowd.

A supporter once said, "Bob Taft has a good smile but does not know how to use it. Eisenhower does, and people fall for it."

Adlai Stevenson did not lack for personal charm. But he resembled Taft in his struggles with television. In part Stevenson was hampered by mishandling: Diamond and Bates called the 1952 Democratic advertising strategy "ideally suited for the radio age." While the Republicans bought commercial spots that did little to interrupt program schedules, the Democrats bought half-hour blocks, killing whole programs. The Stevenson programs, scheduled far in advance, gave audiences plenty of time to find something else to watch. The Eisenhower spots were more likely to catch, and in their brevity keep, viewers' attention.

But Stevenson failed as well. Despite having half an hour to talk—an eternity by nineties political standards—Stevenson was notorious for his inability to finish a speech on time. And because he was laboring within scheduled blocks, any overrun was simply cut off. Historian Kathleen Hall Jamieson has written:

> Although historians quote the eloquent peroration to Stevenson's 1952 election eve speech as if it had in fact been delivered to the nation, the producer had faded to the disclaimer long before.

Stevenson biographer Porter McKeever said Stevenson nonetheless clung to the formal speech even when a more informal, and TV-friendly, "fireside chat" was well received. Other politicians would not be so foolish. When 1952 candidates appeared on a CBS series called "Presidential Timber"—which gave candidates a half hour to show off in a format of their own choosing—the common thread was a carefully staged informality. After watching a couple of shows Jack Gould was thinking, "perhaps television and the world of politics may be a little too preoccupied with techniques."

CBS also held a school for politicians in 1952, teaching them such fundamentals as wearing blue shirts instead of white on camera, avoiding hand-painted ties and wearing Panama hats instead of the straw variety. At the 1952 Democratic convention, venerable politician Sam Rayburn "had makeup smeared on his bald head every day." And, of course, that year saw Nixon's renowned "Checkers" speech, his plea for his family, their dog and his place on the Republican ticket; Ben Gross called it "one of the most artfully contrived and spectacularly melodramatic television shows ever staged. . . . There are few stars of the theater and the movies today who could have equaled it." But I can think of one who might: Nixon's boss, Eisenhower.

Ike's use of television did not end once he got into the White House. Indeed, Gross thought Eisenhower in office "is still at his best not in a set speech but in the informal discussion or question-and-answer type of telecast." And he thought Eisenhower had a chance to improve because of a new man in his camp, the actor and director Robert Montgomery.

Montgomery had been a handsome leading man and a player of psychotics, a daring director (*Lady in the Lake,* in which he also starred as detective Philip Marlowe, uses the camera as Marlowe's point of view for virtually the entire film), and a conservative politician. "He's a wheel in the Republican party," *TV Guide* said of the man then better known as host of dramatic anthology *Robert Montgomery Presents,* "and it was said that if Dewey had been elected in 1948, Bob would have rated a cabinet position." Instead, Montgomery had to wait for Eisenhower's election and for a role that did not include cabinet rank but carried great importance.

Few people in any line of work could match the credit *Newsweek* attached to two TV appearances by President Eisenhower: "supervised by Robert Montgomery." His main accomplishment, the magazine reported, was "relaxing the president and giving him professional confidence." A United Press story a month later offered one example; just before a broadcast Montgomery showed golfer Eisenhower a battered ball and jokingly told him "never do a thing like that . . . again."

But Montgomery also took control of the details of television. He recommended a softer-looking makeup for the president, a higher lectern so Eisenhower would not have to bend his head and show his baldness, new glasses to make him look younger. By early 1955, Montgomery was on a magazine's list of the three men responsible for Eisenhower's speeches. On one speech, Montgomery spent a reported eight hours advising Ike on technique.

When Eisenhower gave that speech, *U.S. News & World Report* said:

> Mr. Montgomery was everywhere in the studio up to air time, checking everything at least twice, keeping an eye on the three dozen people on the floor. . . . During the telecast itself, he stood to the left of the President, handling the 3-foot by 4-foot cue cards.

According to *TV Guide,* the networks at first thought of Montgomery as a "usurper" who was filling a role normally reserved for them. But the magazine said that changed because, one unidentified network representative conceded, "This is the first time . . . that we are perfectly confident nothing will be snafued."

Journalists noting all this manipulation began to stir, and presidential press secretary James Hagerty had to make clear Montgomery was not on the government payroll. (He did, however, have his own office.) But beyond that his presence does not appear to have caused much comment. In his book *Eisenhower and the Mass Media* Craig Allen contends "Montgomery worked in almost total anonymity," a bit strong given several backstage stories about his efforts. But it is noteworthy that even in the early fifties no one seemed to think much about the president having a makeup adviser.

It may be that journalists covering this president decided he had already crossed some arbitrary border between style and substance, since Eisenhower's television campaign and other public-relations techniques had already caused complaint. The pro-Stevenson *New Republic* said during the 1952 election that the World War II hero had

given way to "a synthetic Eisenhower" spouting "platitudinous gener-
alities"; the campaign was reduced to one "between a machine and
a man."

Just as Montgomery's actions were a progression from the 1952
campaign, so the Eisenhower team continued a systematic exploitation
of TV. On October 25, 1954—smack in the middle of heated congressional campaigns—the president hosted the first televised cabinet meeting, which just happened to include a report on progress against the
Soviet threat in western Europe. While the president called the meeting
a matter of national interest, reporters were not fooled. The *Times's*
James Reston said the telecast was pure politics, comparing it to Harry
Truman's tour to boost candidates in the 1950 elections.

Eisenhower's TV moves continued, though, with the first televised
presidential press conference coming in January 1955. But one should
not think that the use of television was occurring solely in the rarified
air of presidential politics. Broadcasting historian Mary Ann Watson
has said that as early as 1956 a young senator named John F. Kennedy
had learned the importance of television, and she mentions Kennedy's
"enviable ease" on television shows even in the early fifties. Kennedy
also used TV in his 1952 senate campaign, and appeared on celebrity-
interview show *Person to Person* with his young bride Jacqueline in
1953.

By the fall elections in 1954, candidates in New York were routinely
scheduling televised pitches. And in Schenectady, a young politician
was supporting his political career (and his family) with TV
appearances.

Samuel S. Stratton, who later spent thirty years in the House of
Representatives, appeared as a newscaster and commentator on a
small station, WROW, from early 1954 until his successful run for
mayor of Schenectady in late 1955. It was a primitive setup: WROW,
which would become one of the first stations in the Capital Cities
chain, had only one studio camera. For set changes, a technician low-
ered a makeshift screen in front of the lens.

But Stratton, who had worked in TV and radio before joining
WROW, enjoyed the forum. His improvised monologues at the beginning of the fifteen-minute newscasts often cut into time allotted for
sports and weather.

"If he finished a minute late, then the next guy just had less time,"
recalled Ralph Vartigian, weatherman on the program. "One night I

had no sooner said, 'Good evening, everyone,' than I got the signal to wrap up."

In one long-remembered report, Stratton went on the air with what he said was a new water meter, supposedly proof that the Schenectady government was about to put meters into city homes. Although one opponent later complained that Stratton showed a standard meter for businesses, not a new one for homes, the TV politician had made his point, complete with visual aid.

Stratton was also in the vanguard for Ronald Reagan and George Murphy, professional actors who took the stigma of their roles into the political arena. He briefly appeared on TV as Sagebrush Sam, the cowboy-outfitted host of Western movies, and viewers remembered that. One friend said after Stratton's death in 1990:

> His opponents thought that was wonderful, because he looked so ridiculous. What they didn't realize was that people would come up to him for years after, saying, "I remember you from that wonderful program when I was a kid." And they'd vote for him.

The real-life politicking on television was so accepted by the early fifties it became part of popular culture as well. Edwin O'Connor's 1956 novel *The Last Hurrah* (the basis for the Spencer Tracy movie) presents an old-time politician brought down in part by his young opponent's use of television to present what one character calls "a parade of banalities." Writer Budd Schulberg and director Elia Kazan were closely watching TV events such as the downfall of Joe McCarthy as they planned *A Face in the Crowd,* the engrossing 1957 movie about a charismatic TV personality who becomes a force in national politics. His tale, the moviemakers wrote, illustrated "the power of television to sell synthetic personalities as it sells the soup and the soap"—although Eisenhower, also called "synthetic" by one detractor, had already illustrated that.

But all of that talks about how politicians were exploiting television. The camera eye was not always guaranteed to be friendly. Television news, as well, had taken shape in the early fifties.

The Ascent of News

In placing fifties TV over nineties TV, the easiest places to make the argument are in comedy and drama. Sustained by strong writing and gifted actors, the productions in both areas had a quality that has proven timeless. But when we turn to news and sports, the case is much harder to make.

You can put on a good drama, or make people laugh, just about anywhere. But in sports and news—both presentations of live and unpredictable events at times taking place in faraway lands—advances in technology make a major difference in the apparent quality of the production. In TV sports (which will be considered in greater depth in chapter 12), the coming of videotape led to the instant replay, not to mention the slow-motion instant replay; this was greeted as an advance by sports fans eager for yet another way to second-guess players and coaches, desperate for the Rosetta stone of error on a single play by which to explain an entire season.

When we talk about news, beaming a live picture from the other side of the world, or even the other side of the country, as quickly as possible is considered a major accomplishment. And that sort of speed was rarely in evidence in the early fifties. When Soviet leader Josef

Stalin died one Thursday in 1953, NBC obtained a set of films that provided a revealing glimpse of life under the dictator; but a documentary was not assigned until Friday, and did not run until Sunday. Such a time lag would be unthinkable for a modern news organization intent on beating its competition.

Competition certainly existed, especially between CBS and NBC, in the early fifties but technology slowed the pace; showing the coronation of Queen Elizabeth II was not a matter of buying satellite time but the slower process of obtaining aircraft and flying film across the Atlantic. The major live TV event of 1954 consisted of congressional hearings conveniently set in a single room in Washington, D.C. But news organizations also went after stories with as much aggressiveness as possible; when Hurricane Edna threatened the Northeast, it was awaited by what one news account called "a vast reception committee of radio and television workers." New York City station WPIX offered a four-and-a-half-hour live report that started atop a Long Island fire station; CBS's owned television station stayed on all night, running movies between storm updates.

Moreover, in comparing news then and now, one measure too often used is sheer tonnage: so many hours of telecasts then, so many now. Even if we just count newscasts, modern TV—with its nightly network half hours (and an hour on PBS), and large blocks of local news, not to mention round-the-clock cable reports—wins going away. CBS and NBC had fifteen-minute newscasts in 1954 (although ABC had experimented with a nightly hour); local news, if it was on at all, might be as brief as five minutes.

But, as the comment from *Business Week* at the beginning of this chapter says, quality of news needs to be considered as well. Given the technological limitations of the time, networks had nothing to be embarrassed about when it came to putting on serious (and, yes, entertaining) news programs. In addition, when we broaden the definition of news to include documentaries, interviews, commentary and public-affairs programs, the quantity of TV news and information was pretty respectable in 1954.

The Sunday interview series *Meet the Press* had seven TV years behind it by then, and *Face the Nation* began late in the year. *Today*, a news show albeit a somewhat quirky one, had two years under its belt, and CBS was getting ready to launch its own morning show. *See*

It Now, in many ways a prototype for the magazine shows now littering the TV landscape, had been on the air since 1951.

Other news programs included *Chronoscope,* fifteen-minute interviews with important people; New York City corrections commissioner Anna M. Kross told viewers that "the world today is quite sick, mentally sick," one reason being "the acceleration of living" caused by airplanes, broadcasting, and other devices. *Background* offered analysis of stories in the news, such as changes in Southeast Asia (which included a report from Indochina, where the French were being driven out and the U.S. was moving in) and the plight of the American draftee. *American Week,* hosted by Eric Sevareid, did a show on Anglo-American relations in which *New Yorker* critic Philip Hamburger saw "grace and wisdom." And, just to prove that tabloid TV is not a recent invention, Los Angeles had a show called *Confidential File* that featured an interview with a pyromaniac, a hypnotized woman giving birth, and other stories the producer frankly admitted were sensationalistic.

News quality is also a matter of intent, a seriousness of purpose that was fully evident in the early fifties. CBS's Sig Mickelson considered early political coverage and thought, "Perhaps we were better off with the inferior technology and more reflective pieces of 1952 than the more superficial content of 1960." Relative standards of quality cannot be divorced from the time in which different productions appear. A viewer considering the available TV news in 1954 did not know the wonders that awaited forty years in the future; his emotional response to a story, and to what seemed in context to be rapid reporting, would be much the same in either decade. Finally, quality can be measured in terms of how news affects the public progress; it has already been shown that television was affecting politics, and in 1954 it played a key role in the biggest political drama of the decade.

The roots of television news go back to the late twenties and a three-times a week farm report in upstate New York. Tryouts continued in the thirties, as Edward Bliss, Jr., chronicles in his history *Now the News;* CBS had regular newscasts in 1931, and television cameras recorded President Roosevelt's opening of the World's Fair in 1939.

In England, television covered the coronation procession of King George VI in 1937, so we've had at least seven decades in which the royals have taken up TV time. TV also witnessed Prime Minister Neville Chamberlain when he returned from a 1938 meeting with Adolf Hitler.

By the early forties CBS was doing afternoon and evening telecasts; Bliss says what may have been the first "instant special" followed the bombing of Pearl Harbor. Still, coverage could be makeshift at best. Bliss described one momentous telecast:

> When President Roosevelt went before a joint session of Congress to ask for a declaration of war, CBS had no video line to Washington. Its television coverage consisted of an audio feed with a camera focused on an American flag. The flag rippled in a breeze from an electric fan.

World War II was dominated by print and radio, with the latter creating a new generation of stars such as Edward R. Murrow, renowned for his radio reports from war-torn London. With the war's end, though, television began even more earnest, if occasionally toe-stubbing, efforts. Bill Leonard, later president of CBS News, has written about taking his radio series *This Is New York* to TV—for one 1947 broadcast.

> We had wanted to show that television could go anywhere and do anything. When we got right down to it, with the limited facilities and money at my disposal, what we could do was bring two or three cameras a few blocks from Grand Central [where the TV newsroom was] to the New York Telephone headquarters and show how the phone system worked. Live. Real nail-biting stuff.

Telecasts of the forties' political conventions (see chapter 7) gave the networks still more hard experience. Former NBC News President Reuven Frank says television news really began at the 1948 conventions; nine cities connected by coaxial cable created a true network telecast, and TV offered gavel-to-gavel coverage at a time when radio did not. (Broadcast TV eventually abandoned gavel-to-gavel reports, leaving the field to its rivals in cable.) And, as was mentioned in chapter 7, 1948 saw a phony event staged for the television audience.

The next major breakthrough for TV news was also in 1948, when CBS premiered its evening newscast with Douglas Edwards; six months later, in early 1949, NBC followed suit with John Cameron Swayze and the *Camel News Caravan*. Both networks, as well as Du Mont, had had earlier programs presenting newsreel highlights, but the modern newscast came into being with the Edwards and Swayze programs.

In a field that tries to redefine as well as reinvent itself, the early newscasts are held in somewhat low esteem. Mike Wallace has dismissed them as "a headline service in the most primitive way." *Camel News Caravan* gets sidewise looks because of its obeisance to its cigarette-company sponsor (Winston Churchill was the lone exception to a rule against showing famous people with cigars) and because of Swayze's later renown as a commercial pitchman. But writer Barbara Matusow for one has said that Swayze's credentials, including a decade with a Kansas City newspaper, "were respectable enough."

A prevailing snobbishness toward TV newsmen also hurt Swayze and Edwards. Reuven Frank's memoirs cites the distaste for Swayze and NBC News often expressed by Pat Weaver, head of TV programming for the network.

> He tried several times to hire reporters whose bylines he had read in the *The New York Times,* portly men in vests with mushy speech patterns who could not say "Howdy" in fewer than a thousand words.

(Weaver in his book alludes to Frank's criticism but attributes his unhappiness not to the people at NBC but to "the technical state of the art of television." But Frank at several points portrays Weaver as someone without expertise in news who repeatedly interfered—not the last time TV's newsmen and showmen would clash.)

Edwards was also the victim of internal dissension. Matusow has written that Edwards was considered a lightweight next to the Murrow crowd; because he had not been among the band of brothers who had overseas assignments during World War II, his writing was considered inelegant and his thinking less than deep. David Schoenbrun said such criticism was unwarranted, that Edwards proved in radio "he was the most able, most professional newscaster on the staff and could pull together all the war reports into an exciting newscast."

Such attitudes had a profound effect on newsmen. Don Hewitt, probably the savviest producer in television news and the driving force behind *60 Minutes,* affects a blue-collar bluntness in interviews. That sets him apart from the high-toned Murrow team for which he worked early in his career, particularly its self-proclaimed leader, Fred Friendly, with whom Hewitt clashed when Friendly ran CBS News in the sixties. His reputation now secure, Hewitt still talks about how it hurt to be shunted aside. But he also turned defeat into triumph—the creation of *60 Minutes*—just as Edwards and Swayze became TV stars despite second-class status among their news brethren.

Where radio had been thought the best field for broadcast news, the future lay in television. Walter Cronkite's star rose because, unlike some old radio hands, he did not try to create word pictures when, as Mickelson observed, "television already had pictures. What we needed was someone who could interpret pictures, give them meaning, and relate them to other pictures"—all skills Mickelson saw in Cronkite early on.

Besides, the early TV newscasts are not as bad as they are often portrayed. They lacked the visual razzle-dazzle of modern TV news programs, but some would consider that an asset. And Wallace is right in criticizing the lack of reporters in the field. But the Museum of Television & Radio has for public view an Edwards telecast from 1949 and a *Camel News Caravan* from 1950 that are perfectly serviceable reports on the events of the day. And the people making television then were already sorting out the fundamentals of a TV newscast, including the importance of pictures to storytelling, and the balancing of hard news with features.

As in the *Camel* newscast, the early Edwards show opened with homage to its sponsor, Oldsmobile, the announcer declaring, "Olds brings you the news." An introduction, or tease, for five of the stories followed. Edwards then read more than a dozen news items, from President Truman's press conference to the Army Day parade, a treaty signing in Panama, the war in Greece, Japan's efforts to recover from an earthquake the previous year, the New York City taxi strike, and the United Mine Workers' plan to lower their retirement age.

The newscast integrated film, which CBS was buying from Hearst's Telenews service, wherever possible: in the parade story, in a visit by the Brazilian minister of war to West Point (which had happened two long days before the telecast) and the treaty signing; the Japan story was accompanied by film of the devastation immediately after the quake. Edwards also touted "some very, very dramatic pictures" of Communist demonstrators in Iceland. "A real pitched battle, stones against nightsticks," Edwards said as footage rolled. "And there goes the tear gas." The show also used graphics, such as a farm fence doubling as a scale to illustrate changes in the federal farm program.

Those who believe television news fell into feature fuzziness only in recent years should be aware that this 1949 telecast included a New York bank that had installed a baby-carriage ramp and still photos of nineteen-week-old Prince Charles of England ("This is my favorite," Edwards said of one). The newscast's closer, introduced by Edwards declaring "now here's one for the books," was about Soviet claims that a Russian invented television. (Russian-born Vladimir Zworykin, inventor of the electronic camera and the picture tube, is considered one of the fathers of television, by the way.)

Even in the short span of fifteen minutes, the CBS newscast aimed to provide a blend of reports, to match pictures with stories (and to enhance the pictures with dramatic narration), and to have the anchor's personality emerge as a natural part of the telecast. During what was supposedly the Age of Seriousness in TV news, this telecast tried to entertain as well as inform, spending some precious time on lighter fare. The *Camel* program, done almost a year and a half later, showed comparable sophistication in presenting what it proclaimed "today's news today."

One of the cracks against *Camel* is its "hopscotching the world for headlines," a collection of brief news items meant to demonstrate the insubstantial nature of TV news. But such wrap-ups are now evident in local and national newscasts, and in 1950 the hopscotching was just a part of a program that had included fifteen other reports before the briefs. Among the longer reports: status of the Korean War, Ford's new raise for workers, Florida bracing for a hurricane, the weekend's baseball scores, and a coming primary election in Nevada.

The program juggled hard news (Korea) with soft (a report on new fashions). It offered a bit of political analysis; Nevada Senator Pat McCarran "faces a real fight. . . . He could be upset." (He wasn't.) The Korea update is followed by a "personalized report" from Philadelphia Naval Hospital, where three soldiers back from the battlefront were interviewed. Other film includes "exclusive NBC aerial views" of British troops arriving in Korea; "a tragic and startling train wreck" with the added twist that passengers were delegates to a model-railroad convention; scenes of the Liberty Bell shipboard for a national tour.

Drawings accompany reports on traffic fatalities and the baseball scores; for the latter, figures meant to represent different teams show smiles when the teams won, frowns when they lost.

From a nineties technical perspective some of the newscast is laughable. But in basic structure it is a modern newscast. More time for news would have been welcome, more pictures a bonus. But the early newscasts pioneered a format still being used in much the same fashion forty years later.

The most important news program of the early fifties was not a newscast as such but a weekly prime-time show called *See It Now.* This is the program that brought Edward R. Murrow into television on a regular basis, demonstrating that radio's dominant days were ending and that the front ranks of broadcast journalism would belong to TV stars. From its title (derived from the radio series *Hear It Now*) and its opening-show display of simultaneous shots of bridges on the East and West Coasts, the show promised the audience a long reach and immediate gratification. Over a season it ranged across subjects in a way that provided the model for TV news magazines (Don Hewitt can be seen at Murrow's side in the first program). And where one can make a nice argument out of the dichotomy of the serious-thoughtful Murrow of *See It Now* against the playful-chummy Murrow hosting celebrity-interview series *Person to Person* (which began in 1953), *See It Now* was no different from other successful news programs in understanding that viewers are more likely to soak up information if they enjoy the way you convey it. That bridge shot, after all, is not so much news as showmanship. But Friendly and Murrow wrote a few years later:

> Until the electronics of television, no man had ever been capable of gazing at both oceans at the same instant. We thought that a medium capable of doing this was capable of providing reporters with an entirely new weapon in journalism.

Well, not entirely new, since people had been working in TV news well before Friendly and Murrow embraced it. And what *See It Now* did best was what news has always strived to do, put stories about major issues in terms of individual lives. In May 1954, eight days after the Supreme Court ruled that public schools must be integrated, *See It Now* showed how citizens of two towns in North Carolina and

Louisiana felt about integration. Even as Murrow insisted "there is no such thing as a 'typical' Southern town," the report particularized and humanized the general debate about integration. To look at *See It Now,* reflective and provocative in equal doses, is to understand why Hewitt, schooled in early television, wrote these words many years later:

> When all is said and done, telling stories is what it's all about. It is your ear as much as your eye—and sometimes more than your eye—that keeps you in front of a television set. . . . People always ask me for the formula for our success, and I tell them it's simple—four words every kid in the world knows: "Tell me a story."

So by 1951, let alone three years later, two basic elements of TV news were in place. In 1952, with *Today,* it took another step, which gave news more visibility and, according to Reuven Frank, doubled the number of news writers at NBC. Television also closely covered the presidential campaign between Dwight Eisenhower and Adlai Stevenson, taking what Mickelson calls its "great leap forward"; on election night, CBS and NBC introduced that boon to coverage (and bane of cautious critics), the computerized projection of a winner. But for television to take what increasingly appeared to be its rightful place among news organizations, it had to pass by some powerful enemies, including its nominal colleagues in print.

In the summer of 1986 I was at a press event that brought reporters together with stars of CBS's prime-time soap operas. It was a combination press conference, photo opportunity, and cocktail party, with the stars dressed to the nines, and reporters standing in shifting clusters around the most popular performers of the day. Naturally, a crowd had gathered around Patrick Duffy, who after leaving *Dallas* the year before had rejoined the cast; I was elbow to elbow with other reporters trying to get a question to Duffy and in hearing range of his answer.

Such situations are not uncommon and professional courtesy comes into play, with reporters nearest the star getting the information they want, then moving out of the way; others stand placidly as hands holding tape recorders reach over both shoulders to capture the dialogue of the moment. In this case, though, a persistent shoving and cries of "Excuse me" began to disrupt the process. Even though Duffy was literally surrounded by print interrogators, a CNN reporter and photographer had decided to push through the group, put their lights on Duffy and at that moment get their clip for telecast. Amid comments loud and soft from the crush of press being pushed aside by the TV tandem, the CNN team slowed their progress a bit; they never considered that the print reporters before them were entitled to more than the minimum of courtesy.

Out of such events comes pure hostility. As it was in 1986, so it was thirty-three years earlier, when a United Nations reporter named A. M. Rosenthal (later top editor at the *New York Times*) wrote a grumpy critique of his television counterparts. He complained that TV "is not interested primarily in news but in entertainment" and that on his beat TV's technical demands created "a hectic, noisy, movie-set atmosphere."

Television was ruining the press conference, Rosenthal said, because officials were shaping their answers for viewers, not to inform reporters. Television had brought "superficiality and phoniness" to interviews, allowing one congressman to read a statement while appearing to speak spontaneously, and then letting him do it repeatedly for different TV news reporters. And TV was getting interviews with people who did not talk to the print press, in Rosenthal's view because a TV interview show was easier on its subjects than a newspaperman would be.

The complaint about access underscores the envy in Rosenthal's critique. There were admittedly lightweights on the loose in TV news. A 1954 *New Yorker* piece said that some newscasters "are nothing worse than cute," according to critic Philip Hamburger:

> impeccably groomed, they just sit around grimacing and grinning and modulating their voices to fit the temper of the item they are reading aloud. An unwary viewer might fall into the trap of thinking that he is watching a keen analyst of the dire events of the day when in all reality he is watching a male lead in summer stock.

However, it greatly underestimates politicians to imply as Rosenthal did that they were somehow preparing answers only for TV, or that their replies to print reporters' "not too friendly questioning" were not meant to reach and persuade the public at large. Where the idea that the television interview was a less formidable arena than a one-on-one with a print reporter has some merit, it also has several flaws.

Print reporters know how to throw softballs, after all, when interviewing someone whose interest intertwines with their own or their publishers'. And those reporters who liked their questions hard, fast, and across the lower right corner of the plate could be found on TV, working on interview shows where they gave no more quarter than they did when the only recording was by pen in a notebook. When Senator Joseph McCarthy appeared on the first *Face the Nation* in 1954, the reporters were so harsh they would have done Sam Donaldson proud. They deferred not a whit to the senator, even calling him "Joe" a few times, an informality generally frowned upon in these supposedly more hostile times.

Lawrence Spivak, cofounder (with Martha Rountree) and host of *Meet the Press* (whose very title emphasized its link to print reporters), "did not conduct the program; he ruled it," said Edward Bliss. I well remember watching the no-nonsense Spivak, a former magazine publisher who had gone into broadcasting in the midforties, pin politicians like butterflies in a collection case. When Spivak died in March 1994, the *New York Times* spoke of his "terrier-like tenacity as an interviewer and what seemed to be a muted but waspish personality."

It conceded the show's many scoops in the late forties and early fifties; that one was the result of a *Times* reporter's question "did not make print journalists feel any more secure." And the *Times* saw a major generational distinction:

> His style and that of the journalists who regularly appeared
> on his program stand in sharp contrast to a later generation
> of television pundits who sometimes used their broadcasting
> time to express their own opinions.

Spivak contended in a fifties interview that no one could determine his politics from his questioning. But he knew that no level of toughness would keep politicians from his door:

> Men in public office live by the voters they attract, and it is
> therefore hard for any politician to refuse to appear on a

program that attracts an audience in the millions—and makes important news across the country the next morning.

Rosenthal's complaint was not new. It came as newspapers were feeling increasing pressure from television, which was not only showing new muscle in its newsgathering but siphoning advertising from print as well. Already in the early fifties the American Newspaper Publishers Association offered to its member papers a series of advertisements attacking TV. "This is a picture, but not the full story," said one ad with a picture of fully clothed women diving into a pool.

> A picture, a headline, a brief announcement can whet your appetite for more, but cannot satisfy your hunger for the whole story. . . . Only the newspaper brings you full stories day after day. . . . This goes for advertising, too. The brief message that hangs in the air . . . or the brief headline here or there . . . may indeed have momentary interest. But the newspaper ad carries the brass-tacks quality, the urgency of the newspaper itself.

Still, one should be clear that Rosenthal's objections came not from financial worry (although broadcasters have routinely over the years blamed print criticism as motivated by advertising competition) but from the war for turf. Newspaper reporters keep well occupied fighting among themselves over scoops without having to open the battlefield to another medium or media. Some print stars used TV to improve their competitive position; when newspaper columnist Dorothy Kilgallen began appearing on *What's My Line?* she became, according to biographer Lee Israel, "the most visible and celebrated journalist of her time." Ed Sullivan maintained dual access to the stars, through his TV show and his newspaper column—and Marlo Lewis said Sullivan thought his newspaper experience entitled him to a place on CBS's news programs.

Walter Winchell, Drew Pearson, and Bob Considine, well known newspapermen all, had also tried TV by the midfifties, albeit with limited results. Considine later praised producer Ann Gillis Slocum who "taught me how to keep my hands out of my pockets on camera" and edited Considine's often overlong interviews. Afraid to hurt a guest's feelings, he said, "I marveled at my superiors who could slice into a guest's prattling like a guillotine."

While individuals were either shifting loyalty or keeping ties to both camps, television as a medium did not receive treatment commensurate with print's until it won two major battles in 1952. The first was gaining access to a press conference by presidential candidate Dwight Eisenhower. The second was fought at that year's Republican convention.

That the TV cameras were even available for Ike's press conference was a demonstration of TV's increasing political role. Eisenhower had befriended both CBS's William Paley and NBC's David Sarnoff, and Paley was backing Eisenhower's presidential run. The two networks put up an estimated $80,000 so they could carry Eisenhower's first campaign speech live from Abilene, Kansas. When the speech (given outdoors during a rainstorm) went badly, Paley encouraged CBS's news team to stay and cover Eisenhower's press conference the next day. According to Paley biographer Sally Bedell Smith, it was one of his few overt interventions in CBS coverage of Eisenhower.

But the print corps objected to admitting cameras to the press conference. Mickelson says the reporters threatened to disrupt the press conference by constantly sending couriers in and out with dispatches for their newspapers; that would unquestionably ruffle the candidate. But CBS stuck to its guns—putting the cameras in place well before the event, it then told those present "you will have to throw us out." Rather than risk a messy public confrontation (as it was, the dispute made news), the Eisenhower forces agreed to let the gathering be televised, although they said at the time they had agreed only to a filming of it while the two networks carried it live.

Television also prevailed at the convention despite an attempt by pro-Taft forces to keep cameras out. But accomplishing that pushed TV news into the same sinkhole as old newspaper interests, cozied up with the very people it was supposed to cover. Such eighties points of contention as commentator George Will's coaching Ronald Reagan and ABC News President Roone Arledge killing a negative documentary about the Kennedys reportedly because of his closeness to the Kennedys—these were foreshadowed in 1952. At CBS, Paley supported Eisenhower and his right-hand man Frank Stanton backed Stevenson so, as David Schoenbrun wrote, "CBS could not lose . . . no matter who won." Schoenbrun had also made a brief attempt to coach then-General Eisenhower in TV performing, and claimed to have coined the phrase "an Iron Curtain in Chicago" for Eisenhower to use in the battle to get cameras into the convention.

The phrase was picked up by news coverage and Schoenbrun wrote that:

> If I had stopped to think about it, I doubt that I would have done what I did. . . . A reporter acts like a reporter, according to the rules of our game. I had no right to invoke my citizenly interests, to breach the rules of objectivity and fairness.

This was not the last time in the fifties anyone would wonder about fairness in coverage; the Murrow-McCarthy joust causes a stormy debate over that issue. But improved access gave networks a chance to show what they could do at a convention, and do it up they did; Reuven Frank recalled that NBC achieved the *ne plus ultra* of coverage—interrupting a special report for another special report.

Election night then brought an array of coverage and network stars—CBS had Edwards, Cronkite, Charles Collingwood, Murrow, and Lowell Thomas; NBC lined up Swayze, radio veteran H. V. Kaltenborn and pollster Elmo Roper; ABC weighed in with Winchell, Pearson, John Daly, Martin Agronsky, and another polling expert, George Gallup. If nothing else that should put to rest a claim later made by ABC's Peter Jennings that in early TV news "there was Murrow, and then there was Murrow, and there was Murrow." But it also showed that the networks were regularly squaring off against each other.

TV Guide in early 1954 described TV's ingenuity in an article called "It's Nice to Scoop the World."

> A few winters back, mountainous snow drifts stalled a train in California's Donner Pass. A CBS photographer, using a rented plane, landed, took pictures and flew back to Los Angeles before the emergency crews had gotten through. That same night, while the train was still stranded in the mountains, Eastern viewers saw the film on the *Douglas Edwards* show.

When a cruise ship rescued survivors of a sinking freighter, a passenger still at sea offered CBS film of the rescue (showing the small movie camera created the amateur TV reporter long before the camcorder craze). CBS sent out a helicopter, the passenger hooked the film to a life preserver and tossed it overboard, the helicopter nabbed it, and the network had a hot story.

"With today's thoroughness of coverage," ABC's John Daly told *TV Guide,* "the most practical hope for a scoop is to hope your competitor's luck runs out." Sometimes it was a combination of aggressiveness, inventiveness, and luck, as at the coronation of Queen Elizabeth II. In a reflection of TV news wars to come, victory was measured in minutes, end runs tried, the coverage a noisy sideshow to the main event.

As *Newsweek* reported, CBS and NBC engaged in a day-long battle royal to be first with footage. A Royal Air Force jet delivered their film to Labrador, where network aircraft were to pick it up, take it to Logan Airport in Boston, and transmit it from makeshift studios there. NBC also planned for its own jet to fly film directly from England, only to see it have fuel-pump problems and turn back. ABC, meanwhile, avoided the air play by picking up a feed from Canadian television for telecast that evening; when NBC fell behind in the airplane race, it arranged with ABC to pick up the Canadian feed live, so both networks beat CBS—by thirteen whole minutes.

Newsweek estimated that CBS and NBC spent $1,000,000 each on the stunt. ABC got by spending a relatively modest $50,000. And, despite the occasional wistful looks at TV's past as a more altruistic time for news, the networks expected to take in some money from all this madness. Contemporary reports pointed out that NBC lost even more money on the deal because it could not run commercials in the Canadian feed. Network coverage generally was criticized for an overload of commercials. And the networks brought show-business flair to the occasion; *Today* show chimp-in-residence J. Fred Muggs was part of its coverage.

People watching TV news at the time did not sense they were always engaged in a high-minded exercise: CBS's venture into morning programming was seen as an attempt to draw sponsors *Today* had enticed into the early part of the day, and CBS's 1954 show originally teamed the estimable Cronkite with a cast of puppets. Jack Gould was already complaining that on nightly newscasts "the emphasis has been on show business, not journalism."

"News shows are getting more room to move around in," *Business*

Week reported in 1954. It pointed to CBS's morning show, more pictures, more live coverage, and increasing speed (in this case meaning an event could be filmed at 6 P.M. for the evening news ninety minutes later). Moreover, CBS at last had a full-scale news department (NBC, thanks to its Camel revenues, had had one for several years). Networks had news bureaus as well as interconnection with local stations. When *Face the Nation* premiered it promised to live up to its title by coming "live from Indianapolis, New York City, and here in Washington." In case viewers missed the implication of television's reach, it was noted that a reporter in Indianapolis was "standing by nearly 800 miles away."

Not too impressive when you watch satellite news from around the world. But for TV audiences in the fifties it was just as clear a sign that the world had gotten smaller. So small, it turned out that people soon sat in their living rooms and watched a political conflict sweep the country.

9

One Man's Subcommittee

> JACK BENNY: I still don't think you should
>   have stolen my pants.
> BOB HOPE: If Eisenhower had done that to
>   McCarthy, the hearings would be over by
>   now.
>
>   TV gag, 1954

O nce upon a time (1950), an evil senator named Joseph swept out of Wisconsin and across the land, spreading fear through sweeping and sometimes false charges of Communists under every bed. People looked under their beds, and when they saw nothing, Joseph said maybe that was because they had been hiding there. The people of the land became most afraid, and shadows blotted out the sun. Then a noble knight, Sir Murrow, challenged McCarthy to a duel; the nation watched on TV as Murrow wounded McCarthy most severely.

McCarthy bled but did not fall, roaring in his pain. When he roared too loud, a wizard named Welch turned on McCarthy and uttered a spell: "Have you no decency, sir?" The gentle breeze from Welch's breath blew McCarthy from his throne. And the people fell on McCarthy, dismembering him, and peace returned to the land.

This, at least, is the public shape of a television myth. It's a real powerful one, and it still has its advocates. When CBS issued a four-tape set of Murrow highlights in 1993, one tape was devoted solely to the McCarthy wars, claiming that:

> Murrow used the fledgling medium of television to expose
> Senator Joseph McCarthy in a series of extraordinary broad-
> casts that led to the end of McCarthy's reign of terror.

Murrow's reputation, with McCarthy its high-water mark, still ex-
erts a hold on people. When in 1993 Dan Rather launched an attack
on the course of television news, including at his own network, he did
so at a ceremony marking the issue of a Murrow postage stamp. "I
didn't want to go before that group on that occasion," he said, "and
tell Texas stories or just toss something off."

Murrow played a major role in the battle against McCarthy, and
McCarthy himself wielded enormous power. But some of the force
time has granted them is symbolic, their confrontation a memorable
duel in a far larger and more terrible battle. In television history it is
a defining moment, perhaps its greatest moment. But even in TV in
1954, Murrow–McCarthy is a *mano a mano* reduction of a complex
series of events.

From his perch as chairman of a Senate subcommittee, McCarthy's
specific work was the pursuit of Communists in the federal government. But he has in public memory absorbed the acts of an army of
Red-baiters of all sorts: newspaper publishers, radio commentators,
congressmen hunting evildoers in the entertainment industry, a grocery
store owner urging blacklists, self-important investigators, contrite in-
formers. They, and people with far less rabid intent, saw legitimate
cause for concern in the Soviet takeover of Eastern Europe, the Communist victory in China, spies stealing atomic bomb secrets, war in
Greece and the Far East, war in Korea—what appeared to be a widespread threat to a United States not even ten years done with World
War II.

Fame and success were no protection from the harsh winds of Mc-
Carthyism. Philip Loeb, a suicide. Jean Muir: cast in a TV version of
The Aldrich Family, she was bounced after being listed in *Red Channels;* although calls in her behalf outnumbered those opposing her, the
sponsor refused to hire her back. Blacklisted and unemployed, Canada
Lee considered setting up a shoeshine box outside a movie theater
showing *Cry, the Beloved Country* in which he starred. Lionel Stander,
later the lovable Max on *Hart to Hart,* defied the House Committee
on Un-American Activities and ended up counting his exile from Hollywood in decades. Pete Seeger, who helped put folk music in the popular

mainstream, refused to cooperate with the committee and eight years later was still banned from a network folk-music series. A producer asked John Garfield's agent for someone like Garfield for a TV drama; told he could have the real but blacklisted Garfield, the producer declined and cast Dane Clark instead. CBS in 1950 ordered all employees to sign a loyalty oath; disgusted and ashamed, newsman Bill Leonard signed anyway. "The paper did not say one would be fired for not signing," he wrote later. "But . . . I signed."

In face of the terror, some stood up—and before Murrow. Liberal newspapers spoke out. In 1952, Jack Anderson and Ronald May put out a book, *McCarthy: The Man, the Senator, the "Ism,"* which said, "It is next to impossible to keep up with all the lies that have tumbled from McCarthy's mouth." They even went after McCarthy on his own turf, accusing him of a "security-without-sacrifice" doctrine in which he regularly voted for federal budget cuts that hampered the worldwide war on Communism. Also in 1952, Merle Miller put out *The Judges and the Judged,* an examination of how publications such as *Red Channels* were driving people out of show business.

Murrow's colleague Eric Sevareid took aim at McCarthy in radio commentaries in the early fifties. Columnist Drew Pearson (for whom Anderson worked) long warred with McCarthy; during the Murrow–McCarthy brawl, Pearson wrote in his diary, "I couldn't help but remember how Ed Murrow vetoed my going on CBS after McCarthy's first attack on me in December 1950."

By the time Murrow struck his hardest blow, there were signs that McCarthy's power was waning, that his own Republican party and president were looking for a way to be rid of him. But even after McCarthy had fallen, anti-Communist fervor had great force. Broadcaster John Henry Faulk found himself blacklisted out of Murrow's own CBS in 1956 and needed six hard years in court to beat the people who had wrongly accused him of leftist leanings.

This became a television series from 1953 to 1956: *I Led Three Lives,* about FBI commie-hunter Herbert Philbrick; TV encyclopedists Tim Brooks and Earle Marsh say the show "contained what was perhaps the most explicit political propaganda ever found in a popular dramatic series on American television." The acclaimed 1954 movie *On the Waterfront* was later seen as a rationale for informing on your friends.

In McCarthy's heyday, his handprints were seen everywhere. In

1953 Elmer Rice looked at the Television Code and saw an example of "entertainment in the age of McCarthy." "Under the code," he said, "Aristophanes, Swift, and Voltaire would have had a hard time finding employment in TV." But McCarthy himself had no trouble commanding air time in the early fifties. One journalist called him "a master of the medium who didn't play by the rules." Because of the vagueness of equal-time regulations and the timidity of the networks, McCarthy demanded time to reply to any perceived attack.

His bullying style was so well known that McCarthy intimidated before the fact. In his 1959 biography of McCarthy, Richard Rovere said:

> Motion-picture and television scripts were often studied by learned men to make certain they contained nothing offensive to McCarthyism. Sometimes projects were abandoned because it was feared that the whole conception was offensive to the man and his hordes.

McCarthy enjoyed hours of television coverage for his subcommittee's hearings and investigations, sometimes to the embarrassment of the broadcasters carrying them. One day in 1953 ABC ended its committee telecasts just as State Department official Reed Harris began reading a statement responding to criticism leveled against him for the previous hour. Although ABC was in violation of the Fairness Doctrine, which called for presentation of both sides of the issues, both ABC and NBC were finding the committee schedule stacked against fairness. *Newsweek* reported:

> For three weeks [NBC] had realized that the testimony of those who appeared on the screen was, of course, more widely circulated than that of the non-TV witnesses. But where newspapers could report on more testimony and also interview witnesses who were not called, television was stuck with the men the committee scheduled [during broadcast hours].

Not every viewer found the McCarthy spectacle as appealing as the senator did. "What can you get out of the McCarthy investigations that you can't get in the paper?" reporter Marya Mannes asked.

"Plenty." She called it "a defective court" where McCarthy "is out to 'get' and not to learn." But McCarthy continued to move against broadcasters on several fronts—including at the Federal Communications Commission.

Theoretically the regulator of television, the FCC would often prove the servant of the industry's most powerful figures. When Edwin Howard Armstrong squared off against the mighty RCA, historian Tom Lewis observed:

> Armstrong . . . watched in disbelief as the Federal Communications Commission dismissed *his* findings, which he had based on empirical evidence, as nothing more than self-serving arguments. Yet the FCC accepted the arguments of the broadcasting industry, which he *knew* to be entirely self-serving.

However it was used, the FCC had the power to help and hurt broadcasters. For years it delayed the merger of ABC and United Paramount Theaters, which would assure the survival of the struggling network, in order to ponder the implications of a theater-network combine at a time when some visionaries foresaw TV programs shown in old movie palaces. The FCC so severely hampered little Du Mont's attempts to buy more television stations, it contributed to the network's demise. When it ended the freeze on television station licenses in 1952, the FCC set aside some channels for educational use over the objections of station-seeking commercial interests.

The FCC also contained a loud voice against commercial broadcasters: that of Frieda Hennock, a lawyer from New York and the first woman commissioner. Appointed by President Truman in 1948, she pretended no initial knowledge of broadcasting; asked at confirmation hearings what she knew about radio, she said, "Only that I've raised a lot of money for radio programs for Roosevelt." She soon proved an outspoken, activist commissioner, voting against the ABC-UPT merger, pushing for educational channels. Former TV critic Lawrence Laurent called her "the great dissenter."

Broadcasters had still more to fear when two McCarthy allies, John C. Doerfer and Robert E. Lee were named to the FCC. The liberal magazine *The Nation* called Lee's 1953 appointment "McCarthy's windfall" since the senator was busily meddling in television affairs.

He had pressured the FCC to deny a station license headed by an anti-McCarthy newspaper editor and intervened to keep a station license sought by the pro-McCarthy Hearst company out of the hands of an educational group.

Still, Lee's association with McCarthy probably generated some unfair criticism. Frieda Hennock had shown that inexperience did not prevent a commissioner from positive action. But Lee was tarred for his lack of a serious broadcasting background. Jack Gould used Lee to complain about

> the assumption that membership on the commission can be regarded as a reward for the politically deserving individual without regard to previous experience in the complex field of communications.

A more germane concern was where Lee had gotten the experience he had: with Facts Forum, an organization that made radio and TV programs, bankrolled by Texas oil billionaire H. L. Hunt. Hunt—who made the *60 Minutes* highlight reel a quarter-century later when he told Mike Wallace, "I would starve to death with an income of a million dollars a week"—was also a hardcore right-winger and an admirer of McCarthy. Facts Forum was a means of getting his message to the masses.

It's tempting to compare Hunt to Ross Perot, another wealthy Texan who used the media to put across his political philosophy. But there was a crucial difference: Hunt was at once a notorious skinflint and shy about personal publicity. Ben Bagdikian, the esteemed media critic and in his younger days a reporter for the *Providence Journal,* once offered to send a telegram to Hunt with questions he wanted to ask. "Don't send a telegram. They're more expensive," Hunt said. "Send it by mail." And when Hunt set up Facts Forum, its purpose was not immediately evident; it was declared a nonpartisan, tax-exempt foundation, which entitled it to free broadcast time.

Bagdikian, who exposed Facts Forum in the *Journal,* pointed to the difference in Perot's and Hunt's methods. But he also acknowledged similarities, since "they were both using the mass media as a way of getting ideas across." Bagdikian said:

> Our mass media is not open to all civic groups. It is open to people with a lot of money, so Hunt was on in '54 and Perot

is on now. . . . With that much money you can gain access for a certain kind of point of view, which is conservative. You don't have too many rich liberals spending money that way, although Norman Lear talks about it.

In any case, by the time Lee came up for confirmation to the FCC in January 1954, Hunt's cover was blown. Facts Forum's radio series was a bully pulpit for McCarthy, Bagdikian reported, with "no record of any criticism of the most controversial figure in American politics." The foundation was also supporting other inflammatory viewpoints, such as "anti-Semitic and racial agitation" by one Allen A. Zoll. A special committee of the House of Representatives began investigating tax-exempt foundations, including Facts Forum. A group headed by Eleanor Roosevelt said it was going to complain to the FCC about the free air time Facts Forum programs were getting. While the threat was not carried out, Hunt—finally "tired of useless and lost causes"— folded Facts Forum in 1956. By which time McCarthy had folded, too.

But not Robert Lee. At his confirmation hearing, he blandly assured the Senate that, friendship with McCarthy notwithstanding, he would play no favorites on the FCC. "I think I'd go so far as to resent any request for special treatment," he said, and he proved it a couple of months later. An even greater comfort to broadcast interests was Lee's probusiness stance; he favored letting competition, not the FCC, determine the nation's color-TV format and wondered why educational programs had to be commercial-free. But neither his loyalty to McCarthy nor his friendliness toward broadcasters had been tested in early 1954. What with McCarthy's sallies, a Senate inquiry into the content of television programs, a just concluded wrangle over an FCC-approved color-TV system, and the FCC's continuing hold on station licenses, even a president who made use of TV but was not yet ready to break with McCarthy—it looked like a time when government and TV were opponents as often as they were collaborators. The final collision was personified by McCarthy and Murrow.

When the first punch was thrown is open to debate. The most commonly cited starting point—notably by Fred Friendly and Murrow's first biographer Alexander Kendrick—is an October 1953 *See It Now* report on Milo Radulovich, an Air Force lieutenant in danger of being discharged because of a shakily established link through his family to leftist causes. But another Murrow biographer, A. M. Sperber, looks back as far as December 1951, when *See It Now* juxtaposed McCarthy's attacks on others with his own complaints about being smeared; the following year, McCarthy sat for an interview with Murrow and, in Sperber's opinion, rolled over the broadcaster. While those telecasts undercut against the myth that the confrontation began later, Sperber also notes that in a world with few televisions, the first encounter with McCarthy had little impact. The Radulovich program, with more viewers and obvious effect, makes for a neater starting place.

Besides, Radulovich was the sort of story people love to hear and news organizations love to tell—a little man against a big, impersonal organization. Murrow editorialized against guilt by association. The Air Force hurt its cause by declining to cooperate with the report, although *See It Now* in the show itself continued to offer "facilities for any comment, criticism, and correction." A month later, the Air Force crumbled and Radulovich kept his commission.

Although Murrow was close to an all-out attack on McCarthy, the time was not yet right. In fact, the same night that *See It Now* reported the Air Force's surrender, it did a neutral report on "an argument in Indianapolis," where groups including the American Legion had pressured the operator of an auditorium in a local war memorial to cancel a scheduled meeting of the American Civil Liberties Union in the hall. Both sides spoke in the piece and Murrow offered no judgment at the end.

Then came 1954. McCarthy's reach was vast but his grip was loosening. Some observers thought, as historian David Oshinsky wrote, that McCarthy was "at the end of his string." Richard Rovere noted that hearings on the Voice of America had "trailed off into nothingness." An overseas junket intended to root out Red influences in U.S. libraries overseas had proven an embarrassing farce. Then there was the matter of G. David Schine, a McCarthy protege for whom counsel Roy Cohn was seeking favorable treatment by the Army. And even as his enemies saw weakness, McCarthy began to turn on the man who headed the Republican party, who held the White House, and who had been consistently silent about McCarthy thus far: the tough old general Dwight Eisenhower.

The beginning of the end for McCarthy came on March 3, 1954, when Eisenhower took a vague swipe at McCarthy in an untelevised press conference. McCarthy fired back full bore, discomfiting even his allies. Then Adlai Stevenson, the Democratic presidential candidate in

1952 and a contender for 1956, gave a televised speech which, ironically, offered the Republicans a way of breaking with McCarthy.

On Sunday night, March 6, television viewers had a fair number of late-evening choices; in New York City the options included *Spotlight on Harlem, Your Hit Parade,* a movie, wrestling from Chicago, and a show hosted by actress Lilli Palmer. The most important telecast, direct from Miami Beach, was Stevenson's scorching attack on Eisenhower and McCarthy.

> When demagoguery and deceit become a national political movement, we Americans are in trouble; not just Democrats, but all of us.

Because CBS had televised the speech (and NBC carried it on radio), McCarthy immediately demanded air time for a response. But the Republicans were ready for him. They maintained the attack had not been on McCarthy specifically and the Republican party should get the reply time. Robert Lee, McCarthy's old friend now on the FCC, backed the party's proposal. It accordingly fell to the vice president, Richard Nixon, to answer Stevenson and protect the White House. "This was not," Nixon said in his memoir *RN,* "a speech I looked forward to writing or delivering." Still he did so, on March 13. But before that happened, with minimal advance notice, *See It Now* presented a crisply harsh attack on the senator.

There was no pretense of fair play. Although the broadcast offered McCarthy time to reply afterward, this was not parallel to the Radulovich program, where the Air Force had been asked for comment beforehand and refused. In fact, since McCarthy took a month to assemble his response to Murrow, *See It Now* slipped in another attack on McCarthy in the interim.

The Murrow broadside is remembered because it tackled McCarthy. Almost as important—and much discussed at the time—was that the piece was real television, using pictures as well as it used words. Naturally it had film of the sneering McCarthy but people had seen that face before. It also varied the visual image so that is not merely the talking heads of McCarthy and Murrow.

For example, when an audio tape of McCarthy speaking ran, the camera focused on the turning tape reels. Instead of simply having Murrow quote from mainstream papers opposing McCarthy, the program displayed a stack of them (in the process reminding viewers past and present that a large journalistic body was arrayed against McCarthy before Murrow). When Murrow read newspaper excerpts, the camera shot over his shoulder to show the front of each edition; it also made him resemble the viewer at home poring over his own paper.

Then after the virtuoso TV moves, the report retreated to Murrow's first love, the spoken word for a radio-style summation. Murrow warned that "we cannot defend freedom abroad by deserting it at home" and ended with a line from *Julius Caesar* that for a time would belong to Murrow more than Shakespeare: "The fault, dear Brutus, is not in our stars but in ourselves." Stirring to viewers at the time, it now seems a bit windy, a superfluous call to action to already mobilized troops.

After the broadcast Murrow would insist, "I didn't say anything that I haven't said many times before on the radio and the Radulovich show" and maintain that the show's impact lay in McCarthy's own words and image. But that is too modest. The broadcast was artfully structured, benefited from not having a McCarthy reply, tapped latent public sentiment against McCarthy—and was good TV. *See It Now* hit a lot of hot buttons at once.

Which meant some viewers were hot under the collar. Pro-McCarthy forces protested against Murrow, *See It Now,* CBS, and the show's sponsor, Alcoa. The controversy became an unending stomachache for CBS Chairman Paley, especially since Murrow had crossed a line on fairness. Just as the Kefauver hearings in 1951 had crystallized some questions about TV in society, *See It Now* created a basis for additional discussion. *Newsweek* said:

> Never before had so many people wondered about the rules
> and regulations that affect the broadcasting industry. Every-
> one was suddenly aware of the problems of "equal time" and
> "editorializing" and the networks' obligation to the public.

Not even admirers of the program would argue that it was balanced. *New York Times* critic Jack Gould contended "the alternative to not handling the story in this manner was not to do the story at all, by far a greater danger"—a questionable premise at best. The danger was not journalistic but strategic; in offering the senator a chance to reply in advance, *See It Now* would have had to tip their hand to McCarthy, and risk putting Murrow in the ring with a man who by Sperber's account had already mauled him once.

But in offering time to McCarthy after the fact, CBS established a precedent the ignoring of which it would come to regret. When General William Westmoreland sued CBS over what he considered a slanted 1982 documentary about Vietnam, CBS News executive Burton Benjamin recalled the McCarthy situation and asked, "Why would this not be the right thing to do for Westmoreland?" He also suggested the telecast of a Westmoreland press conference attacking the documentary. CBS did neither, the case went to court, and lawyers racked up $15 million in fees.

The fairness issue aside, the unique medium of television was being called to account on unique issues. In one of the most pointed criticisms of *See It Now* (not least because it came from a Murrow admirer), John Cogley in *Commonweal* argued that the TV images of McCarthy in the show were all negative—when positive images were also available. Murrow and company had used television skills against McCarthy, and their foe might be overmatched when it came time to respond.

> On the one hand, Mr. Murrow had all the know-how and resources of one of our great networks to set up his case; and on the other, there was an individual Senator with nothing to call on but his own speech and whatever film he might lay his hands on. Of its nature such a contest would be unequal.

Cogley overstates a bit on both sides. *See It Now* had resources but it was a troublesome duchy within Paley's empire, not the empire itself; one can only imagine the audience for *See It Now* if the network had put its full promotional power behind the program. But save your tears for McCarthy; as has been detailed, politicians had been closely studying television. And a man as powerful as McCarthy was not without his own resources—columnist George Sokolsky helped write McCarthy's TV remarks, and the senator proposed that William F. Buckley, Jr., act as his on-air surrogate. (Murrow said the reply would be by McCarthy or no one.) And the senator billed Alcoa for production costs on his program—adding to the controversy the question of who should pay for a rebuttal.

Still, the broad principle behind Cogley's concern stands today. You see it any time a station offers citizens a chance to reply to an editorial; the reasonably able station announcer gives way to people whose nervousness and TV difficulty became a ripe topic for Johnny Carson parodies. And McCarthy did not prove very effective on TV; critic Gilbert Seldes wrote in *Saturday Review* that it was "a feebly handled newsreel talk illustrated by two or three unanimated maps."

Cogley's concern also worked toward the larger point that television's growth had raised, whether Murrow and CBS had not only used the power of television but abused it.

> When the channels of communication are controlled by private corporations, these corporations are necessarily big. Since they are big, their personal interests are the interests of similar giants. . . . So far, speaking generally, we have escaped the use of network resources for private interests. Both CBS and NBC have tried to present both sides fairly. I am sorry to say that I truly believe the Edward R. Murrow show has set a potentially dangerous precedent.

At about the same time, *Newsweek* examined the Murrow–McCarthy question for a cover story and asked, "Is it right in principle for television to take a clear stand on one side of a great issue?" Given that networks employed commentators of various stripes, given that the major TV networks were built on a foundation of commentator-laden radio, the answer should have been a simple yes. Instead it was decidedly mixed, even from CBS's top brass, which bounced from a declaration of the right to editorialize—albeit with opinion clearly separated from fact—to a proviso that "the execution of a policy cannot be reduced to a mathematical formula or even to a set of rigid rules." Two months later, though, Paley gave a speech reasserting that there were rules and that CBS would be objective in its reporting.

Although the issue consumed the national attention for a time, television history to that point showed the naïveté in assertions such as Cogley's about networks not serving their private interests. An obvious example was Paley's urging coverage of Eisenhower's Abilene press conference in 1952. And it was certainly in the cause of self-interest that CBS and NBC accepted the Republican demand for time to reply to Stevenson's Miami speech while brushing off McCarthy's complaint. (The senator thundered at the rejection but got nowhere and resorted to petty revenge, refusing to pose for NBC and CBS cameras at a press conference.)

Richard Nixon delivered the official reply on March 13. As was common in Nixon's approach to crises, he later wrote of being "calm and low-keyed" in presentation so he could reach the middle-of-the-roaders in the audience. It also says something about the prevailing attitude toward Communists that his main metaphor involved hunting rats; people needed to shoot straight, Nixon said, so that they did not risk hitting someone else hunting the same rats. No one had to ask who was firing wildly.

See It Now reentered the struggle a few days later, showing McCarthy and Cohn badgering Annie Lee Moss, a clerk whom the McCarthy crowd, based on secret testimony, had declared a Communist with access to secret Pentagon codes. Amid Moss's professions of innocence and ignorance, McCarthy and Cohn appeared to have brought in the wrong Moss. Murrow compounded their embarrassment by replaying it on *See It Now,* and accompanying it with a 1953 Eisenhower speech about an individual's right to confront his (or in this case her) accuser, something McCarthy with his secret information generally did not permit.

The serial continued in early April with McCarthy's reply to Murrow, which fulfilled every concern Cogley had expressed. Having thrived on TV with bullying and speech making, McCarthy assumed the practice would work in his rebuttal. Drew Pearson, no friend of McCarthy or Murrow, called it "a savage and effective job" and it might have been so delivered before a hall of McCarthy faithful; as a telecast, and in contrast to the artfulness of *See It Now,* it was the flop Seldes described. Moreover, Murrow did not let the matter drop, replying to the rebuttal a week later.

Not long before, McCarthy had thought he was riding high. *Life* magazine in early March devoted nine pages to him, most of it about his triumphs, the last page filled with a photo of the man himself. "Efforts have been made in the past to control McCarthy," the magazine said, "but he has always fought his way out." Since then he had suffered setback after setback, some of his own making, most of them conveyed to the television nation. Donkeys and elephants alike were trampling McCarthy and the circus hadn't yet come to town.

The tents were pitched in late April, in the form of hearings on whether the McCarthy claque (and mainly Roy Cohn) had unduly pressured the Army in the matter of David Schine. McCarthy's own subcommittee did the investigating, with the beleaguered chairman stepping aside for the duration to become—as he would be reminded—not the boss but a witness at the proceeding.

From the beginning the hearings were made for television. Although they did not provide as polished a view as sophisticated legislators would prepare in later TV generations, the participants knew enough to joke about wearing makeup and camera-friendly blue shirts. Strict time limits were set for each question period. And the seating changed daily, McCarthy's team and the opposing group from the Army switching according to one newspaper report "to equalize their opportunities to be picked up by the three cameras that will be televising."

Pool cameras were to serve the four networks (ABC, CBS, NBC, and Du Mont) but in short order only two networks were presenting live coverage. While in retrospect one can wonder why any network would want to give McCarthy more free air time, even for something that proved to be his downfall, financial rather than political concerns were a major factor in the network decisions. CBS opted for late-night filmed reports (and of course material in its newscast) so as not to interrupt its high-paying daytime schedule of soap operas and variety series (*Arthur Godfrey Time, Art Linkletter's House Party,* and so on). Not only would CBS lose the ad revenue from those shows, but the subcommittee eliminated the chance to recoup even part of the investment by refusing to allow commercials while the hearings were in progress.

NBC carried the hearings for two days, then cited loss of income (a reported $125,000 in advertising just to that point) and low ratings as justification for dropping live coverage in favor of entertainment programs such as its month-old *Home* show. That left ABC and Du Mont to shoulder the burden, which they did, and not only for their affiliated stations. ABC began live feeds to some NBC and CBS affiliates wanting coverage. Such feeds indicate that the audience for the telecasts was far stronger than NBC had surmised—or that it wanted to surmise.

Figures at the time said that after a few days the hearings were being watched in about 10 percent of TV homes, a poor showing compared to the 32 percent the Kefauver organized crime hearings achieved in 1951. But the number of television homes had more than doubled in the ensuing three years, and it could well be that the raw number of viewers for Army–McCarthy was as high as for Kefauver, but a smaller percentage of the total audience. In addition, because of CBS's decision, some viewers who wanted the hearings might not have been able to get them, especially in markets served by one station committed to CBS's lineup, or by a dominant VHF station carrying CBS programs and a harder-to-see UHF with Army-McCarthy. Besides, there was anecdotal evidence of viewer interest. ABC's Chicago affiliate estimated at least 300,000 viewers were watching the hearings there, sales of TV sets went up in some cities, and in Los Angeles—where the live telecasts began at 7:30 A.M.—people were showing up late for work.

Much the way broadcasters would approach special events in the cost-conscious eighties and nineties, they checked their wallets before deciding what to do about the Army hearings. In some cases, local stations cut in and out of the hearings for their own programs. Some interrupted coverage for commercials in defiance of the subcommittee. In May the subcommittee finally gave ABC and Du Mont a bit of relief, allowing "limited sponsorship"—the equivalent of a modern PBS underwriting announcement—"in recognition of the value and services of the live coverage." In light of all this, Gilbert Seldes posed questions that are still pertinent.

> Would *all* the networks be justified in refusing to carry the proceedings? . . . If not, aren't the ones who refuse taking advantage of the fact that someone else is doing the work? . . . Is the cost . . . too great for the industry to bear without sponsorship, or is this cost part of the price which stations pay for their license to broadcast? . . . How big does an audience have to be to justify the cost of broadcasting to it? . . . Why didn't the networks get together and form a pool, dividing the time so that no single one took a disproportionate loss?

That last idea came to pass almost twenty years later when the networks rotated live coverage of the Senate Watergate hearings; one can nonetheless argue that it was a so-so solution at best since viewers did not receive all stations equally well; the emergence of cable has not resolved the issue either since a cable channel carrying an important hearing while the broadcast networks do not is of no help to a viewer who does not have cable. But broadcasters' concerns also had merit as hearings, however important, could drag on for weeks; Marya Mannes, a month into Army–McCarthy, prematurely complained it was "a drama wholly without catharsis: a plot without form, a story without end." Others questioned the value of live coverage not only of Army–McCarthy but of any such proceeding.

People began anew consideration of problems first raised during the Kefauver hearings. When the Federal Bar Association asked Vice President Nixon for his thoughts on the issue in 1954, he repeated comments from a 1952 speech:

> Televising hearings tends to create a circus atmosphere which diverts not only the witnesses but even some committee members from the serious business at hand of getting the facts. Too often temptation is to play to the television audience. . . . In addition, televising hearings places an unreasonable burden on the average witness. . . . The physical and mental discomfort which television lighting and production entails is, in my opinion, in effect a kind of third degree to which he should not be subjected against his will.

Nixon's assessment can be applied to the Kefauver hearings, to the witnesses dragged before McCarthy in his heyday, and finally to the Army–McCarthy hearings. They were, after all, high drama and low comedy. With their careers on the line, McCarthy and Cohn went to extreme lengths to defend themselves, such as presenting a photograph that appeared to help their case—until the Army showed it was cropped from a larger and less beneficial scene. The low point in comedy came from Army counsel Joseph Welch, McCarthy's nemesis, who twitted the senator with remarks alluding to rumors of Cohn's homosexuality.

"As law the comment was improper; as humor it was unjust," said a reporter for the liberal *New Republic,* but "as drama it was beyond anything the theater could conceive or reproduce." And Welch was baiting McCarthy at a time when homosexuality, real or rumored, was considered exotic and dangerous. In 1952 a TV columnist noted Hollywood complaints about "the alarming influx of queers on TV"; when an avowed homosexual appeared on TV in 1954, he was fired from his job the next day.

But the hearings did not have to rely on Welch's tasteless remarks for humor. Comedy writers feasted. Humorist Goodman Ace looked at the hearings' running in slots normally reserved for soap operas and hypothesized "One Man's Subcommittee" complete with organ music and absurdly intricate plot synopsis. *Newsweek* said "a comedy show wasn't a comedy show without some mention" of catchphrases from the hearings. Such attention ensured that no one at the hearings forgot they were in the camera's eye; McCarthy at one point handed a note to photographers asking, "Could I have time off from cameras for 10 seconds to use handkerchief?" Ace's soap opera and Mannes's drama were just two of the TV metaphors for the hearing; a Denver TV executive compared it to sports: "'Who's winning it?'—that's what people say."

The winner, history says, was Welch. Fred Friendly described the long hearings this way: "They took almost two months and involved two million words of testimony, but all that most of us remember now is the thirtieth day." McCarthy, weary of Welch's jabs, tried to stop him with the accusation that a Welch aide had Communist links. The attack boomeranged, Welch shifting it to McCarthy's own credibility in an impassioned speech about the "cruel and reckless" attack. When McCarthy tried to return to the point about Welch, the attorney struck the final blow:

> Let us not assassinate this lad further, Senator. You have done enough. Have you no sense of decency, sir, at long last? Have you no sense of decency?

Marya Mannes had gotten her catharsis. As Lately Thomas said in his McCarthy book *When Even Angels Wept,* the sincerity of Welch's performance is suspect. But it was marvelous television, the avuncular, indignant Welch overcoming the suddenly stunned McCarthy.

And if this were simply a television production, we could end it at that moment—freeze on the two adversaries, slap up a note that McCarthy was later condemned by the Senate and roll the credits. But the implications for television did not end with McCarthy's comeuppance. Consider the notion, much repeated up to that time, that television was a conveyer of truth; the debate over *See It Now*'s treatment of McCarthy centered on the art of television. Nor did the telecasts of the hearings present an absolute truth. McCarthy admirer Harold

Lord Varney thought they did. But he contended that anti-McCarthy newspapers "went on a smear binge, with every trick of phony headlining, slanted story leads and news column editorializing" while TV showed people the true nature of the players: the "Uriah Heep–like" Welch whose decency remarks were "a tawdry exhibition of anti-McCarthy hokum"; a McCarthy whose gallantry and sportsmanship "have endeared him to millions." McCarthy, he concluded, would make a "swift and certain" comeback.

Which he did not. And television could rejoice in the cementing of its position as a powerful political medium, a place where the nation gathered to watch momentous events unfold. But McCarthy had not left TV unbloodied. The long, costly Army hearings validated the concerns of CBS and NBC about the cost of covering such proceedings. ABC lost a reported $600,000 from its coverage; Du Mont's costs added to a host of other problems that drove it out of the network business in 1955.

A little more than a decade later, CBS refused to offer live coverage of the Senate foreign relations committee hearings on Vietnam. Fred Friendly, then president of CBS News, resigned over the issue and wondered if any network would have carried the Army–McCarthy hearings had they occurred in 1966. The answer is by no means clear. NBC after all showed the hearings Friendly could not get on CBS, so the possibility remained. But in 1994? Most likely the commercial networks would leave the grunt work to PBS, CNN or C-SPAN— unless McCarthy was accused of sexual harassment, or had assaulted a figure skater.

The brouhaha over *See It Now* increased Murrow's stature and won him an armload of awards. But in the real television world, Paley's stomachache was as important as Murrow's reputation, and the controversies *See It Now* continued to pursue undoubtedly contributed to its loss of both its sponsor and its weekly time slot in 1955. Moreover, the success of the McCarthy broadcasts could be interpreted in a way that narrowed television's news focus.

Humanizing the issue—Milo Radulovich, Annie Lee Moss, McCarthy, and Murrow themselves—made good storytelling of a sort that television news magazines still rely on. But the search for the human story can turn attention away from the details of large institutional stories, such as the savings and loan crisis, except in those situations where it can be personalized—and the story of a robber baron or of a family that lost its savings, while compelling, does not explain the how and why of the crisis. Other sorts of personal stories, for instance the seemingly endless parade of stories about legislative perks, are nice at putting an individual on the spot or conveying a broad impression of political arrogance; but they do not really address more pressing political issues, including the federal deficit in which the cost of congressmen's Caribbean vacations is a pittance.

Government learned from McCarthy and television would not like all the lessons. In June 1954 a Senate rules subcommittee began discussion of ways to avoid what one senator called the "undemocratic, high-handed, and tawdry manner" in which some committees had operated—meaning McCarthy's. But a further rub to the speaker, Democratic Senator Thomas C. Hennings, Jr., of Missouri, was Army–McCarthy, which he called "tawdry, tedious, and shameful" and "an affront to the people of this country." The *New York Times* reported:

> Had this inquiry been conducted behind closed doors, Mr. Hennings told the subcommittee, it could have been brought to a solution in a week. In general public sessions, he maintained, ten days would have brought it to a conclusion. Under the lenses of television, he said, the inquiry was stretched into weeks of "a race that went only to the hams" trying to outdo one another in "amateur histrionics."

The fault, dear Brutus, was not in ourselves after all. It was in the electronic witness to our worst selves. Although many agreed with Gilbert Seldes when he wrote in the wake of Army–McCarthy that "the right to televise whatever is being otherwise reported will not be challenged from now on," the Senate appeared to believe Hennings's theory. And when it prepared hearings on a motion to censure McCarthy, print reporters were allowed in but radio and TV were barred.

Given the seeming triumph of television in the McCarthy story, the decision was a shocker. The American Civil Liberties Union protested. CBS President Frank Stanton called it "grossly discriminatory." Senator Karl Mundt, who had been acting chairman of McCarthy's subcommittee during Army–McCarthy, said TV and radio "are a great and mighty conscience for the press." *Collier's* magazine said the broadcast ban "transgresses the American doctrine of equal rights."

Yet the Senate had allies. A committee of the American Bar Association, long opposed to cameras in courtrooms, claimed broadcast coverage caused a "circus atmosphere"; the full ABA later voted in favor of broadcasting only if individual witnesses could ask that their testimony not be shown. Federal Judge Harold Medina said—in rebuttal to a CBS editorial, by the way—that cameras and microphones "constitute a psychological and very real barrier which, for all practical purposes, makes it impossible to get at the truth."

The cameras were kept out. Although the public rationale for that move was the distraction and discomfort created by broadcast equipment, there is no doubt the senators did not want a reprise of the semiprofessional wrestling at the Army hearings, at least not while the public watched. A few senators had improved their images with their behavior at the Army hearings, but the game was a risky one as McCarthy had shown. If you don't want people to call you a ham, best not to let them see you oink.

But where obstruction was the order of the day in 1954, manipulation was the ultimate guiding principle. McCarthy and Welch were just the latest figures showing how people's images were formed on and by television—and that politicians had better learn how to use the medium. Indeed, David Oshinsky has argued that the problem for McCarthy was not the crystallizing confrontation with Welch but

> the cumulative impression of his day-to-day performance—
> his windy speeches, his endless interruptions, his frightening
> outbursts, his crude personal attacks.

The novelist John Steinbeck revealed one TV metaphor for McCarthy in his 1955 essay "How to Tell the Good Guys from the Bad Guys." Steinbeck observed that his son Catbird, seemingly a zombie before the set, was in fact accumulating information and impressions. He had, for instance, quickly learned to distinguish characters in Westerns—the good guys wore white hats, the bad guys black, the in-between guys ("if he starts out bad he ends good and if he starts out good he ends bad") wore gray. Steinbeck himself realized that bad guys wore dirty clothes, seldom shaved, and (unlike the stoic good guys) had expressively nasty faces.

Steinbeck told this to a friend, who applied it to the hearings. Mc-

Carthy, the friend said, "sneers. He bullies, he has a nasty laugh and he always looks as though he needs a shave. The only thing he lacks is a black hat."

Steinbeck went to Catbird and asked about McCarthy. The child's answer: Bad guy.

THE PRICE OF SUCCESS

· · · · · · · · · · · · · · · ·

The growth of television changed how people thought of it. The more viewers there were, the more cause for celebration by those who wanted to use television and the greater reason for worry by those who believed it was having a negative impact on society. From either point of view, the next step was obvious: make sure television's agenda was your own.

To Hollywood, which had long hoped television would go away, that meant becoming a full partner with television, an act that would dramatically change what appeared on the small screen. Professional baseball, on the other hand, saw the growth of the television game as a threat to its collective well-being and for a time resisted TV's attempts to bring the game to the nation; TV not only prevailed, it left a trail of rooftop antennas to the West that major-league teams would follow.

Others, dismayed by what they saw as inappropriate content on television, turned to Congress for help; by the end of 1954 both the House of Representatives and the Senate had held hearings about how television was influencing children, and whether the TV industry was acting responsibly. As commercial television's mission focused increasingly on revenues and less on responsibility, people sought relief in a new, noncommercial form—educational television, later known as public TV. But a poor funding base would force educational television to face the same problem its commercial counterparts had—how to generate an audience large enough to justify the financial investment necessary to keep it going.

But let's begin with the audience most likely to be drawn to television, and the constituency on whose behalf television has faced recurring protests: the littlest viewers, children.

Sex, Violence, and
Ladies Pouring Cocktails

Television, a new gadget in the majority of
American homes, arouses hot argument
among those who can take time from
watching it to discuss it.
American Mercury, 1954

In his 1957 book *America as a Civilization,* Max Lerner looked at the complaints about television (such as columnist Harriet Van Horne's contention that "the grandchild of the Television Age won't know how to read this") and pleaded for calm.

> Every new medium has been hailed as a worker of miracles
> and dreaded as a destroyer of the ancient virtues. Neither the
> salvation nor the doom has been fulfilled.

But Lerner was swimming against a tide of criticism that continues to wash over television—at times justifiably. By the time Lerner's book appeared TV had been under attack for close to a decade—an attack that went far beyond judgment of the newest comedy or drama, or objection to some obnoxious commercial, to fundamental considerations of what TV was doing to society in general and children in particular.

It's fun to imagine that the first child to have television babysit was a little Sarnoff or Du Mont resting in the glow of a tiny screen in the thirties. Even if that is not the case, by the late forties the video nanny was very much on the scene. Bob Considine, the Hearst newspapers columnist, wrote a series of tales of bringing up his children in 1947 and 1948 and included his original reaction to television:

> a varnished, dial-laden robot that would soothe colic, delight, bemuse, drug, and finally pack the young 'uns off to bed by means of a finger-wagging, chuckling Uncle Don. We turned the thing on, chained the kids to it, and forgot it and them.

Considine soon discovered, like John Steinbeck and many other parents, that television does not merely slip children into suspended animation. They absorb images and ideas and projects (Considine's home was overrun by puppets and little cowpokes). And this was no time to be fooling with ideas.

"Reactionary politicians have managed to instill suspicion of all intellectual efforts into the public by dangling before their eyes a danger from without," Albert Einstein wrote in refusing to testify before the House Un-American Activities Committee. "It is shameful for a blameless citizen to submit to such an inquisition." But people were afraid, of the Red menace described in chapter 10, and of other apparent threats to their society.

The movie industry, for example, was waging an intense internal battle over censorship. Between 1952 and 1955, as Geoffrey Cowan has written, the Supreme Court restricted state and local censors' ability to suppress films. In 1953 the movie industry was considering a quiet overhaul of its long-standing Production Code, which put tough restrictions on film content, but was thrown for a loop when Howard Hughes—and other filmmakers later in the year—released films without the code's seal of approval. Because of Hughes's action, one report said, "vociferous pressure groups might get the idea that some deep, dark plot was afoot to overthrow the code."

Powerful and seemingly contradictory messages abounded. For one, you had President Eisenhower participating in the American Legion's "Back to God" movement. For another, you had 10,000 young people flocking to disk jockey Alan Freed's rock 'n' roll concert at the Newark Armory—the culmination of a musical movement that had been building since the war. People were breaking free and pulling back in almost the same breath. Popular-culture writer Nick Tosches has said that rock 'n' roll—which for hitherto unaware listeners was just arriving in the person of a former Memphis truckdriver in 1954—was dying that same year:

> Bill Haley, the first white rock 'n' roll star, came, turned to shit, and went, all in one fell swoop, by the summer of 1954. . . . The beast of rock 'n' roll had been tamed for the circus of the masses by the time Elvis . . . came along. Elvis played out the cycle again, in the span of six months: In "Milkcow Blues Boogie," his third record, made in December 1954, raw power has already turned to schmaltz.

Whether in the schools, where the Supreme Court had ordered integration, or in the darkened movie houses where kids watched motorcycle-riding Marlon Brando in *The Wild One,* change loomed. And someone had to take the blame. It couldn't be that change was needed. It couldn't be that the forces in power had brought this on themselves. The nation played the blame game just as Senator Hennings did after the Army–McCarthy hearings. While some people looked into their souls, others looked in the living room—and saw the culprit in the corner, in a French Provincial cabinet. It was all the fault of television.

Well, some of the fault anyway. Geoffrey Cowan lays moviemakers' defiance of censors (and theaters' willingness to show the films) in part on the success of television and the need to offer audiences "material that they couldn't find on television, such as sex, violence, and rough language." And the movie industry did its job well, creating an appetite for uncut movies that still-censored television would not run, but that premium services like Showtime and Home Box Office would, and video stores would rent. When producer Steven Bochco defended the content of his excellent but controversial series *NYPD Blue,* he said it would not be possible to compete with cable "unless we can paint with some of the same colors that you can paint with when you're making movies."

And by 1954 television was presenting regular testimony as to its power to reach and influence viewers. When a play on *Studio One* used a little known song by a just as little known singer, "Let Me Go, Lover," sold half a million copies in five days. When daytime TV host Garry Moore asked viewers to send a nickel to a Mt. Pleasant, Michigan, woman in his show's audience one day, she received 8,000 letters in 24 hours. Estimates were that she would end up with 200,000 letters and about $12,000 in nickels. "This is the second windfall she's had," an envious neighbor told a reporter. "Last year she and her husband learned the rumba."

Moore had originally been making a point about *Strike It Rich,* a program that had regularly tugged at viewers' heartstrings and in the process became one of the most reviled shows of the period. Trading in the same sort of human misery that would fuel daytime talk shows in the nineties, *Strike It Rich* was most likely the worst series—and one of the more successful ones—in 1954.

Starting in radio in 1947 and moving to TV with both prime-time and daytime telecasts in 1951, *Strike It Rich* presented contestants who told about the terrible problems in their lives. They were then asked a series of questions to win cash and prizes to help them out. After the questions, they were taken to the "Heart Line" area, where a telephone awaited calls from viewers offering still more assistance.

TV director Kenneth Whelan, briefly associated with *Strike It Rich,* said Heart Line calls sometimes came from businessmen who promoted their products on the air. Staff from the show would also make calls when things were slow, using the opportunity to plug other goods. For viewers, the attraction was the unflinching, even enthusiastic, view of suffering. Whelan said a director on the show quit after his boss insisted on a tight shot of the crutches and legs of a paraplegic hobbling to the Heart Line. "It suddenly occurred to me," Whelan wrote in his memoirs, "that I was working on a Geek show."

When *Television,* a trade magazine, asked critics their views of TV, *Strike It Rich* topped the list of worst shows. (Runners-up included *Stork Club, The Pinky Lee Show,* and *My Little Margie.*) But it also did well on another list: the twenty-five most popular prime-time shows; in its second season it cracked the top twenty. The show was so popular that in 1954 it ran afoul of Henry McCarthy, New York City's commissioner of welfare; he claimed *Strike It Rich* was an unlicensed welfare agency—and that needy people were traveling to New York in the hope of getting on the show.

The commissioner had been gunning for the show for some time, having also criticized it in a 1953 speech. But press attempts to find these hordes of indigent game-show aspirants were unsuccessful. Pro-TV writer Max Wylie, who had also worked on *Strike It Rich,* spoke up for the show as a public service that "gives money to people who badly need it, and right then and there." (Sounds like an *efficient* welfare agency.) Wylie also called it "the most revealing social commentary that television is offering anywhere" precisely because it showed people going through hard times.

In any case, *Strike It Rich* withstood the legal challenge and remained on the air until 1958. But the viewers' appetite for such wallowing in pain has continued. The modern TV schedule provides plenty of ammunition for a discussion of "Daytime Talk: Social Commentary or Geek Show?"

Getting back to public concerns about television, the power attributed to *Strike It Rich,* and to TV generally, was exactly why people were wondering if it had done deep damage to society. The worries fit under three headings: sex and other matters of taste, violence, and the effect on culture, including reading skills in children. Television was not alone in being attacked—comic books took an even harder hit from social critics in 1954—but it was rarely left off the list of trouble-makers. No less prominent an observer than Pope Pius XII said:

> Television programs are, for the most part, made up of films and theatrical spectacles, and the number that fully satisfy Christian morality is still too small.

Television, which was supposed to have been an advance from radio, which was supposed to serve an elite audience, which was seen as a glorious educational tool, had become a launching pad for a radio monologist named Arthur Godfrey and an aging comic named Milton Berle. In his 1950 book *The Great Audience* Gilbert Seldes complained:

> the audience television will create if it excites and feeds only one group of appetites will be lower in the scale of human values simply because so many natural human wants will go unsatisfied and so many capacities will atrophy from disuse.

Then again, when Max Wylie came to write his book-length defense of television, *Clear Channels,* he said that "after many hours of patient study" of Seldes's book, "I could not make any more out of it . . . than that its author is a true snob and a sports hater." Contrary to

Seldes's concerns, a *New York Times* examination of television in 1951 reported:

> In a remarkable unanimity of opinion . . . state superintendents of school systems, principals and school teachers agree that at first children may look at the screen excessively or neglect other activities, but that they soon return to their old habits and maintain their scholastic standing.

The newspaper also reported that children may have been reading more, not less, since the advent of television because TV "appeared to be stimulating the youngster's interest in books, especially Westerns and adventure stories of the type generously represented on video schedules."

In an article the next year, Ohio State Librarian Walter Brahm said, "Our fear of harm is more likely to harm [libraries] than television." He produced an article from *Library Journal* in 1924 that blamed a seeming drop in book circulation on the automobile, radio, and movies.

An analysis of "televiewing by pupils, parents and teachers, 1950–1953" in *School and Society* magazine was also guardedly optimistic, saying "the strong interest of children and youth in television may become either a liability or an asset in education." It urged that teachers and parents find ways to assimilate TV into the learning process, for example by turning attention to science and history shows.

> The almost universal appeal of television offers an unparalleled opportunity for influencing children and youth in positive ways. If this is to be accomplished, programs must be planned and developed through co-operative efforts.

And, as Edwin Broderick had put the issue of TV's content in the context of parental responsibility, so a prominent psychiatrist said parents who complained about their children's viewing were "unconsciously confessing their own abdication of reasonable parental authority." Overall you can see the framing of an argument about television that would remain essentially the same through the rest of its history. On one side were the critics who believed the medium must be rid of bad influences on viewers. On the other were those who thought the viewer, or the viewer's parent, needed to control content by the simple act of choosing what to watch and what not.

Naturally some observers balanced both elements—Broderick's fifties guide *TV and Your Child* said "responsibility for TV's impact upon juvenile delinquency is divided between the industry itself and parents"—but extreme positions were more common. In 1950 a radio—yes, radio—host in Cincinnati told his young listeners to raise their hands but neglected to tell them to put them down. Critic John Crosby had no doubt about whom to blame for the resulting furor.

> More and more during the last couple of decades, the parent has had to behave with the utmost circumspection to avoid bruising his child's psyche. . . . It's come to the point where any clown on the radio demands and receives more respect than mummy and daddy.

Which is not to say television was simon-pure. In the early nineties a prominent critic wrote, "During the 1950s and early 1960s vigorous self-regulation made the world of television a sexless place." Since that opinion is commonly held, it's surprising to see what television was actually offering. Here's how wide-eyed Gracie Allen proposed raising money for her club.

> GRACIE: We can raise the money the way my sister Bessie did. . . . Every time her husband kissed her, she made him put a 10-cent IOU in the piggy bank. And after two weeks she had 90 cents in IOU's and 65 dollars in cash.
> FRIEND: Well, where did the cash come from?
> GRACIE: Well, you don't think she'd take IOU's from strangers!

Early television personality Guy LeBow, recalling articles about sleazy TV from the forties (one titled "The Sinking Video Standards") into the early fifties, reeled off problems from the period.

> You know the stuff. Blue jokes, busty girls and sight gags that concentrate on breasts, buttocks and legs. Double-entendre jokes. . . . Lots of lap-sitting, ass-pinching, tit-touching. Bosoms galore in plunging necklines.

(Before anyone cries about sexism, LeBow also said "directors of wrestling matches ordered crotch shots for female fans.") Television would not have needed a censorship code if there was nothing on worth censoring. Some female stars became successes thanks to their bosoms, among them Dagmar of *Broadway Open House* (whose fame irked Robin Morgan) and Faye Emerson, an actress and TV personality.

In 1950 John Crosby gave Emerson a publicity bonanza by calling her "the plunging neckline Woollcott" (a reference to critic and man-about-town Alexander Woollcott), adding that she "fills a ten-inch screen very adequately. Very adequately." Although Crosby attributed the Woollcott line to another publication, Emerson went on the air and told her viewers that Crosby disapproved of her decolletage. She got, as Crosby admitted, "bushels of mail, much of which she read over the air and 95 percent of which upheld the low neckline." Crosby backtracked, telling readers that he felt not disapproval but "helpless admiration." Then he addressed the actress:

> It is one of the functions of criticism, Miss Emerson, to outline to the readers the general nature of the entertainment and the entertainers. To have avoided outlining your own spectacular outlines would have been a shameful neglect of my duties.

Although New Yorkers apparently took this cleavage contretemps with good humor, the folks in Washington found such affairs all too serious. The FCC was logging increasing numbers of complaints. In May 1952 the House of Representatives voted to investigate offensive matter in print, radio, and TV, a crusade *The Saturday Evening Post* dubbed "Congress vs. the Plunging Neckline."

E. C. Gathings, the Arkansas congressman who had called for the hearings, was really more worried about print than TV. *Newsweek* reported that Gathings in his research had accumulated more than a hundred offensive items, including

> playing cards picturing nude women, nudist magazines, and art books showing nude men and women on the beach, in the shower, or just talking; pseudo-scientific volumes on such subjects as the sex life of the bachelor; homosexual novels, and literary sex shockers by the dozen.

But TV had trouble spots: the already mentioned sex, immorality (a South Carolina representative complained about seeing "beautiful ladies demonstrating the techniques of pouring cocktails"), and violence. A watchdog group in Los Angeles claimed that one week of programs between 6 and 9 P.M.—supposedly children's hours—contained:

> 91 murders, seven stagecoach holdups, three kidnappings, 10 thefts, four burglaries, two cases of arson, two jailbreaks and a murder by explosion . . . [and] a suicide, a case of blackmail, many instances of assault and battery, and "numerous" instances of drunkenness and brawls.

Still Gathings's mission was greeted with more than a little skepticism not least because he seemed to be bringing the government to bear against free speech. The inquiry into publications explicitly excluded newspapers, to avoid interference with freedom of the press. Nondenominational magazine *Christian Century* said existing laws seemed sufficient to forbid obscenity and "it is virtually impossible to give . . . censorship boards power without giving them too much power." And the National Association of Radio and Television Broadcasters had shown its willingness to censor itself, with the Television Code, which had gone into effect about two months before the House voted to hold its hearings.

Even worse for Gathings's case were the many ways in which he and his supporters were made to look foolish. When Gathings testified before the committee investigating TV, he acknowledged that the new code had apparently affected Dagmar's costumes. "Give us a little detail," a congressman on the panel asked. "Just how low did it get and how high has it gone?"

"I think the waistline is a little higher," a flustered Gathings said, assuring reporters covering the hearing at least one juicy quote for the next day's editions. And he wasn't done. Gathings also told the committee he disliked seeing a dancer do the samba on TV, and tried to demonstrate the offensive movements. "He did not succeed in doing the samba," Max Wylie wrote a couple of years later. "He did succeed in making a fool of himself and was enthusiastically photographed during these bony convulsions."

But let's not just pick on Gathings. Joseph R. Bryson, the representative alarmed over cocktail techniques, claimed his two-year-old grandson knew when "Howdy Doody" came on and could turn on the set and tune it in himself, at a time when tuning was by no means automatic; just imagine what a tyke that smart could have found with cable and a remote control! Oren Harris, chairman of the committee, reported "complaints about commercials in which cigarette smoke is blown out of the screen"—a physical impossibility.

Such nonsense obscured the real threat TV felt from the hearings, one it blunted for the time being with the code. The House report in December 1952 said "self-regulation is making substantial progress and . . . is preferable to government imposed regulations." But history has shown that any attempt at censorship, however well motivated, will come under criticism on principle and the code was no exception. The American Civil Liberties Union called it "stultifying and illegal censorship" that "would create conformity and reduce TV to dull mediocrity," something TV did not need a code to accomplish. On a more practical level, Frank Orme wrote in *The Nation* that the code was almost impossible to enforce and had been violated pretty much from the moment it came into existence.

Television did show some signs of self-regulation, at least on innuendo and cleavage. *TV Guide* said in early 1954 that "the plunging neckline has pretty much gone out of style." Violence was another matter. In May 1952, a year after NARTB adopted the code and three months after it had gone into effect, Orme and a monitoring team checked just crime shows (police, detective, and the like) in Los Angeles for a week. They found 852 major crimes, including 167 murders, and 85 percent of the mayhem was before 9 P.M., when children could be watching. Orme further said that the number of crime shows (along with Westerns the most criticized for violent content) had gone up from a year earlier, before the code. "Day by day our television stations are piling up a record of the failure of the NARTB code," he wrote.

Although Congress had for the moment let TV off the hook, a drumbeat of complaint continued amid alarming TV images still available in video stores: violent early episodes of *Superman,* kinks in the mean streets of *Dragnet* (one episode called "Big Girl" involved a mugger who turned out to be a man in drag). A paper trail of worry formed.

Christian Century, cautious in 1952, sounded fed up in 1953. "Parents have taken up arms against the indoctrination of their children in murder and violence by television," it said in an editorial that was reprinted in the National Education Association's magazine. When the Chicago *Daily News* reported on local surveys of violence in TV, *Christian Century* said it brought "a roar of angry confirmation from parents, teachers and pastors."

Cosmopolitan in 1953 said this:

> Many parents, educators and doctors regard the appalling crime wave regularly beamed at 70 million American viewers as anything but entertaining. . . . Almost the only group that seems completely undisturbed about the TV criminals-at-large is the television industry itself.

"The toll mounted last week," an issue of *Time* magazine reported in January 1954:

> One man was brained with a monkey wrench as he lay sleeping. A woman, tied to a chair, was tortured with a carving knife until she died; two strip-teasers were sliced to death with razors; four gangsters were shot down in a columnist's living room; a bartender was murdered in his own saloon, and a small boy was killed by a hit & run driver. . . . More people are killed each year on TV's crime shows than die annually by murder and non-negligent manslaughter in the six largest cities of the U.S.

A nineties TV viewer may well wonder how bad these violent acts in the fifties could have been. The answer is, pretty nasty. Because of technological limitations—not only in TV but in the weaponry available to criminal and crime stopper alike—you did not get the sort of artistic slaughter that marked, say, *Miami Vice*. But the violence was still there in some detail. Consider *Casino Royale*, a 1954 live drama that is credited with being the first adaptation of one of Ian Fleming's James Bond stories. It's not that good a production—Barry Nelson plays "Jimmy" Bond, an American spy who comes on more like a hard-boiled private eye—and the emphasis is on suspense built around a game of chemin de fer. But it does have its share of brutality, from four opening gunshots through a beating, a fistfight, a couple of shootings, and a scene where Bond, tied up in a bathtub, has pliers taken to his bare feet by chief villain Peter Lorre.

That goes to the question of degree of violence and the effectiveness with which it is portrayed on the screen, a question crusades against TV violence tend to ignore. The use of statistical counts of violent acts, whether in the fifties or the nineties, validates the assumption that presentation of any violent act is on its face unacceptable. But that assumption means, as has so often been pointed out, that telecasts could not include parts of the Bible, Shakespeare's plays, or American history, including its wars.

The point was not lost on some fifties observers. In the report on TV violence mentioned above, *Time* magazine acknowledged the relativity of violence, that some crime shows' inept production "makes it impossible to take them with any more seriousness than so many Punch & Judy shows." A National Council of Churches of Christ study of families in New Haven, Connecticut, in 1954 found 69 percent of those surveyed considered the available children's shows acceptable; only 26 percent disapproved.

Robert Lewis Shayon showed more generally "the frustrations of subjective measurement" in writing about two viewer-opinion surveys. In one a viewer rated *My Little Margie* "poor" while another respondent called it "good." *The Pinky Lee Show*—like *Margie* on a critics' worst-show list already mentioned—was "excessive bad taste" in one analysis, "just plain funny" in another. And TV ratings indicate viewers made clear subjective distinctions among the violent shows. *Dragnet,* often nonviolent and consistently of high dramatic quality, was the only crime show in the top ten for the 1953–54 season; the only other crime show in the top twenty-five, for that matter, was *Treasury Men in Action.*

Such data was drowned out by the loud, sustained cries that something be done about TV. Congress, looking at a turbulent society that it could not well control, was more than willing to find somewhere to point a finger. A Senate committee investigating the causes of juvenile delinquency provided the vehicle.

As was the case in 1952, the new hearings, which began in April 1954 and continued off and on into 1955, went beyond TV to examine radio, movies, and comic books. Horror comics, repeatedly attacked by bluenoses and academics, ended up being destroyed by the hearings. Dr. Frederic Wertham, who had issued a broad attack on the causes of juvenile delinquency in his book *Seduction of the Innocent,* told the Senate that "comic books are an important contributing factor in many cases." The comics industry, lacking the clout of TV especially when it came to helping politicians' careers, made an ideal target. Comic-book publisher William Gaines became a legendary figure when Senator Estes Kefauver asked him whether a comic cover showing a man holding the severed head of a woman was in good taste—-and Gaines said yes.

"I think it would be bad taste," Gaines added, "if he were holding the head a little higher so the neck would show with the blood dripping from it."

"You've got blood dripping from the mouth," Kefauver replied.

By comparison television could not help but look mild. And one has to wonder if television was helped when its part of the hearings did not get going until October, after television had played a positive role in bringing down Joseph McCarthy. But Thomas Hennings, who had loudly complained about the cameras' presence during Army–McCarthy, was on the subcommittee holding the TV hearings; the violence issue created another opportunity for payback against TV.

That may explain why the television industry received mixed messages from government. Before the hearings began the subcommittee—Kefauver, Hennings, William Langer of North Dakota, and the chairman, Robert Hendrickson of New Jersey—was "strongly opposed to censorship." Then, when the hearings began, Hendrickson proposed a "TV czar" to police programming. Similarly the FCC came out against government censorship of shows during the hearings—"We believe it would be dangerous, as well as contrary to our democratic concepts," said FCC member Rosel H. Hyde—but Hyde said the FCC would consider program policies and content when station licenses were up for renewal, a clear warning that somebody better be censoring shows.

Not that everyone was on the anti-TV bandwagon. Esteemed psychologist Erik Erikson said television and comic books were being made scapegoats for juvenile delinquency. In a statement that should be laid before any legislator planning a hearing on television, Erikson said:

> When people get worked up, they often look for something or someone to blame. That makes them feel better but it doesn't mean they have found the cause. They fool themselves into believing they have found an immediate cure, with no evidence whatever that it will work now or has in the past.

Goodman Ace, a veteran comedy writer for television as well as a print commentator on the medium, gave a mocking assessment of the antiviolence crusade in his *Saturday Review* column.

> When I was a child—which was pre-television, for that matter pre-Marconi—I played fireman one afternoon and flooded the basement of our home. My parents called a meeting and it was decided that my stereoscopic slides of Niagara Falls would have to go. And so, having been deprived of my three-inch screen, I began wandering around town and soon became a juvenile delinquent.

Television, meanwhile, knew what it had to do in the hearings: take a public flogging from critics and promise that it could solve its own problems. And so it went. On the first day of the hearings the subcommittee saw what one report called "juicy film excerpts" of violent acts on TV. A CBS vice president spoke up for "self-regulation and self-discipline." Al Hodge, better known as kiddie-show star Captain Video, assured the senators "we don't even use the word 'kill.'"

An ABC vice president said television "is a very young industry, while juvenile delinquency is very, very old." The president of the National Association for Better Radio and Television, said NAFBRAT "is alarmed and dismayed over the volume and degree of violence which dominate television programs for children." Clara S. Logan said:

> We believe that upwards of ninety percent of all teachers and administrative educators are convinced that crime programming on radio and television is harmful. We *know* that millions of American parents are alarmed at the present situation.

But the TV industry had a hole card. Harold E. Fellows, president of the National Association of Radio and Television Broadcasters, spent much of his statement to the subcommittee on the broadcast code and how it worked.

> In the Television Code . . . we have the machinery to act quickly and effectively in a manner that would justify the

Federal Government's confidence in broadcasters to regulate themselves.

Fellows said NARTB planned to increase staff and monitoring of programs, to underwrite a study of the impact of TV on children, and to increase the number of stations subscribing to the code (almost half the stations on the air did not). The trade magazine *Broadcasting* said, "Industry feeling was that television acquitted itself well."

But not well enough, apparently. Under continued pressure, NARTB in late 1954 announced it would try harder to avoid violence in programs. While Hendrickson praised the NARTB for showing "intelligence and responsibility," he took the action as TV's admission of "some validity in our criticism of certain crime-horror films now shown for children on television." And there had been other signs that television knew it had overstepped. *Superman* for example had retreated from the violence of its early episodes (largely drawn from the radio version of the show); in 1955 the show further took pains to remind youngsters tempted to imitate the Man of Steel—especially by flying leaps from rooftops—that "no one, but no one, can do what Superman does."

The subcommittee, meanwhile, ended up walking both sides of the street in its final report, admitting there was no proof that television harmed children but contending that there was "reason to believe" it could do harm. In one passage the report said of TV's crime shows:

> Life is cheap; death, suffering, sadism and brutality are subjects of callous indifference and judges, lawyers and law-enforcement officers are too often dishonest, incompetent and stupid.

That's almost verbatim what Frank Orme had written in *The Nation* in 1952:

> Life is cheap; death, suffering and brutality are subjects of callous indifference; judges, lawyers, and law officers are dishonest, incompetent, and stupid.

Opinions were so fixed, a three-year-old comment was still considered applicable. Heck, you could make the first half of that comment today and still get nods of agreement. Television and its adversaries have kept going to the same dance.

11

The Mouse That Flinched

I don't care how big a star is, every one
of 'em is a ham at heart.
                                TV producer, 1954

When *Disneyland* premiered in October 1954 it made official what had long been anticipated: Hollywood's surrender to television. That the white flag was held by a twenty-six-year-old, three-fingered rodent named Mickey hardly mattered; he just stood in for moguls who had long known that when it came to television they would have to play or pay.

The idea of a partnership between television and movies is as old as TV itself. In January 1928 RCA, the General Electric Company, and Westinghouse announced plans to work with Joseph P. Kennedy's FBO Pictures "for the purpose of developing sound reproduction and synchronization, radio broadcasting and television in connection with motion pictures." Film and television historian Michele Hilmes, in her book *Hollywood and Broadcasting*, details extensive collaborations between television and the movie industry in the years leading to 1954. Du Mont was partly owned by Paramount from the late thirties on. Twentieth Century-Fox and Warner Brothers both considered mergers with ABC in the late forties and early fifties; MGM began advertising its movies on TV in the late forties. Ed Sullivan worked his Hollywood connections on his variety show, as in a 1954 tribute to MGM. Small, independent production companies anxious for any way to make a buck were more than willing to funnel their productions into TV. By 1950 motion picture producer Samuel Goldwyn had declared

Motion pictures are entering their third major era. First there was the silent period. Then the sound era. Now we are on the threshold of the television age. . . . There is no doubt that in the future a large segment of the talents of the motion-picture industry will be devoted to creating motion pictures designed explicitly for the new medium.

But that thought was anathema to others in the movie industry, who had built their fortunes on a theater-based system; even Goldwyn devoted a large part of his article for the *New York Times Magazine* to how movies would compete with television. Goldwyn suggested among other things that it would have to turn out better pictures. Hollywood preferred to try to strangle its competitor, for instance refusing to sell its old movies to TV or only movies made before 1948 (the modern made-for-TV movie was long years away). But that only worked to the advantage of companies that did sell movies, and of old stars such as William Boyd, who became a TV sensation when he sold his *Hopalong Cassidy* Westerns to TV in the late forties.

By 1951, it looked as if movies, not TV, were strangling. Movie houses around the country were reporting attendance declines of 20 to 40 percent, and television was a likely culprit. Still, any Agatha Christie reader will tell you to beware of the likely culprit—and the *New York Times* cited many other problems for the motion-picture business: the troubled national economy, the indifferent quality of some movies (as Goldwyn had warned), and shifts in population from cities to the suburbs. While an alarming number of theaters had closed, the *Times* said many "were outmoded buildings in distressed neighborhoods"; new theaters were opening elsewhere and the nation's 3,000 drive-ins were doing a booming business.

Hollywood tried to answer the threat. In 1952 it introduced 3-D and Cinerama, a wide-screen technique; 1953 saw CinemaScope, another fancy way of showing movies; the late fifties brought Aroma-Rama and Smell-O-Vision, two systems for pumping movie-appropriate smells into theaters. The Academy Award, a barometer of what the movie industry liked about itself, went to full-color, wide-hipped extravaganzas impossible on a TV screen, *An American in Paris* in 1951 and *The Greatest Show on Earth* (unfortunately about the circus and not the movies) in 1952.

Around that time, though, Hollywood began making overtures to the TV-loving audience; in 1953 the Academy Awards ceremony was televised for the first time. The best picture that year, *From Here to Eternity*, is on one level a big-screen epic with a star turn by Burt Lancaster, an actor so energetic it seemed difficult for a movie screen to contain him, let alone television's; it also had that famous smooching-on-the-beach scene (memorably parodied on *Your Show of Shows*). But *Eternity* is also a highly focused, intimate drama, where audiences are drenched in closeups—Lancaster, Donna Reed, Deborah Kerr, Montgomery Clift, Frank Sinatra, not to mention the cruel gleam in Ernest Borgnine's eyes. Granted the movies had used closeups before television, the use of it was comforting and familiar to the televiewer accustomed to big faces on a small screen.

Then, in 1954, *On the Waterfront* won the Oscar with an intimate, talky story full of the grit people associated with the "kitchen sink" school of television drama. The filmmakers may have known they were working in a manner influenced by the neorealists coming out of post-World War II Europe; the audience at large sat in theaters (or their station wagons) and watched the black-and-white progress of something like what they saw at home. They were sure to notice Eva Marie Saint, winner of an Oscar for her performance in *Waterfront*, and long an acclaimed television actress.

The final capitulation was *Marty*, an adaptation of an acclaimed television drama by Paddy Chayefsky, and winner of the best-picture Oscar for 1955. The simple story of a butcher and his search for love had touched television audiences with Rod Steiger in the lead role, and did likewise in a gentler big-screen version. And the institutional acclaim for *Marty* was just part of the picture; clear-eyed commercial considerations motivated both a theatrical version of *Dragnet* and a Lucille Ball–Desi Arnaz feature, *The Long, Long Trailer*, both released in 1954. Hollywood had taken to television for its own purposes (and moviegoers had already started complaining about people bringing their TV–viewing manners into theaters). All that remained was what form its help to TV would take.

Again, there were signs before 1954. Lucille Ball had had a movie career. So had Burns and Allen, Jack Webb, Robert Montgomery, Jack Benny, Groucho Marx, Ann Sothern, Abbott and Costello; Martin and Lewis made movies and TV appearances. Not only Hopalong Cassidy but Gene Autry and Roy Rogers were bringing Western flair to TV. Dick Powell had hosted *Four Star Playhouse*, which regularly called on movie actors, since 1952. Loretta Young, winner of a best-actress Oscar in 1947, began hosting her own drama anthology series in 1953. *Time* magazine noted the trend but added "the big-studio, big-star antipathy toward television still exists," and explained why:

> Most term contracts at the big cinema studios still forbid TV appearances, except for special walk-ons to plug a new picture ... and most top-ranking free-lance stars are too wary or too weary for television. Explains Cinema Tough Guy Humphrey Bogart: "I got a helluva good racket of my own. ... I don't have the time and I don't trust the medium yet."

At least one actor worried about adjusting to the new system of series TV. Bing Crosby, in an as-told-to-Pete Martin memoir published in 1953, said he would go to television eventually but "anybody who goes into TV should be sparing in how much work he does." Crosby noted:

> If a new motion picture of mine were released each week for fifty-two weeks—or even for thirty-nine weeks—I soon wouldn't have many friends coming to the theaters to see me. And they'd drop the flap on me at home, too. They'd weary of my mannerisms, my voice, my face.

After a few appearances here and there, Crosby formally broke into television with his first special in January 1954. But he appeared sparingly, as an actor and as himself, over the years; while that could be attributed to Crosby's worries about overexposure, *TV Guide* further pointed out that "TV is hard work. Crosby's idea of hard work is to lie out in the shade of a poolside tree." Bogart, meanwhile, did a guest shot on Jack Benny's show in order to promote his movie *Beat the Devil* and in 1955 acted with wife Lauren Bacall and Henry Fonda in a TV adaptation of his thirties breakthrough, *The Petrified Forest*. But that still amounted to an appearance by an actor, albeit a very popular one; more significant was the entry into television of producer David Selznick, who in *Gone with the Wind* had made the epitome of the grand-scale movie.

Selznick's involvement in TV proved to be on a grand scale, too, as producer of *Light's Diamond Jubilee,* a two-hour special that ran on all four networks, sponsored by power companies in celebration of the invention of the electric light. Selznick biographer David Thomson notes the impresario had a standing interest in TV; a friend of CBS's William Paley, he sent kibitzing letters to the network boss. But Selznick claimed in a 1956 memo that Paley told him to stay away from TV, if only because Selznick could make more money with less effort in the movies.

Selznick said he took on the spectacular, which boasted an array of stars and an appearance by President Eisenhower, "for the express purpose of learning what the medium was about" without taking on the long-term obligations of a series. He appears to have enjoyed experimenting "for the purposes of my own education," such as by blending filmed and live segments. But the cost of the program was far more than the $350,000 budgeted, "a lesson in the cost of a first-rate show" to Selznick. Thomson mentions other headaches, including the ultimately successful battle to include an adaptation of a short story by Irwin Shaw, who in the words of his brother, writer David Shaw, "was sort of graylisted."

The special did come together at last, and was well watched (which you would expect since every network was carrying it). But Selznick never did another TV project. Thomson speculates that the cause was "the insignificance of the people who made TV. . . . TV was so modern, it was as if it simply happened, without makers. There was no room for a personality like Selznick." Strange words about a world where great personalities strode through the stages, control rooms, and executive suites, among them Selznick's friend Paley; that description better fits a changing Hollywood, for which Selznick would make just one more film before his death in 1965. Television was showing movies a relative cheap path to audiences in which the extravagance of a Selznick would fall into disfavor for a time. Interestingly, though, it was another self-indulgent visionary who would bring movies and television together.

Walt Disney was his name. His passion in the early fifties was a theme park called Disneyland, a financial sinkhole where costs had started at $4 million and risen to almost four times that. In his search for more money, as Richard Schickel wrote in *The Disney Version,* Disney also had to battle the deep skepticism toward an amusement park without a roller coaster. But Disney persisted and came into contact with ABC's Leonard Goldenson, then searching for programs for his network and making the studio rounds.

Accounts of what happened next vary. Sterling Quinlan's book *Inside ABC* says Goldenson got a verbal commitment from Jack Warner of Warner Brothers over a long dinner in 1953, then reached agreement with Disney. Goldenson's memoirs place the Disney deal first, then the Warner dinner. And Michele Hilmes says that other studios were on the way, that "by the end of 1953, all the major studios either had on the air, or had announced plans for, their own television production."

But nothing like *Disneyland*—a big budget, filmed series drawing on every skill the Disney organization could muster—had happened up to that point. The Disney–ABC deal was also a complex interweaving of the two companies' fortunes; ABC bought into Disney's company to give him a much-needed cash injection, agreed as well to help him get other financing, and let him use his show to plug the living daylights out of his theme park and other projects. If it worked, the potential reward was enormous. If not, the implications went beyond financial disaster for Disney. The company was, if nothing else, a stalking horse for the rest of Hollywood. Certainly Jack Warner would have thought twice about proceeding with its ABC deal if *Disneyland* had been a quick, expensive failure.

Early signs were ominous. "Davy Crockett," a three-part story that began on *Disneyland* in December 1954, went over budget when bad weather hit location shooting in the South; an already large $450,000 price tag ballooned to $600,000. The company also went through careful (and time-consuming) editing to reduce the seventy-five-minute feature *Alice in Wonderland* to a television hour (with commercials). *Television* magazine called it "a painstakingly edited show with single-frame deletions made in places so that the flow and continuity would not be disturbed." Disney himself remained unperturbed by the adjustment to television (or distracted from it by the building of Disneyland). If you doubt his wisdom, though, just ask any fortysomething in reach what comes after "Born on a mountaintop in Tennessee."

"It's wonderful," critic Jack Gould said of the *Disneyland* premiere, which like other shows drew on four program categories—Adventureland, Frontierland, Tomorrowland, and Fantasyland, which just happened to be the four sections of the planned theme park. Although Gould conceded the first show was really just a preview for forthcoming installments—selections included a clip from "Davy Crockett"—"enough was shown to lure back viewers of all ages next week." Especially in view of the telecast of some vintage Disney cartoons, Gould said:

> To hear all members of a family laugh out loud is not something that happens very often in watching TV. But it must have occurred in millions of homes on Wednesday night. More need not be said of the genius of Disney.

Disneyland was just one show, just one of twenty-five prime-time hours each network could fill every week. But the impact was inestimable. As ABC's biggest hit—it ranked sixth in prime time its first season and was only the second ABC show, after *The Lone Ranger,* ever to crack the top ten—it probably saved the network. It definitely saved Disney. *Disneyland* was an early demonstration of the success of counter-programming—going against shows appealing to similar audiences by putting on a show that reaches to a different viewership—by reaching out to children in a time slot where shows like Perry Como's and Arthur Godfrey's targeted the old folks; it also encouraged ABC's pursuit of young viewers in opposition to the other networks' more adult lineups, which became even more evident in later programs like *American Bandstand, The Mod Squad,* and *Happy Days.*

Disneyland served as another reminder of the marketing possibilities in television, even winning an Emmy for an episode Schickel derides as "hardly more than a promotion piece" for the feature *20,000 Leagues under the Sea.* It tried new things—critic David Bianculli points to "Davy Crockett" as one of the earliest miniseries; it was also a precursor of the adult Westerns about to take over television. (The Crockett saga, which included additional episodes when the first three proved a success, was also edited into feature-length movies in 1955 and 1956, which can still be found in video stores—and still intrigue a child or two.) And the error-laden live telecast of the opening of the Disneyland park would be seen as a writing on the wall to proponents of live TV, who already had reason to fear from *Disneyland* itself, a filmed series with high production values and seemingly endless repeatability.

Finally, *Disneyland* proved to Hollywood filmmakers that a partnership with television would work. That led to additional involvement in TV—Warner Brothers began putting series on ABC in 1955—and a shift in creative power away from the New York-based, stage-oriented writers, producers, and directors (who to survive often found themselves logging many airplane miles, or simply moving west) and toward a Hollywood-centered, movie-studio-style system that was far more amenable to artistic compromises in reaching the largest possible audience. Moviemakers had been reaching such compromises for years.

It made sense in some respects. As has been mentioned, comics from movie and radio had a stronger sense of how to tailor their acts to the vast, unseen audience than did early New York performers used to an urban audience that was becoming a smaller and smaller fraction of all TV viewers. At the same time, the Hollywood crowd had no qualms about endlessly duplicating a successful formula to achieve still more success, even if the copies were less inventive than the original. By the sixties some productions had become generic, Hollywood certain that it could create a star as it had always done—not from a performer's gifts but from an act of studio will. When Warner's detective show *Bourbon Street Beat*—a knock-off of *77 Sunset Strip*—was a flop, the studio took two characters from it (and the actors who played them) and transplanted them to the real *77 Sunset Strip* (Rex Randolph) and a second knock-off, *Surfside Six* (Kenny Madison).

While Hollywood also took television out of the intimacy of its interior sets and into the great outdoors, too often the open air was filled with a posse on the gallop or a patrol car with siren screaming, instead of the sound of the marvelous words the TV playwrights had composed. The writer had never been held in high regard in Hollywood, nor would he be in Hollywood-ized TV. The frustration that generated was summed up by Reginald Rose.

> The whole thing deteriorated in terms of how much fun it was and how exciting it was. And the writers were no longer the stars. . . . People turned on *The Defenders* to watch the defenders, not the people who wrote it.

Does that mean only bad television came out of Hollywood? Of course not. And were only good shows produced in New York? No to that, too. But television had made a major change in orientation. It's not unusual these days to hear television producers talk about their series as "little movies." It's an offhand phrase but a telling one to those who came up in early television; then you didn't have to make movies because you made a unique thing called television. The Hollywood forces coming into TV saw it not as a unique medium, but as a unique distribution system for their old-style product.

The Dark Age
of Television Sports

In the matter of television . . . I do not
believe that it was ever the intent of the
Congress of the United States that any law
should be interpreted so as to permit one
industry to grow fat on the lifeblood of
another.

Baseball Commissioner Ford Frick, 1954

In the early eighties I was covering a public hearing on the local
cable franchise, and one citizen stood up to complain that the cable
system did not carry SuperStation TBS. The cable manager mentioned several other services the system offered, and each was greeted
with the reply, "I don't care about those." Nor did it matter that the
cable system had two New York City stations and one from Boston
carrying sports, and ESPN, and the network sports programs. This
fella wanted Braves games from Atlanta and would not be satisfied
until he got them. It seemed that for him the only reason to have
television was to watch sports.

That man had about forty years—now fifty—of similarly inclined
viewers behind him. They do not want reason, they want sports. More
important for our purposes, they are disinclined to revel in ballpark
ambiance; they just want to see the game. Steve Allen spoke for millions of fans when he described attending a college bowl game, having

a great seat, then leaving before the game was over because he could not see the action as well as he could on TV. These are the fans who prompted a then-struggling CBS to bid $1.1 *billion* for baseball rights in the late eighties and the Fox network to open its wallet for football in the early nineties. It encouraged ABC, on one of the rare occasions it outbid one of its larger counterparts, to make a deal for college football in 1954. Although some of these deals across the decades proved unprofitable, dedicated sports fans consistently sent a message: If you show it, we will come.

Because television sports has exerted such a powerful pull, 1954's place in television sports is less about the court than the courts— where sports fought to control where and how often their games might be seen. From 1953 to 1955, both professional baseball and football were embroiled in legal wrangles over TV sports rights, and the National Collegiate Athletic Association members fought among themselves about how to administer football telecasts of their games.

Television and sports had long intertwined. The first telecast of a baseball game—a college match between Princeton and Columbia— was in 1939, with the first major-league telecast two years later. By the mid forties New York TV viewers had also seen hockey, basketball, track, and boxing. What came to be known as trash sports, like professional wrestling and roller derby, were TV mainstays in the late forties and early fifties; Dennis James, long a popular game-show host, got his first real taste of fame as a wrestling announcer on TV.

"It was commonly said, when television was beginning," Gilbert Seldes wrote in 1950,

> that the great problem was not the size of the screen or the cost of production or the reluctance of sponsors; the essential thing was to get into Madison Square Garden.

The reason for the sports-TV marriage was evident, and no better put than Ron Powers did in his book *Supertube: The Rise of Television Sports:*

> Television needed something live, something conspicuous and established as a field of human interest; something that could be transmitted from a relatively small, highly defined field of activity. Television sank its teeth into sports.

Powers strikes a chord we have already heard in this book—the notion that television's fundamental power lay in the presentation of live events. When people considered the reality of home reception of television signals in 1928, their vision of the future immediately included the chance to see faraway sports events *as they happened*. The localness of television in the early years, presenting sports to the local fans, came into play as did the visionary power a sponsor could exert; as has been mentioned, Gillette with its *Cavalcade of Sports* and Falstaff, which pioneered the national baseball game of the week, are two examples. When *TV Guide* gave its first program awards in 1954, the three shows it cited were *See It Now,* drama anthology *U.S. Steel Hour,* and *Cavalcade of Sports.* Looking at the previous season *TV Guide* praised *Cavalcade* for bringing viewers

> the outstanding sports programs of the year, including the World Series between the New York Yankees and the Brooklyn Dodgers; the Rose Bowl game between U.C.L.A. and Michigan State; the Kentucky Derby and a weekly series of Friday night boxing bouts. . . . *Cavalcade,* through its initiative in pioneering sports coverage and its willingness to spend large sums for such major events as the World Series, has made a tremendous contribution to the growth of television.

Inventiveness beyond the networks was essential because, as both Powers and Seldes have written, the idea of television as an elite medium did not mesh with the rough and tumble of sports. Especially in those early years when televisions were in few homes, Seldes wrote that sports moved TV "from the atmosphere of the home . . . to the saloon."

Where sports still like to pretend to a certain toughness, one can easily imagine the alarm with which TV-fixated high panjandrums of pro football today would greet the likes of Hardy Brown, a defensive linebacker for the San Francisco 49ers from 1951 to 1956. Extolled in a 1987 NFL Films presentation as possibly "the most destructive hitter of all time" in an era when "every team had a notorious hit man," Brown took credit for knocking players out seventy-five to eighty times over his career.

Downstate rivals the Los Angeles Rams once put a $500 bounty on Brown; he said he colluded with a college classmate, then playing for the Rams, to fake being put out so they could split the bounty. And what did Brown say about the heavily padded, protection conscious, chill-fear-at-every-injury pro football of the television age? "A sissy game."

Boxing caused similar discomfort, even among some of its fans. Daniel Lord, writing in *America* in 1953, recalled listening to a fight on the radio where "boxing sounded an exciting, glamorous and pretty thrilling business. But you can't broadcast blood and cut eyes and the faces of an audience." Watching boxing on television, he said, presented "the brutal reality . . . the bloody, brutalized, beaten, pulpy faces of the boys in the ring," as well as the hard faces of the spectators. Noting the sponsor, Gillette, urged viewers to "look sharp, feel sharp, be sharp," Lord examined the fighters and found "little that was sharp about their looks."

Small wonder that men's products—blades, beer, and butts—were the principal sponsors of sports telecasts. And in a business hungry for revenues, the assurance of sponsor support for sports put it into prime time six nights a week in the fall of 1953. A fundamental change in sports was taking place, not in the games so much as where people watched them. Benjamin G. Rader describes it in *In Its Own Image: How Television Has Transformed Sports:*

> After World War II, when millions of Americans moved to the suburbs, their spare-time activities moved with them. In suburbia residents might bowl more, play softball, attend church, go to the beach or a nearby lake, or hunt and fish, but they often left behind them public entertainment located in the inner city. Above all else, suburbanites spent more of their spare time at home.

In January 1954, *Life* profiled "the new American domesticated male"—mowing the lawn, building a barbecue, entertaining colleagues at his at-home bar, even going to the grocery store and minding the baby so "wives can have their hair done, shop, go to club meetings." (*Life* was apparently slow to clue into the working woman.) Paint, lumber, power tools, and other goods were enjoying increased sales thanks to the male homebodies; *Life* also reported that "home economists guess that more kitchens are remodeled the day after a husband gets supper than after years of wife's complaints."

The article ignored television in this new household, save for the rooftop antenna in one drawing, but TV was unquestionably part of this domestic agenda. When a family lived in the city, the stadium was easily accessible by mass transit; not so when the family faced the necessity of a trip from the suburbs. One midfifties examination of sports said:

> The difficulty of getting to the ball park, and the problem of parking their cars, keep more fans from attending ball games than does TV.

Television provided another kind of access to sports. For a struggling organization, that was a boon. The National Basketball Association signed its first league contract in 1953, with Du Mont, $39,000 for thirteen games. "It was good exposure for the game, and that $3,000 [per game] was a nice little revenue in those days," said one NBA official.

For better-off sports, such as football, college athletics and, the preeminent game of the era, baseball, television was at best a mixed blessing. To be sure, it brought millions of fans to individual sports and to sports generally (1954 saw the launching of a new magazine, *Sports Illustrated*); but those fans were not putting their money directly into the pockets of the sports teams, and the income from broadcast rights was abysmally small by modern standards—in 1953, regular-season broadcast revenues for major league baseball totalled less than $6,000,000; pro football that year took in just over $1.2 million.

On the other hand, even that money helped to compensate for other problems. Nine of twelve pro football teams made a profit in 1953, but for two, TV income made the difference between profit and loss. Major league baseball, at almost 21 million spectators in 1948, was down to 17.5 million in 1950, then 14.4 million by 1953—and that last figure was inflated by an attendance boom in Milwaukee, where the Braves had moved from Boston.

The minor baseball leagues were in free fall; fifty-nine leagues in 1949 dropped to forty-nine by the end of 1951 and to thirty-eight just two years later. In 1950 pro football also suffered a decline in attendance, although one coach blamed not television but poor publicity by pro football itself. Indeed, as sports historian Ira Horowitz has written, it was after the televised 1958 championship-game thriller between the Baltimore Colts and the New York Giants that "professional football was firmly established."

Whether TV was in fact helping or hurting sports is a question that has as many answers as does the same question regarding TV and the movie industry. Certainly, it was culpable in one respect, bringing major league baseball into minor-league towns. Just as the locally produced television shows suffered by comparison to more extravagant and star-laden network productions, so the not-ready-for-prime-time ballplayers slipped into the shadows when the big show came to town. Other factors may also have come into play—Rader points to the rise of stock-car racing in the South as drawing fans away from minor-league ball—but TV cannot be ignored.

Still, TV was far from alone in causing trouble for sports. The whiff of corruption had long been around boxing. College basketball, pure gold for television these days, had been rocked by a 1951 scandal, where thirty-three athletes from seven colleges admitted fixing ninety games. With shifts in population, some teams tried moving to where new fans were: when the Braves moved from Boston to Milwaukee in 1953, they suddenly had a million and a half more fannies in the seats. In 1954, the new Baltimore Orioles pulled about 700,000 more spectators than they had as the St. Louis Browns in 1953.

Even though the country was moving South and West, baseball was dominated by three New York teams—the Giants, Yankees, and Brooklyn Dodgers (who, incidentally, benefited from both large local TV audiences and high ballpark attendance). And while baseball had its thrills, such as the Giants' Bobby Thomson home run to win the National League championship over the Dodgers, maverick baseball analyst Bill James calls fifties baseball "the most one-dimensional, uniform, predictable version of the game that has ever been offered for sale."

J. Leonard Reinsch, a broadcaster and political consultant (and author of the 1988 consideration of campaigning and media, *Getting Elected*), in 1954 proposed that baseball reinvent itself for television. Reinsch called for a two-platoon system where each team had nine offensive and nine defensive players. Time would be saved in the game, since outfielders would not have to make the slow trot in to bat each inning; instead they could, as Jack Gould reported, "sit on an outfield bench and catch up on their reading" while their offensive team was

1. Fred Rogers and Josie Carey work on *The Children's Corner,* which began in 1954 on then-new educational television station WQED in Pittsburgh. The show was an early home for some of the puppet characters later made famous on *Mister Rogers' Neighborhood.* (Courtesy Fred Rogers)

2. LEFT: Robert Montgomery—producer, director, actor, and political activist—was generally credited with helping President Eisenhower perform more effectively on television. (NBC)

3. RIGHT: Richard A. Mack is seen at the 1958 congressional hearings during which he was urged to resign from the Federal Communications Commission after serious questions arose about his financial conduct. Mack had replaced Frieda Hennock on the commission in 1955. (Associated Press)

4. Sid Caesar, comic genius of TV's golden age, saw his series *Your Show of Shows* end in 1954, but went on to still more acclaim on *Caesar's Hour* later that year. (Archive Photos/Pictorial Parade)

5. New York Governor Thomas E. Dewey poses with his family—and a television—in a New York hotel during his 1948 presidential campaign. The
television was more than a prop; in coming years Dewey would use television
in novel ways that politicians would be aping more than forty years later.
(Associated Press)

6. This Associated Press photograph shows President Eisenhower "facing a group of bothersome microphones" in July 1953. By early 1954, AP reported, "he feels and looks better in TV appearances. The change resulted from the addition of an unpaid adviser, Robert Montgomery."

7. Bing Crosby and Jack Benny were two big stars who approached TV somewhat reluctantly. Both worried that viewers would tire of seeing them regularly on TV. (Crosby, Photofest; Benny, HBO)

8. David Sarnoff, top man at RCA, saw in color TV a chance not only to upgrade television but to sell new color sets to the viewing audience. (David Sarnoff Library)

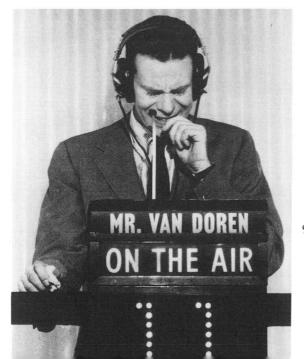

9. Quiz shows became a TV sensation in 1955 but exacted a high price, speeding the demise of *The $64,000 Question* and leading to one of the worst scandals in TV's history. (Fred Wostbrock)

10. *Amos 'n' Andy* was, and is, a funny show but became a lightning rod for criticism about how black characters were presented on TV. (Photofest)

11. Television and politics had come a long way by the early fifties. In 1952, a computer—here being checked by CBS's Walter Cronkite, right—was used to project presidential election results. (Harry Wulforst)

at bat. Pitchers could stay warmed up at all times, rather than have to cool off to bat and then warm up again. The game would also be livelier since teams could stack their offense with heavy hitters rather than have to worry about putting good fielders up to the plate. Overall, Gould said, "More action in less time is the keynote."

Baseball has taken tiny steps toward Reinsch's vision, notably with the introduction of the designated hitter in the American League in 1973. But in the fifties rather than adapt their games, many preferred to force concessions from TV. One historian even said TV had made the game dull. By 1951, the *New York Times* reported, "severe restrictions and outright prohibitions on the televising of athletic contests are spreading across the nation." The NCAA was considering a plan to ban large-scale telecasts of college football in favor of a single national game, or selected regional games—a policy it adopted in 1952. Professional football banned telecasts of home games that year and would fight in coming seasons to exercise even more control. Boxing was experimenting with "theater television"—what later became known as closed-circuit, where viewers had to watch the game in theaters, after paying an admission charge, and no broadcast signal was available.

In Atlanta, the *Times* reported, high-school football was no longer televised after attendance dropped. Hockey and professional basketball in Boston were not televised. Minor-league baseball in Los Angeles was not telecast until forty-five minutes after the game started. In Houston, only the early matches on wrestling cards were televised; the main event was not.

In baseball, the dominant sport of the era, some trouble might have been avoided. Historian David Quentin Voigt has said:

> Major league baseball of 1946 was positioned to gain large profits from television. All that was called for was bold leadership, but, instead, owners responded with timidity and selfishness.

Televised baseball stood poised for its greatest years when open warfare broke out on several fronts. In late 1952, Bill Veeck, the antiestablishment owner of the St. Louis Browns, made several proposals to deal with the minor-league problem and the Balkanized approach to television contracts. Where the minors were concerned, he suggested that minor-league teams should share in the revenues when major-league games were televised in their areas.

With TV, Veeck wanted visiting teams to get a share of a home team's TV revenues; Veeck said in his 1962 memoir that he threw that grenade "as an opening wedge for coming to grips with the whole problem of television." He wanted teams to black out all home games to protect attendance, and wanted TV revenue sharing across the board to correct imbalances already being felt by teams. (He also tried to increase the visiting team's cut of gate receipts.) As Voigt has said, teams' refusal to share revenues equally "mocked official claims of competitive balance."

Losing on all points, Veeck tried to force the issue again by refusing to sign agreements that would allow teams to televise games in St. Louis back to their home markets (the Browns themselves had no TV deal at the time). In retaliation, in early 1953 three teams—the Yankees, Red Sox, and Indians—announced they would only book the Browns for day games, when attendance would be lower than at night games. Veeck claimed to the press he had a "secret weapon" to get his way but in his memoir admits he was doomed since the Browns, a terrible drawing home team, depended on road revenues. In March, Veeck gave up the fight; by year's end he would be in one of his periodic exiles from baseball—and the Browns were headed to Baltimore.

Veeck's defeat may well have steeled the resolve of the minor-league teams, who were suffering from their major-league compadres' televised expansion. Their plight got some lip service; baseball Commissioner Frick spoke up for "limited control" of radio and television in June 1953 "protecting our minor league clubs against the constant, perpetual encroachment of major league radio and television." But that encroachment was coming with the approval of Frick's employers, and they were moving inexorably toward more expansion, not less.

In early 1953, as Powers describes, an ad man named Edgar Scherick started putting together a national package of baseball games for his client, Falstaff beer. Instead of dealing with the league, he had to go from team to team and only three—the Philadelphia Athletics, Chicago White Sox, and Cleveland Indians—agreed to participate in the package, to be shown on ABC. It was not a glamorous assemblage, although all three teams finished in the first division of the American

League in 1952 with over .500 records. For the teams still trailed the era's dominating, dreaded Yankees.

Worse yet, the major leagues forbade any telecasts of games into *any* city with a major-league team, wiping out the television-heavy Northeast. The good news, it turned out, was that the South, where television was beginning to boom and drawling announcer Dizzy Dean was a dose of home, and the Far West were wide open. The broadcasts proved wildly successful for two seasons—so naturally CBS came in and took the games from ABC.

It was a few months into the second season of ABC baseball that the minor leagues were fed up. At the National Association of Radio and Television Broadcasters meeting in May 1954, minor leagues President George Trautman said television was strangling the minors; but instead of blaming his hosts, Trautman cited "the expansion of major league club networks"—individual teams selling their games to stations across a region. Frank Lane, general manager of the Chicago White Sox, concurred, saying, "If all the major league clubs discontinue their networks, it will be a great help to minor league baseball"; Lane did not reconcile that personal position with the White Sox's charter membership in *Game of the Week.*

In September 1954, the president of the minor-league Portsmouth (Virginia) Merrimacs announced that a group of minor-league owners was going to sue the major leagues for $50 million for damages caused by TV and radio incursions. By the time the suit was filed two months later, Portsmouth was alone and the suit was for $250,000 but a point, however futile, was being made. A week later the minor leagues as a body voted for a ban on all commercial broadcasts of baseball from outside a ball club's territory, knowing as they did that "the major leagues will toss the matter out of the window." Which is exactly what the majors did the following week: they offered the minors other forms of assistance but television rights—and revenues—remained, unmolested and undiluted, in the majors' hands.

Other indignities awaited the minors, including the majors' invasion of the lush western farmlands in the late fifties. But a mortal blow had been struck. And it had come, not from television, but from the greedy major league owners eager to stuff their pockets with TV's cash.

Nor did the battle over TV revenues end there. The players fought for a share of the TV money for their pension fund, winning modest concessions in early 1954. That same year members of the Chicago

Cubs (led by future broadcaster Ralph Kiner) said they wanted $100 to appear on any sponsored pregame or postgame baseball shows. Senator Edwin C. Johnson of Colorado, a minor-league baseball executive, introduced legislation in 1953 to restrict baseball telecasts; he cited not only the threat to baseball but to small brewers who were being swamped by the major beer makers' advertising in baseball around the country. But the Supreme Court late that year affirmed baseball's special status among sports; although the decision did not specifically deal with television rights, it was immediately cited by pro football as protecting them.

Pro football was going through a TV battle of its own. The games were available—Du Mont was carrying forty-eight to fifty in the 1953 season, in prime time and on Sunday afternoons, nineteen through the whole network, the rest on a regional basis. But football wanted control of where those games went, and the Justice Department did not see that football had it (not until 1961, when Congress broadened certain antitrust exemptions to include football, basketball, and hockey, were league sports able to operate as true cartels). In 1953, a federal judge gave football a limited right—to ban telecasts in a team's home market when that team plays at home—but far fewer options than baseball had in its sweeping decisions for and against TV. An attorney for the National Football League had claimed early in the trial that a Justice Department victory "would surely be the death knell of professional football in the United States." The partial defeat, it now appears, was somewhat less than fatal.

I could try to slog through other wrangles over rights in the early fifties, including the NCAA's, but I suspect you are growing as weary as I am. What, after all, does this have to do with the argument I started at the beginning of the book, about 1954 as television's greatest year? Can one say that television sports, technologically primitive and fighting their way through their own prejudices and greed, were really all that great in that year?

Not entirely. Ron Powers has said TV sports went into a Dark Age in 1948, when the FCC freeze on station licenses squelched ABC and Du Mont, which had blazed trails in the early years of sports TV. And by his account, things got progressively worse in the midfifties as Du Mont failed and entertainment programs took over prime time.

Indeed, the six nights of sports in the fall of 1953 was down to two in 1955. And the phrase "Dark Age" has another connotation, that of the blackouts that the leagues were using to protect their sports. Certainly such restrictions were apparent in 1954. But this much of an argument can be made for television's greatness in the early fifties: in wielding the blackout bat, sports interests were conceding the massive power of television. And when the revenue potential in television became more evident, as the 1953–54 success of ABC's baseball telecasts brought major teams and a major network into the fold, then fears about gate receipts were soothed.

The question then became who would benefit. In 1955, the NCAA began to modify its single "game of the week" TV strategy in favor of regional telecasts because major conferences were threatening to bolt in favor of separate TV deals. As has been mentioned, players and owners fought over shares of TV revenue in baseball; Voigt writes that "as a divisive influence, television pitted players against owners, and rich clubs against poor."

Over time, of course, players would reap the rewards of big-time TV money, and be castigated for doing so. People complaining about the players' harvest should recall that the earliest TV windfalls went to the owners, who shed only crocodile tears as their TV complicity dealt a blow to the minor leagues.

As for the long haul, you've heard the complaints about television manipulating sports, about slickness and marketing taking over games (where are you, Hardy Brown?), about how the need for more and more television revenue led to unnecessary expansion of leagues and gerrymandered playoff systems embracing "wild cards," about TV-pretty AstroTurf curtailing careers. One day while I was working on this in March 1994, a group of sportswriters were on TV arguing about the new playoff system in baseball and whether it was ruining the glorious pennant races of days gone by; the following May the fine broadcaster Bob Costas continued the complaint on Dennis Miller's show.

But the nineties fan who has some wishful memory of a childhood when the sports pages were full of scores and highlights, should have to slog as my research consultant did through all the fifties stories on the issues discussed here. The fans today include me, who sat in upstate New York rooting for the Pittsburgh Steelers in football and the Boston Red Sox in baseball, both of whom I got to see on television. Given the nature of the Steelers in recent years, I follow the wild-card hunts as closely as any pennant race, because that's how my team gets in;

driving back from vacation on the last day of the 1993 season I kept the radio hopping, looking for updates on games that affected the Byzantine formula by which the Steelers got into the playoffs. And if it takes a wild card to extend the Red Sox season, then a wild card is the one I will play. Like that fan at the hearing who wanted to see the Braves, I don't want to be confused by logic and reason. Praise the tube and pass the Falstaff.

The Blurred Vision
of Educational TV

Educators are the hardest people
in the world to educate.
John Crosby, 1950

F red Rogers has amusing stories to tell about his days as a floor
manager at NBC in the early fifties. About seeing singer Snooky
Lanson, one of the stars of *Your Hit Parade,* shooting craps with
the crew between numbers. About working on tests of color broadcasting—until he had to confess he was color-blind. But he turns very
serious when he considers the direction television was already taking.

"I floor managed things like talent shows that people would bring
their kids in, and the mothers would push them so," he said one day
in early 1994.

> And there were other programs in which people would throw
> pies in each other's faces, and things that I felt were starting
> to be demeaning. And I just thought, you know, that I can
> floor manage and I was in direct line to be a director . . . but
> I'll always be either floor manager or director of somebody
> else's material.

As was discussed in chapter 10, a lot of people worried about the
content of television. Still other concerns went beyond who did what
to whom to television's commercial basis. Children's programs, what-

ever their merits, both included commercials and were parts of larger business ventures; the makers of early children's series *Rootie Kazootie* ran an ad in the *New York Times* listing sundry products—pajamas, hats, rainwear, handbags, watches, comic books, musical instruments, and so on—while asking:

> Are your products listed here? Rootie Kazootie and his friends can sell your merchandise from coast to coast.

Better yet, the ad promised, "Rootie Kazootie appeals equally to boys and girls."

Still TV at times mounted eloquent defenses of its content. TV "was more like a combination of public TV and commercial TV," director Kirk Browning recalls. "Few people realize how much superior programming is on the air," an editorial in *Television* magazine in late 1954 argued,

> So much of it seems to be passed over by the critics in favor of an amusing column on the crying need for intelligent fathers in situation comedies or a profound analysis of what's wrong with *December Bride.*

The magazine ran off a list that included a special presentation of *Macbeth* with Maurice Evans and Judith Anderson and fifteen series: *Meet the Press, Face the Nation, See It Now, Chronoscope, College Press Conference, American Forum, New York Times Youth Forum, Omnibus, The Search, Adventure, Johns Hopkins Science Review, You Are There, Camera Three, What in the World,* and *Opera Cameos.*

Most of them were very thoughtful shows. *The Search,* for example, followed the progress of research at American universities. Alex McNeil, author of the encyclopedia *Total Television,* called *What in the World* "perhaps the most erudite game show in television history," saying academics had to identify archeological artifacts; Tim Brooks and Earle Marsh in their TV encyclopedia say the identification involved works of art. Either way, no one had to buy a vowel.

But by 1960, all but three of the series—*Camera Three* (which lasted until 1980) and the enduring *Meet the Press* and *Face the Nation*— were gone. In fact, *New York Times Youth Forum* was done by the time the editorial ran; by the end of 1955, four shows—*Chronoscope,*

The Search, Opera Cameos, and *What in the World*—were off the air entirely, *College Press Conference* had been dumped from prime time to Sunday afternoons, *See It Now* had lost its weekly time slot and been turned into a series of specials, and *Johns Hopkins Science Review* was on a twenty-month hiatus.

(*December Bride,* by the way, made new episodes through the 1959 season, and was rerun in prime time in 1960 and 1961; it also yielded a spin-off, *Pete and Gladys.*)

Television had long dealt with two impulses: the vision of it as an inspirational medium and the demand for it to reward its owners and advertisers. Sometimes they would try to make awkward accommodation, even within the same program; when *Studio One* did *Macbeth*—with Charlton Heston in the lead—in 1951, it not only trimmed the production to fit an hour time slot, it added a grisly bit of business at the play's end: MacDuff holding up Macbeth's severed head. (One can only wonder if William Gaines thought it in good taste.)

While the wish to use television to enlighten audiences was not gone in 1954, it was certainly taking a back seat to the commercial urge. As has been discussed in other chapters, some programs survived because they were in time slots the networks considered consistently unprofitable—such as Sunday afternoons—and a few others benefited from a sponsor-patron.

But the success of shows such as *Today* in the early mornings and *Tonight* late at night were indicating that the public hunger for television would take it into almost any time period if the program was appetizing enough; Sundays, as we now know, eventually became the province of sports broadcasts. At the same time, networks looking at their schedules as a unified whole where programs flowed one into the other, would prove increasingly reluctant to cede control of time periods to sponsors whose interests might not coincide with the total schedule. Pat Weaver, the programming head of NBC (and, to be fair, someone who saw television as far more than a source of income), made a major inroad into the single-sponsor system in 1954 when he set aside time slots previously reserved for series to televise NBC's spectaculars.

But that sense of a unified schedule did not work to the advantage of many of television's most acclaimed shows. Because they had small audiences even as the total audience for television grew, they were seen not only as faring poorly in their own time slots but hurting shows around them. *Johns Hopkins Science Review* enjoyed six years in prime time, most of them on Du Mont as a "time-filler," as Brooks and Marsh put it.

> During its long run ... it was scheduled against such hit shows as *Break the Bank, Milton Berle, Arthur Godfrey* and *Dragnet,* programs from which its network had little chance of luring away viewers.

As television grew, as the possibility of financial gain from every time slot became evident, opportunities for special shows diminished; better to rerun *December Bride.* What, then, could someone like Fred Rogers do?

He went into educational television.

Noncommercial, educational TV—what is now known as public TV—was finally being realized in 1954, close to four years after the Federal Communications Commission held its first hearings on setting aside stations for a higher purpose than selling deodorant. To those who saw stations as the path to profit, such thinking was heretical. The National Association of Radio and Television Broadcasters opposed the allocation of educational licenses as well, contending that "educational institutions could never make a financial success of telecasting and might 'waste' their alloted channels."

Educators also proved lukewarm to the opportunity before them. John Crosby wrote in 1950:

> In the hearings opening today, there will be no representatives from Yale, Harvard, Princeton, Columbia; there will be few representatives from any of the great educational institutions of this country. They are letting go by default the greatest educational medium ever devised as they let radio go by default to the commercial interests.

Television was seen as a menace to education, not a tool for it; in 1951, one academic dismissed it as a "wasteful and dangerous toy." The following year, at a seminar on the application of television to education, Western Reserve University President John S. Millis acknowledged his colleagues' hostility and ambivalence.

One of our great failings, I think, is to underestimate the interests, the aptitudes, the potentialities, the capacities, of the mass audience. We do it with the movies; we do it with the radio. I think we tend to do it with television. We even do it in our lectures and discussion groups. We are so keen to simplify, to keep to facts and to simple concepts and ideas, and to use one-syllable words, that we miss a large part of our opportunity.

At the same seminar, vocational education administrator William F. Rasche said, "The medium is here, and we'd better use and test it out." But commercial broadcasters' reservations were not merely spiteful; trying out television cost money. Although estimates varied wildly—a *Time* report in 1954 put start-up costs between $33,000 and $754,000 and annual operations at $25,000 to $500,000—it was still money that had to come from somewhere. The University of Missouri was one of several educational organizations that asked the FCC to allow stations to run commercial programs part-time to pay for noncommercial programs the rest of the time.

With problems of both practice and principle weighted against educational stations, it took someone extraordinary to bring them about. Frieda Hennock, the FCC's firebrand, dragged educational television into existence. Crosby wrote that she "crusaded almost singlehanded for the setting aside of TV channels for education." "If it hadn't been for Frieda Hennock, I don't think we would have all these channels set aside for educational television," Fred Rogers said. Through her tireless campaigning, when the FCC lifted the freeze on station licenses in 1952, 242 of the licenses were made available for education.

Hennock still was not satisfied. She said there should have been more educational licenses, since many cities were not assigned any and the 11 million people of New York City were assigned just one. Others had reason to fear the allocation of educational frequencies in the UHF band when commercial television was on VHF, making it harder for programs to be seen once they got on the air. And the FCC had not simply turned the airwaves over to education; it also made available about 1,800 licenses for commercial stations, the equivalent of starting a TV range war then dropping the sodbusters of education in the middle of it.

But educators were publicly content with the challenge put before them. American Council of Education President Arthur S. Adams said:

> Educational institutions must now meet, in concrete terms, the challenge of using [TV] so wisely as fully to justify the allocation of educational channels.

The FCC had made that challenge even tougher by not putting any mechanism for funding the new stations into the law. It also turned down the proposal for part-time commercial broadcasts because, as the *New York Times* reported, it "would tend to vitiate the difference between commercial and noncommercial operation." Groups wanting the educational licenses also knew that they could not hesitate, since the original announcement reserved the educational licenses only until June 1953. One expert said:

> Commercial broadcasters will attack the reservations just as soon as petitions to that effect will be entertained by the [FCC] . . . particularly so in the large cities where the channels have high commercial value.

There were some early funding sources, including Ford Foundation grants; the foundation also funded the Educational Television and Radio Center, which supplied programs to educational stations and was the first step toward the national Public Broadcasting Service. Others explored alternative methods; WQED in Pittsburgh, the first educational station to rely on community instead of school support, sold a program guide to its viewers for $2 a year. But stations searching for individual or corporate sugar daddies sometimes ran into trouble.

Historian Erik Barnouw points to KTHE, founded with a grant from oil tycoon Allan Hancock, a member of the Board of Trustees of the University of Southern California; his support meant "one of the station's features was a Hancock string quartet, in which Captain Hancock played violin." The station was reportedly well received in the community, but after Hancock had a falling-out with other USC trustees he withdrew his support of KTHE, which spelled its doom.

Houston's KUHT, the first educational-TV station, went on the air in 1953 and had major money troubles by early 1954. The University of Houston, which had backed the station in partnership with the regional school district, faced a loss of income because of declining enrollment; the school district meanwhile had expanding enrollment and had to put available funds into dealing with it. Even more ironic, given the FCC's position on commercial-educational mixing, the school district did not put its programs on KUHT, where it would have to pay a fee, but on a local commercial station that made time available for free.

When *TV Guide* reported on educational TV in April 1954, it said "most of [the organizations] must run a never-ending financial obstacle course." That same month *Time,* noting the problems both of cost and of the UHF situation, said 195 of the 242 available licenses "are still going abegging." Among the six stations on the air at that time, the University of Wisconsin's station telecast just two hours a day, and KQED in San Francisco no more than thirty minutes a night; its immediate goal, according to *Time,* was "to find the money for a daily 2½ hour schedule." Once again money was an issue, and a damaging one; federal funding of public television did not begin until 1975, forcing individual stations to function like frontier outposts dependent on themselves alone for survival. TV critic Les Brown has said that at the creation of a public-television system in 1967, many stations "were opposed to surrendering any of their sovereignty to a national system."

There are conflicting views of what this led to. Looking at the state of public television in the early seventies, Brown argued that public television had become too meek, unwilling to tangle with commercial broadcasters who assisted it from time to time and who could out-lobby public broadcasters in Washington; too beholden to powerful local and national businesses whose support of public television would be endangered by programs such entrenched interests deemed too controversial; and not a true alternative to commercial TV but a supplement to it. Brown called for public television that ended station autonomy in favor of a strong national network modeled on the commercial ones—and fully willing to compete for audience with the commercial broadcasters. "*Superior* television, and not a self-congratulating cultural service, should be the goal of public television," Brown said.

Not long after, journalist Martin Mayer wrote that in essence public television had done at least part of what Brown had envisioned. He thought the current hits on public television "would have been entirely plausible commercial products." He said:

This is not a criticism of programs or of public television; it means that some way is needed to get such programs onto commercial stations, where they would be entirely suitable and more heavily viewed. They don't seem to do public television any good, and it doesn't help them.

Under just about any scenario, actual or imagined, public television from the fifties on had at once to provide the public with something it could not find in commercial television, whether that meant different shows or simply better ones; and to present those programs in such a way that audiences would want to watch them. Without the former, there was no reason for public TV to exist; without the latter there was no reason for anyone—government, corporation, or viewer—to provide financial support.

The point was not lost on people working in educational television, since there were regular reminders that television viewers saw it as something apart from the things they liked (hence the shift to the label "public" television in the late sixties); *TV Guide* said of the early stations, "their prime purpose is education rather than entertainment."

Educational programmers knew that sort of thinking, within and without their operations, could be fatal. At a 1952 symposium on educational TV, Lynn Poole, producer of *Johns Hopkins Science Review,* said as much in talking about Johns Hopkins University's entry into television in the late forties.

> There was no past experience from which to draw. All we had was a conviction that on television, informational programs could be exciting and dramatic.
>
> We believed that programs could be devised which would entertain, delight, and hold audience attention while giving out worth-while information. I ask you to note that I said entertain. . . . Television is an entertainment medium for the most part, and if informational programs are to survive, they must be planned and presented in such a way that they can hold their place in competition with the mystery drama, variety show, and quiz program.

But making a program that entertained and educated was another matter. To this day public-television programs run a risk of being too entertaining—and raising questions of why they are doing something commercial TV might do—or too educational—a nice way of saying dull. Sometimes things come together in a marvelous way—*The Civil War, Eyes on the Prize, The American Experience, American Masters, The Great Depression,* and *The Secret of Life* are all shows that have been meaty and dramatic. Other times, though, in the concert specials by aging baby-boom rockers, in the pledge-drive compilations from Lawrence Welk's old commercial shows, in the marathon talks by the feel-good *guru du jour,* the meter tilts toward entertainment without purpose or information without amusement.

As it was in the beginning. Lynn Poole described a *Science Review* about sunburn that was spiced up with "a beach scene of curvaceous cuties and muscled males . . . without destroying the inherent dignity of a scientific program." Uh-huh.

Children's Corner, an educational show for children on which Fred Rogers was working for WQED in Pittsburgh, was a better example of providing entertainment and education; in fact, it was entertaining enough to enjoy a commercial network run as well (see chapter 4)— and no one has ever questioned Rogers's "inherent dignity." Plus on WQED the show ran without commercials, a practice Rogers still prefers. No fan of "enhanced underwriting announcements" and the prolonged pledge breaks that mark public TV, Rogers said, "I think we must preserve what Frieda Hennock set out to do, and that was to have some channels that were completely noncommercial."

But to get back to Mayer's point, *Children's Corner* says as much about the failure of commercial television as it does about the success of its educational counterpart. A *Children's Corner* should have been available on commercial broadcast TV; Luciano Pavarotti should be performing on a contemporary *Voice of Firestone; The Paper Chase* and, more recently, *I'll Fly Away,* should have had long network runs instead of having to turn to cable and PBS for continued telecast; Supreme Court confirmation hearings should be allowed to preempt daytime soaps. But by the midfifties commercial networks were drifting away from television's need to be important as well as watched.

And educational television, from the beginning a poor cousin to its commercial counterparts, spent precious years struggling for survival that could instead have been used to establish a clear identity—and a strong bond with viewers; instead public television stations were equivalent to struggling Du Mont and ABC—only those networks had more options in finding an income.

So how does that fit into television's greatest year? For the audience at large, all those good programs that *Television* cited were still available to commercial audiences. In the long term, though, the emergence of public television merits consideration not as a great thing for viewers but as one for the television industry, suddenly blessed with an excuse to become ever more mercenary in its practices and narrow in its programming.

TROUBLE AHEAD

· · · · · · · · · · · ·

Having scaled the heights of public acclaim, having reached out to audiences on a grand scale, having made itself the dominant entertainment medium in the nation, where could television go but down?

Not down in terms of audience attention; the day had not yet come when virtually every home in America would have television. Nor when the yardstick was financial success; millions and billions of dollars were still to be had. Some would argue it became even more important to public life; as grand as the triumph of *See It Now* and the Army–McCarthy hearings was, having assisted the last president of the fifties, television would get considerable credit for electing the first one in the sixties, thanks to the Kennedy–Nixon debates.

But when you look at what television had done, and what it might have done, and what it did instead, the years following 1954 were by no means a march to glory. Previous chapters have talked about some of the ways television was changing. The following will fill in a few more blanks—what happened to Du Mont, the gutsy fourth network of TV's early years; what technological advances, including color TV, did to the creation of good television programs; and finally, a sweep through some of the events over the rest of the fifties that brought television not merely to the end of its first golden era, but to a low point of criticism from which it would never truly rebound.

. . . . .

The Little Network
That Couldn't

We're never going to look back.
We're going to look ahead.
Allen B. Du Mont, ca. 1951

I n April 1954 the executives of the Du Mont Television Network
were talking enthusiastically about the future. A year and a half
later the network was no more.

Du Mont is the Jesse Garon Presley of networks, a sibling that died
young and was lost in the mists of memory: a "partial network,"
sniffed one old TV hand, "the Atlantis of television," a TV critic said
thirty years after Du Mont's demise. Although it has been paid homage
from time to time—the Museum of Broadcasting (now the Museum
of Television & Radio) put together a Du Mont retrospective in
1984—the attention fades almost as quickly as the network did; even
that museum tribute coupled Du Mont with Metromedia, a chain of
stations started from Du Mont's remains. The victors in the early
network wars, ABC and CBS and NBC, are still around to congratulate
themselves in prime-time specials about programs past and present;
for most viewers Du Mont is as forgotten as *Faraway Hill* and *Rhythm
Rodeo* and *Chicagoland Mystery Players*—Du Mont shows one and
all.

It should not be so, because Du Mont was as bold a program service
as television would have. "It set standards in terms of versatility, range

of programming, and public service," critic Ron Powers has written. It was home to the first network soap opera, the first hour-long network show, the first network newscast originating in Washington, the first live prime-time telecasts of the National Football League (seventeen years before Roone Arledge, who worked briefly at Du Mont, created ABC's *Monday Night Football*), and live presentation of the Army–McCarthy hearings, which as has been said were carried by the little networks, ABC and Du Mont, while the far better off NBC and CBS passed. Du Mont had Jackie Gleason before CBS (he did his first "Honeymooners" sketches on *Cavalcade of Stars* in 1950), Bishop Sheen before ABC, *The Original Amateur Hour* before NBC; that also demonstrates that almost any sign of success on Du Mont prompted another network to steal its thunder.

But success as defined by Du Mont was exceedingly small; after 1950 it never had a prime-time show among the twenty-five most popular, let alone the top ten. Its last show to rank that high was the variety series *Cavalcade of Stars* in the 1949–50 season, which took a tumble after NBC wooed away both its original host, Jack Carter, and his successor, Jerry Lester. (At least that opened the door for Gleason). Du Mont was a network that marked its twentieth anniversary with a thirty-minute special done in a few spartan sets. When the actor playing network founder Allen B. Du Mont said, "I've got $500 and a place in my basement," viewers arriving late may have thought he was talking about the show's budget and location.

Du Mont the network started because Du Mont the man wanted to sell television sets. The story goes that Brooklyn-born Allen Balcom Du Mont had polio as a boy and was bedridden for months; as a present his father bought him a radio and so began a lifelong fascination with broadcasting. After college and four years with Westinghouse (where he was in charge of producing radio tubes), Du Mont went to work for the De Forest Radio Company, a manufacturing firm owned by Lee de Forest, the self-proclaimed "father of radio" whose place in history would stem as much from his litigation as his inventions.

Du Mont's assignment was television, far from de Forest's strong suit. He made some strides there—one, according to Du Mont historians Craig and Helen Fisher, was "the first broadcast of synchronized picture and sound." But de Forest stuck with a crude early system of making television (the Nipkow disk), while Du Mont saw the future lay with an electronic system.

"You're not going to begin touting that electronic theory again!" a colleague argues in the Du Mont anniversary production. Indeed, the show—as well as at least one major obituary of Du Mont in 1965—says that he left de Forest in 1931 to work on his electronic idea. But even that obituary concedes "economic conditions were quite inauspicious for innovators," lending credence to a less adventurous version of the story, summed up in Du Mont's entry in the 1946 *Current Biography*.

> His work [on electronic TV] . . . was halted by the depression; when he returned from a vacation he had taken in Bermuda in 1931, he learned that the concern had failed and that he was without a job.

Whether driven by his vision or his unemployment, Du Mont started his own laboratory in his Passaic, New Jersey, garage (as a result, Passaic is among those mentioned as a birthplace of television); he then developed a cathode-ray tube, essential to electronic TV, which was cheaper and longer lasting than those available up to that time. In 1937, Du Mont applied for a construction permit for a station in Passaic, which after years of experimentation evolved into New York City's Channel 5, WABD (and later WNEW and WNYW). In 1939, Du Mont began selling the first all-electronic TV sets for home use; as the Fishers point out, it was pretty fancy furniture, "ornate wooden cabinets in a vaguely art deco style."

Broadcasting continued in New York during World War II; at one point the only TV stations operating in the city were Du Mont's and NBC's, and Du Mont's put more hours on the air. In 1946, Du Mont put his second station, in Washington, D.C., on the air and the Du Mont network was born. (Two stations do not seem like much of a network, but it was the same as NBC had when it started linking stations.)

Although Du Mont was a visionary about many aspects of television, programming was not one of them. Critic William A. Henry III called Du Mont "an engineer, not a showman . . . far more concerned with how a picture came in than with who or what was actually on the screen." That left his programmers to their own devices, which often consisted of not spending too much of the boss's money.

The best and worst of Du Mont, as well as an extreme example of how television worked in the early fifties, was *Captain Video,* the first space serial on television, which ran from 1949 until shortly before the network's demise in 1955. The story of what the show's opening called an "electronic wizard, master of time and space, guardian of the safety of the world," *Captain Video* was admirably (if talkily) written by esteemed fantasists such as Damon Knight and Arthur C. Clarke, and very sophisticated compared to Westerns and other children's adventure shows of the day. One early episode contains a protracted discussion of how to deal with a recently conquered planet; the analysis begins with a call for reparations reminiscent of what happened to Germany after World War I but ends with a more benign, United Nations–like structure.

The gadgetry on *Captain Video,* the interplanetary politics and exotic villains allowed for the kind of detail that science-fiction fans keep discussing long after the last light's been turned out at a *Star Trek* convention. But the futuristic flourishes accompanied sets where the desks, clothes, and telephones were basic fifties functional and reused from scene to scene; the controls on a spaceship were painted on; the special effects budget was $25 a week. The exposition in the dialogue had to be intriguing because just about all the characters did was talk. And "secret agents" of the captain, seen on missions via a monitor at his mountain retreat, actually consisted of performers in old Westerns and adventure movies; their scenes were used as a break in the action on *Captain Video* and as a cost-free means of including outdoor action. (Star Al Hodge's claims notwithstanding, the shoot-outs, fist fights, and gunplay in the movie clips also pushed the violence level in the show pretty high.)

Still, critic Tom Shales once said, "The special effects were pretty tacky, but when you're a kid you don't require much to prick your imagination." *Captain Video* became one of Du Mont's biggest hits, spawning toys, comic books, and a movie serial. When Al Hodge appeared before the Senate committee investigating TV violence, the chairman called him "Captain."

A few more shows like that might have kept Du Mont afloat but a wave of problems ultimately sank it. Unlike CBS and NBC, Du Mont had no radio network from which to take talent and program ideas for TV. The lack of radio was even more painful when AT&T, which controlled the coaxial cable linking stations in the presatellite days, made networks buy radio as well as TV lines—charging Du Mont a premium it could ill afford for a service it could not use. A cash-poor Allen Du Mont, trying to finance his television research, in 1938 sought salvation from an investment by Paramount Pictures. It proved to be a pact with the devil when the partners had a falling out and Paramount, despite Du Mont's requests, refused to sell its shares in the company; even worse, the FCC counted two stations owned and operated by Paramount toward the maximum of five stations Du Mont was allowed to own, effectively hindering its growth.

But wait, as the commercials say, there's more. The FCC freeze on station licenses from 1948 to 1952 hindered the growth of Du Mont as the major networks (better known because of their radio background) strengthened their ties to the few stations on the air. While Du Mont could boast many affiliates, the stations with which it affiliated often had other, and stronger, relationships with other networks, leaving Du Mont with a far more difficult time getting its programs seen. In addition, when the FCC did lift the license freeze, *that* hurt Du Mont— just as it did educational TV—because the FCC mingled new UHF channels with established VHF stations in the same market. Du Mont had unsuccessfully recommended a system where an individual market would be all-VHF or all-UHF. In his book *Fifties Television: The Industry and Its Critics,* William Boddy explained the resulting dilemma.

> UHF operators in intermixed markets were unable to attract network and advertising affiliations given the low penetration of UHF-equipped receivers; without advertising revenue and popular network programming, UHF operators were unsuccessful in attracting viewers or convincing the public to purchase UHF receivers.

Although Du Mont took in money—$12.3 million in advertising revenues in 1953—that was one-eighth of what CBS was getting from its TV operation. And it took a crazy quilt of deals for Du Mont to make that much. Acting more like an advertising agency than a national network, it sold sponsors ad time on its shows in as few as a dozen markets carrying the program, then sold time to other sponsors in other markets, and so on.

As was already mentioned, Du Mont took on a huge financial burden when it offered live telecasts of the Army–McCarthy hearings, which though intended to run ten days lasted more than three times that long. ABC, which also carried the hearings live, was strapped as well but had two things Du Mont did not: a sounder financial base thanks to its 1953 merger with United Paramount Theatres, and the upcoming relief from the success of its new series *Disneyland*.

Amid all these other problems, the Du Mont company saw its main business—selling televisions—take a hit. "Du Mont television sets were the Cadillac of the industry," the Fishers wrote.

> But GE, RCA and Westinghouse soon established high-volume, low-profit operations with which Du Mont did not successfully compete.

Du Mont sold its Pittsburgh station, which gave it cash in the short-term but eliminated a steady, long-term revenue source. The advertising situation worsened, until the network's revenues for the first six months of 1955 were less than half what they had been two years before and its competitive position was awful. *Broadcasting* reported that Du Mont's six-month take was about one seventh of what a newly healthy ABC grossed in the same period, about a fourth of what NBC averaged *each month* and a fifth of what CBS did each month.

Du Mont's stockholders demanded something be done in mid-1955. The company announced in August what it called a spin-off of the network into a new corporation. Approved in October, the spin-off actually killed the program network and left a company owning two television stations (the original New York and Washington properties) and a production center in New York; from those remains came Metromedia and, in the eighties, the Fox network. The proud Du Mont company, which had grossed almost $92 million in 1953, sold off its remaining interests in 1958 and 1960.

The end of Du Mont established a three-commercial-network universe that remained firm despite occasional challenges (such as the United Network in the sixties, and Operation Prime Time in the seventies) until the emergence of Fox. And in some ways, Du Mont was the model for that successor. Fox executives in the early years talked about their lean staffing and the resulting flexibility and speed in decision making—a contrast to what it liked to portray as its older, fatter, slower network siblings. In 1954 Du Mont, led by what one magazine called "a small group of experienced, hard-working men," represented the old story of the small company that can move faster and adapt itself to a new situation more quickly than a giant firm with heavy commitments.

The differences between Fox and Du Mont lay in the former's deep pockets, courtesy of Rupert Murdoch, and its ability to stay out of the federal government's way, and the rise of cable. Where Fox proved willing and able to pay big bucks to take things it wanted, Du Mont did not even pay enough to protect the stars and shows it had. Where Du Mont lost a prolonged battle with the FCC, Fox programmed just few enough hours not to be considered a network under federal regulations, allowing it to make money in ways the Big Three, as networks, were forbidden. And cable removed the disadvantage of being on a UHF station, as Du Mont had been and many Fox affiliates are, by putting UHF and VHF alike no farther away than the button on the cable control.

The loss of Du Mont struck an incalculable blow to television, removing not merely a competitor from the game but one whose own daring kept the networks from becoming too comfortable and confident, bringing ideas into television that might not have been imagined under other circumstances. (In some ways it filled the role Les Brown once imagined for public television, mentioned in chapter 13.) To some extent ABC ended up taking risks that CBS and NBC at first did not, but many of those risks were matters of marketing instead of creativity—its youth strategy, for one, just remodeled traditional program forms to appeal to a younger audience.

Had it survived, Du Mont might well have taken a less audience-obsessed path than its counterparts. When the other networks began dropping their live dramatic anthologies, Du Mont could well have given them a home—and the audiences who still loved them a new place to turn. It might have found visionary young leaders; imagine Roone Arledge returning from military service and finding not that Du Mont had folded in the interim, but that he could take up his small job there and rise through the ranks at a network as open to innovation as Arledge would be. Then imagine the impact of Arledge competing against ABC instead of molding its sports and news divisions.

Struggling independent stations over the years, not to mention station licenses that went untaken for years, would have had a better chance with a fourth network to provide them programs—as Fox showed. And something like the Western-show explosion of the late fifties, where close to a third of prime-time hours were taken up by sagebrush and shoot-'em-ups, might have been curtailed by a thoughtful counter-programming strategy of a network disinclined to join the wagon train.

Then again, Du Mont might have just saddled up with the rest of them. *Cavalcade of Stars,* after all, was an attempt to duplicate the success of rival networks' *Texaco Star Theatre* and *Toast of the Town,* and Du Mont's programs overall resemble the grasping of program straws as much or more as they look like a strategic plan. The network might even have become the House of Reruns simply carrying replays of the other networks' shows. Leonard Goldenson said ABC was offered a chance to do that and refused; to ensure its survival Du Mont might have been more willing.

Concoct your own what-ifs for a world with a fourth network after the midfifties. This much will still be certain: Du Mont had its honorable place in television history, it went boldly where others would not, and its demise took an innovator out of a medium already being criticized for its lack of innovation.

The Mixed Blessings
of Technology

Still driving a Model T?
Headline on color-TV article, 1953

At various points in this book you've probably written me off as a video Luddite decrying every advance TV has made since 1954. Well, here's another reason to feel that way: I think color technology hurt television programming.

An extreme position, granted, but one that follows a course similar to other issues covered already. Whatever the perceived benefit of a change in television, however much something is seen as an advance, it has a price. And the price may outweigh the advantages. For example, when Hollywood surrendered to television there were certain benefits in financial terms and in the access to an established production system; on the other hand, Hollywood brought in on a large scale a different way of making television that placed the emphasis less on creativity than on churning out product.

When television started slouching toward Hollywood, it sped up a technological shift that proved a mixed blessing: the increased emphasis on filmed production (and later videotape) and the downplaying of live programs. To some, this was an improvement. Bill Dana, the actor and writer, was part of some of the live glory days, including a stint as a writer on Steve Allen's *Tonight* show; still he prefers recorded TV because it can eliminate technical mistakes, blown lines, and other flaws that afflict live TV. For Dana (who continues to market his sixties series *The Bill Dana Show*) and the industry at large, recorded productions also mean long-term financial benefit, since they can be replayed and resold for networks, syndication, cable, and home video; and on a simple practical level it took pressure off broadcasters who would need to find replacements when their live-series stars took vacations.

But recorded TV is not the same as the live variety, although television has tried at times to make the two seem indistinguishable, as in CBS's dramatic but taped presentations of the Winter Olympics. To this day the unexpected and spontaneous in TV generate talk about the medium that the prerecorded often does not: comedian Martin Lawrence's excesses on *Saturday Night Live,* and the live *Tonight* show following the series finale of *Cheers,* however alarming they were to some viewers, remained something that would not have survived an edited videotaped production. Tom Hanks's acceptance speech at the 1994 Academy Awards seemed over the top to some viewers (I happened to like it) but the outpouring of emotion in it could not have been duplicated if, immediately after Hanks finished, a producer could ask, "Would you like to try that again?"

Sweeping technological changes affect not only what we think about what we see, but the very thing we do or do not see. Think about the period when television stations became able to do live on-location reports during newscasts. Conceived as a great tool for covering breaking news, live remote capability became an obligation; we paid for the truck, now we have to use it. Throw in a television consultant waving research concluding people like live reports, and you end up seeing what I've seen a lot: reporters standing in the dark and cold, hours after something has happened, just so the report will be live from the scene.

Instead of freezing, that reporter could be off doing another, warmer story while videotape of the earlier event rolled. But what should just be another television tool turns telecasters into Tim Allens gone amok. And like Allen's *Home Improvement* character Tim Taylor, they go looking for tasks for the tool to perform, instead of just adding it to the devices they already have to perform existing tasks.

Which in a roundabout way brings us to the time that television, as one magazine described it, "harnessed the rainbow." Color TV, after a pitched and prolonged battle, took its place in the television tool kit in 1954; it did not take over the television schedule right away but, thanks in particular to NBC owner RCA's desire to sell color TVs, the certainty that color would eventually take over was absolute. The price, though, was high.

Color might have come to TV sooner but for conflict between two network titans. RCA and CBS developed rival, incompatible systems for transmitting color programs. CBS at first carried the day, winning Federal Communications Commission approval in 1949, but its system fell victim to a major flaw and bad timing.

The flaw was that CBS's color system was not compatible with existing black-and-white technology; if CBS went to color, you could not see the programs on your own set, while you could watch the same show in black-and-white or color with RCA's system. Timing included the FCC freeze on station licenses, which forced a station-hungry CBS to pay inflated prices for available stations, in the process diverting revenues that might have gone into its color planning; in addition, the federal government at one point asked for a delay in color development because it used materials supposedly needed for the Korean War effort ("supposedly" because, as journalist Sally Bedell Smith has written, the U.S. had been fighting in Korea for a year when the delay was sought).

While CBS was stalled, RCA and other set manufacturers flooded the market with black-and-white sets, creating a world of black-and-white set owners whose needs the FCC could not ignore. Lawrence Bergreen has written that CBS was probably doomed even in 1949, when there were already some 3 million black-and-white sets in the U.S.; although CBS and the FCC prevailed over RCA in the Supreme Court in 1951, by then 12 million black-and-white sets had made their way into American homes.

RCA also continued to make improvements in its system and to lobby fiercely for it. Pat Weaver, then a vice chairman of NBC, remembers the effort made at a theater the network used for color presentations.

> We herded people in and out constantly, selling them hard on what we considered not only the best but the only practical conversion to color. In the meantime, I made speech after speech, especially to our affiliates, preaching the importance of color in the continuing growth of our industry.

Color was important to television's growth, since the movies—then battling television for audiences—had color when TV did not. *Time* magazine, in fact, called color TV "the industry's answer to 3-D," a significant comparison. 3-D, after all, was one of the many gimmicks the movies were using to distinguish themselves from TV (see chapter 11). And 3-D would demonstrate the pitfall of putting all your faith in technology. Ephraim Katz wrote in his *Film Encyclopedia:*

> Most films of the 3-D crop were low-quality quickies whose sole attraction was technical gimmickry. Within a year or two the 3-D frenzy had subsided in the face of growing public apathy.

Color would face, and cause, similar problems once a system was established. In fact, the demands of implementing the technology were already taking a heavy toll on CBS. Faced with the prospect of turning out color programs no one would be able to see, it chose to get around the problem by acquiring a set manufacturer to turn out its model. It first considered buying Du Mont (which had sided with RCA in the color-format battle) but Smith says Paley and Allen Du Mont did not get along; CBS settled on another company, Hytron, which did not remotely live up to expectations. It ended costing CBS $50 million, "the largest financial disaster in CBS history," Bergreen wrote in 1980. (Later deals would surpass that total—the unsuccessful CBS Cable venture lost $60 million by the time it was folded in 1982; CBS's billion-dollar deal for major league baseball in the early nineties lost hundreds of millions.)

In 1953, with the marketplace swimming in black-and-white sets, the FCC finally endorsed the RCA format over CBS's. Then resistance from TV dealers (some complained that all the talk about color would hurt sales of the black-and-white sets filling their stores) and consumers had to be overcome. RCA at first figured to sell 70,000 color sets in 1954 and 10 million by the end of 1958—a not entirely unreasonable projection given that about 10 million TV sets had sold between 1946 and 1951 and more recent sales had averaged about 5 million a year. But actual sales went much slower—only 10,000 color sets were in use by late 1954, and it would be the late sixties before they hit the 10 million mark.

The few color sets that could be found were expensive—$800 to

$1,000—and small-screened compared to the larger black-and-white models, a significant problem in an era when TV viewing was a group activity. Many people were still paying off their new or nearly new black-and-white TVs. Besides, there wasn't much color programming.

In all of 1954 there were sixty-eight hours of network color broadcasts. An April trade magazine report said "only NBC and CBS-TV are doing anything color-wise. . . . Du Mont is testing via closed circuit and ABC is 'watching' developments." Although there were color series to be found—syndicated series *The Cisco Kid* and *Superman,* Hume Cronyn and Jessica Tandy in *The Marriage,* believed the first network series done entirely in color—the effort at first centered on one-time-only "spectaculars," or specials, which NBC launched in a big way in the fall.

And whatever rainbows the networks harnessed could not reach viewers unless local stations had the equipment for color broadcasts. Stations that were part of RCA or General Electric, companies with a financial interest in color-TV sales, could expect to move fairly quickly. But all stations faced the expense of conversion to color: about $22,000 for transmitting network shows, three times that to produce local shows in color, at a time when many struggling stations' annual revenues were only about $80,000. As a result, many of those interested in color phased it in, network transmissions first, then upgraded their production equipment.

Producers also faced additional costs: color added about 30 percent to a show's budget. Independent producer Frederick Ziv told *Television* magazine:

> In addition to the actual expense of color film and processing, color adds a great deal in shooting time, in set and costume preparations, and in lighting.

One estimate had a color show taking twice as much technical planning as one in black-and-white, and lighting alone had to be three to five times as bright. *Life* magazine said a CBS color studio "carries enough current to light the town of Danbury, Conn." And problems continued down the line. *Life* said:

> Actresses become doubly fussy about costumes and makeup. Stage designers, knocking themselves out to create eye-filling

sets, turn their studios into jungles of color, hung with cables and ablaze with light.

Color took up time, energy, focus. *Television* gave considerable space to a discussion of "the psychology of color," contending:

> The color TV expert must understand more than lighting. He must have a knowledge of the physical and psychological aspects of color as well, and the esthetic sense to know what colors go together. He must have the ability to plan color patterns, maintain color control from scene to scene while keeping hot colors down, and to plot out too rapidly changing colors.

Talk about having your colors done. But all this attention (and money) for color had to come from somewhere. Just as high-tech would-be blockbuster movies of the eighties and nineties spent so much time on special effects that little things like plot got lost, so color created an environment less conducive to straightforward storytelling. If, as Dinah Washington sang, TV was the thing in 1953, color was more in 1954. It can be seen in reviews that focus on color more than more basic program issues. In 1952, Jack Gould wrote a scathing review of New York City Easter Parade telecasts, presenting a long list of the product plugs that had consumed coverage. In 1954, writing about the Tournament of Roses parade, Gould devoted much of his review to the quality of the color. He not only reviewed what was on the screen but how it had to be watched.

> In the broad daylight and sunshine it was necessary to draw the shades and cut out all the glare if the colors on the TV screen were not to be washed out. This, frankly, was a nuisance.
> Another difficulty related to the size of the picture. The disadvantage of a small color image—roughly 12½ inches—was much more noticeable with the parade than with earlier studio programs. And, since it is necessary to sit much farther away from a color screen than from a black-and-white set . . . finding a happy compromise between picture size and viewing distance could be tricky for the engineer and the

viewer, particularly if the latter must start rearranging the furniture again.

I remember even into the sixties, as neighbors began getting color TVs, the tricks that sometimes had to be done to get the color right. Any time you're focusing on such issues—trying to get the skin tones a little less green, for example—you're not really watching the show. And what you're watching may have had misplaced priorities. When Gould reviewed *Sunday in Town,* a color spectacular that boasted Judy Holliday, Steve Allen, and a promising young comic named Dick Shawn, he called it "as labored and heavy-handed a show as seen in many a day. Before worrying about color video, it may be first necessary to retrieve black-and-white."

By 1955 there were suggestions that color might not last, but other assurances that the marketing possibilities made it a sure thing. *U.S. News & World Report* said:

> Psychologists believe it will be next to impossible to keep attention away from a color set. . . . It will increase TV's impact on the minds and emotions of viewers. Already you can hear people saying, after seeing a color-TV program sponsored by a meat-packer: "I can almost taste that bacon."

But color TV, like other changes in the medium, is no great boon once viewers are used to it. In a television universe where almost everything is in color (including some things originally made in black-and-white), producers try to break out of the pack by shooting in black-and-white. Moviemakers, with an even longer history of color production, also return occasionally to monochrome—witness *Schindler's List.* Unfortunately such efforts are seen as exceptions to common practice rather than a perfectly understandable use of an available tool in a context where producers use black-and-white or color, whichever suits the production at hand.

Any producer with a lick of sense can look back at *Marty* and see that its story of drab little lives is enhanced by its black-and-whiteness, but it's certain that any TV-movie remake of it would be in color. In the scurrying world of live drama, black-and-white helped mask some of their limitations (even later series, after being colorized, tend to have a shopworn look); but the contrasting color productions, so determined to present the glories of the new technologies, could not help but indicate there was something lacking, even false, about black-and-white. The build-up for color told viewers that good storytelling was no substitute for flashy appearance, exactly the opposite of what it should have taught. That in turn added to the chronic urge in television to substitute flash—quick cuts, fancy effects, loud music, all designed to get attention quickly (as psychologists said of color)—for quieter pleasures—subtle storytelling, intimate dramas that require the viewer to pay close heed; while people still try to tell simple, affecting stories on TV, they have to fight through a garish TV mob even to be seen and heard.

Color was not the only area in which TV technology was being explored. The New York police department in 1954 used television to closed-circuit a lineup from Brooklyn to its Manhattan office. TV security cameras were in place at the city jail in Houston and the Watertown Arsenal in Massachusetts; the Sands Hotel in Las Vegas put in television cameras to monitor gamblers; and the Beverly Hilton was planning a TV system that would let guests read menus on their screens. *Time* magazine spoke ominously of TV as "little brother," spying on people at every turn; although it all sounded a bit speculative in the fifties, the question being asked would be repeated with more forcefulness in the eighties and nineties as video cameras made a spy out of any person who could afford one.

For all its enthusiasm about color, broadcasters were less thrilled with another technological possibility—paid telecasts. These took two forms: theater television, where events or programs were shown in old movie houses, with an admission fee charged; and various forms of pay-per-view or subscription television, where viewers at home paid a fee to see a broadcast program whose scrambled over-the-air signal was straightened out by a converter.

Theater TV had an obvious limitation—you still had to persuade viewers that the telecast was worth leaving the house to see—but it had a relatively long life among free-spending sports fans wanting live access to big events such as championship boxing matches. But its luster began to fade as pay-per-view finally became a reality.

Pay-per-view, in the fifties called "pay as you see" and "feevee," among other names, had long been imagined. In the late forties Phone-vision, a system where viewers could order programs by telephone and then watch them on their home screens, was already in working order. And it had some strong proponents, such as the movie industry, which could sell its films to audiences no longer willing to go to theaters; and the weaker television stations, which saw it as a way out of the red without having to wrestle advertising from their dominant competitors.

For that matter, subscription TV might have been another way of supporting educational and cultural programming on noncommercial stations; viewers could either be asked to pay directly for such programs on pay-per-view, or stations could provide some paid programs as a revenue base for their noncommercial lineup.

But strong broadcast stations and the networks, wedded to an advertising-based, over-the-air system, treated pay-TV not simply as another tool for delivering programs (which they might also be able to exploit) but as a threat to their well-being. In tandem with theater owners who did not want the movie industry to feed TV instead of them, broadcasters lobbied fiercely against pay TV with both the public and the government. (This is the sort of rhetorical battle, still seen, in which broadcasters counterpose themselves to pay services by declaring themselves "free TV," as if there were no price to be paid in commercial interruptions and the arbitrary editing of programs to eliminate offensive matter or just make room for more ads.) The FCC, siding with broadcasters, stalled pay-TV and, as Michele Hilmes has written, opened the door to a more potent threat: cable.

In fact, broadcasters made the same mistake with cable that they had made with subscription TV, treating it not as a tool that could help them but as a force that could hinder them. By the time broadcasters understood that the best way to deal with cable was to exploit it, a new generation of entrepreneurs, most notably programmer Ted Turner and cable-system magnate John Malone, had seized the high ground. Since cable proved a far more formidable foe than subscription TV (if only because, as an over-the-air signal, subscription TV was far more easy to trap in a maze of federal regulation), broadcasters only achieved a belated and ironic victory. After decades of resisting other means of delivering programs to homes, and declaring themselves "free TV," they proved the right they really wanted was to make more money—by cutting themselves in on cable's delivery system, either through cash compensation or putting their own channels into cable packages.

Such a battle was long in the future in 1954. But the shape it would take was already evident in the use and marketing of color TV. In each case, television had a marvelous and potentially rewarding tool at its disposal. With color, where the potential reward from selling color sets was obvious, the major TV powers took advantage. With pay-TV, where a little imagination and flexibility were required, the increasingly inflexible broadcast interests let opportunity slip away.

16

·····

TV Goes to Hell, 1955–61

I think the way things have been going, up a
blind alley, that television has so completely
lost its interest, they're losing their audience.
                                    John Crosby, 1961

When 1954 came to an end, television had not merely reached a crossroads. It faced a simultaneity of courses more like a freeway cloverleaf—this way to New York, that way to Hollywood, film on this off-ramp, live TV around the bend, culture here, crassness there, advertiser desires or viewer needs, local shows or network spectaculars, and oops, just missed the turn for pay-TV.

In just about every case, the medium took the wrong, one-way street, heading single-mindedly in a fixed direction rather than trying to encompass all the possible pleasures the medium held. Believe me, even if you do not agree that 1954 was television's greatest year, it does not take a great leap of faith to see 1955 as its worst. Being important was by then far less a goal than being profitable; as a reward for that stance, government decided that abetting television had far more appeal than directing it.

In May 1955 President Eisenhower did not reappoint Frieda Hennock to the Federal Communications Commission. As has been seen in this book, Hennock was a gadfly stinging powerful broadcast interests; as such she made things uncomfortable not only for broadcasters but for an administration headed by a man who had cultivated the two most powerful men in television, and who was taking pains to use the medium to his advantage.

Although Hennock was often on the losing end of issues, in the FCC she had had a bully pulpit. "Having fought the interests, I was not the least bit surprised that I was not reappointed," she said of Eisenhower's dumping her. "Monopolistic forces control the entire field of TV." We could argue that statement a lot of different ways— broadcasters did attempt to monopolize the airwaves, as their fight with subscription TV and early resistance to educational television showed, but they also fought bitterly among themselves, as in the color wars—but it does not matter in light of Hennock's successor. Richard Mack, a former member of the Florida railroad and public utilities commission, proved ready to do business with broadcasting; unfortunately, his way of doing business became part of a major scandal at the FCC.

In 1957 Mack voted with the commission to award a Miami television license to a subsidiary of National Airlines even after an FCC examiner had recommended that another applicant receive the license. Mack also happened to have received loans and gifts from a Miami friend who was working for National on the station license; during House hearings in 1958, it was also shown that Mack owned an interest in a Miami insurance company that had sold a large policy to the new station. Asked to explain his friend's financial help—which extended through Mack's terms on the Florida commission and the FCC—the commissioner replied, "Well, I was having a hard time making ends meet." Mack was making $20,000 a year on the FCC.

Representative Oren Harris, chairman of a House subcommittee investigating the FCC, told Mack, "The best possible service you could render now . . . would be to submit your resignation." A few days later, under intense pressure from the White House, Mack did so. But the scandal did not end there. John Doerfer, the old friend of Joe McCarthy and since 1957 the FCC chairman, was accused in 1959 of what Les Brown called

> undue fraternization with the broadcasting industry, of taking trips paid for by organizations regulated by the FCC and of receiving honoraria while being reimbursed by the Government for his expenses.

While there was no evidence of formal wrongdoing by Doerfer, the furor over his activities forced his resignation in 1960.

There had been examples before this of the FCC playing favorites. But the public scandals of Mack and Doerfer created the picture of an FCC for sale to the highest bidder at a time when the growth of television underscored the need for a powerful viewers' advocate. And no longer was Hennock there to provide a voice and a vote for the disenfranchised.

After leaving the FCC and resuming her law practice, Hennock continued lobbying on broadcast issues where possible; Drew Pearson's 1958 diaries note "she has been yapping at me for a couple of years about the inequities and scandals of the TV industry." During the hearings on the FCC she reminded Pearson that

> the subcommittee was treading very gingerly regarding the most important thing of all, namely the manner in which the big networks dominate the TV industry and the FCC.

But her time was short. She died in 1960 after surgery for a brain tumor. She was fifty-five years old.

While Congress may have skirted the TV industry's role in the FCC scandals, a major stain on the networks' reputation occurred while Americans watched. In June 1955 CBS had premiered *The $64,000 Question,* the first of the big-money quiz shows and an immediate hit. Successful quiz shows up to that time had had fairly small pots—*You Bet Your Life,* Groucho Marx's show, had a three-figure payoff—but this new one started with questions worth $64, then rose in perpetually doubling sums; contestants also had repeated, cliff-hanging opportunities to walk away with their winnings or risk them in the attempt to win still more. Finally, in its most memorable stroke, for $8,000 questions and up contestants answered the increasingly complicated queries while in a cramped, seemingly hot, isolation booth.

"The summer of 1955, on Tuesday nights, the nation's crime rate drops," Maxene Fabe has written.

> So do movie, baseball and bingo attendance, water consumption and long-distance calls. Two things rise: *The $64,000 Question*'s ratings and [sponsor] Revlon's profits.

Louis G. Cowan, the producer who dreamed up the show, became a top executive at CBS. Spin-offs and imitations appeared, notably

Twenty-One and *The $64,000 Challenge* (which featured winners from *Question*) in 1956. The success of *Question* also hastened the demise of the prestigious *See It Now,* that followed it on the air. Fred Friendly later recalled how the journalistic team, waiting to do the second part of a report on cigarettes and lung cancer, watched the new quiz show. Murrow, Friendly said, "was riveted and horrified by what he saw." By the night of *Question*'s second sensational telecast, Murrow was asking Friendly, "Any bets on how long we'll keep this time period now?"

The answer was, not long. Having already lost its sponsor, and still controversial, *See It Now* could hardly take advantage of the huge lead-in from *Question*. CBS wanted a show that would appeal to the quiz show's viewership and would attract a sponsor eager to pay the premium high ratings would demand. *See It Now* had its last telecast as a weekly series in July 1955; that fall, its time slot went to the situation comedy *My Favorite Husband.*

Although *See It Now* continued as specials, the clout that comes with appearing in people's homes weekly was gone. As Murrow said after being congratulated when the specials found a sponsor, "It won't be like the old days." The show's future lay in broadcast histories and in *60 Minutes,* which old *See It Now* hand Don Hewitt concocted from his own smarts and pieces of other shows, including *See It Now.* Hewitt told Edward Bliss in 1989 that people watched *60 Minutes*

> for the adventures of six reporters. It was that way in the 'fifties with "See It Now." It really was "Let's watch Murrow."

Murrow himself would never match that glorious moment in 1954. His name would be attached to another landmark in TV reporting, the documentary *Harvest of Shame* in 1960, but the withering examination of the plight of migrant workers was not really his handiwork; as A. M. Sperber pointed out, the program was "first and foremost the creation of [filmmakers] David Lowe and Marty Barnett. . . . Murrow had come on the scene only after months of shooting."

Murrow's last great moment—the one that keeps him remembered as the conscience of broadcast news and made Dan Rather feel he had to say something special while standing in Murrow's shadow—would be not in a TV studio but at a lectern. In October 1958, he spoke to a convention of radio and TV news directors, and called on the great corporations to put some of their advertising dollars toward "a most exciting adventure—exposure to ideas and the bringing of reality into the homes of the nation.

> To those who say people wouldn't look; they wouldn't be interested; they're too complacent, indifferent and insulated, I can only reply: There is, in one reporter's opinion, considerable evidence against that contention. But even if they are right, what have they got to lose? Because if they are right, and this instrument is good for nothing but to entertain, amuse and insulate, then the tube is flickering now and we will soon see that the whole struggle is lost.
>
> This instrument can teach, it can illuminate; yes, and it can even inspire. But it can do so only to the extent that humans are determined to use it to those ends. Otherwise, it is merely wires and lights in a box.

When Edward Bliss edited *In Search of Light: The Broadcasts of Edward R. Murrow 1938–1961,* he deviated from the title just enough to include two speeches, one after Murrow received a citation for his stand against McCarthy, the other the 1958 speech. The line about "wires and lights" still has resonance and relevance; I worked it into a few talks in 1993. But as much as the passage above, the most famous from the speech is a call to action, one has to believe that at that point Murrow believed the cause was lost. He ended the speech with a line from a great warrior in a famous lost cause, Stonewall Jackson: "When war comes, you must draw the sword and throw away the scabbard." Murrow's conclusion: "The trouble with television is that it is rusting in the scabbard during a battle for survival."

Those dismal words echoed across a TV landscape mired in scandal, wallowing in imitation. By 1958 the quiz shows were collapsing under repeated, documented charges: that contestants received questions in advance, that they were coached in how to act on the air, that an unpopular contestant had been urged to lose deliberately so a more appealing contender could continue on the air. Like television itself, the shows had become too big to be left to chance; the TV industry wanted their popularity to remain high and their coffers filled, and some people were willing to do anything to keep it that way. Kill *See*

It Now, coach a contestant, what difference did it make if the viewers were happy and the advertising still coming in?

If one could not expect happiness from a world where cynicism extended to the rigging of quiz shows, then it should be no surprise that people looked for satisfaction in an earlier, simpler world—the Old West. The fall of 1955 saw three new heroes ride into TV-land, and they came with goodies not only for the young 'uns who'd been riding the TV range for years, but for their maws and paws as well. *Gunsmoke, The Life and Legend of Wyatt Earp,* and *Cheyenne*—the last show part of the Warner Brothers deal with ABC—premiered as part of a surge in Western programs that would reach landslide proportions by 1958, when the three networks among them had thirty-one Westerns in prime time.

Although some of the shows had considerable merit—and *Gunsmoke* would become one of the longest running prime-time shows in TV history—their appeal to the TV industry was not really about that. As filmed shows, they had a repeatability that made their economic potential far greater than live shows (*Gunsmoke* was still in rerun, on cable, in early 1994 and available on home video); as outdoor shows they brought a visual quality to TV that the studio shows lacked; they were a natural genre for Hollywood studios coming into TV. As series with regular characters, they provided a week-to-week continuity for viewers that the ever-changing stories and people in the dramatic anthologies lacked—but in the context of the rambling West, which allowed other figures to enter and leave week to week. A Western like *Gunsmoke* is a canny transition from the anthology to the series, presenting continuing characters but giving considerable story and air time to the guest star of the week. That technique, used to a limited degree in *Medic* (which had only one continuing character and so was more of a pure anthology), would be picked up with varying degrees of effectiveness by other Westerns, medical shows, and such oddities as *The Love Boat.*

The Westerns had an additional virtue from the TV industry's point of view, in that they practiced what is now called "historical violence." Tim Brooks and Earle Marsh say that "TV violence took its first major upswing during the era of the adult western" but as we have seen, television had already gone through two rounds of congressional hearings about violence by 1955. Unlike the heavily criticized crime shows, the Westerns had a rationale for violence because it was part of their historical fabric, especially when it came to the justice system; in addition, in contrast to the early TV Westerns targeted at children (and therefore susceptible to antiviolence body counts), the new Westerns were designed explicitly for grown-ups.

You can see that in the first episode of *Gunsmoke* where John Wayne, introducing the series and his friend James Arness, says the show is "honest, it's adult and it's realistic." Arness's character, Matt Dillon, walks through a cemetery and imagines how some of the dead would have survived had they talked issues over instead of resolving them with guns. In the episode's story, a man on the run for murder has come to Dodge; before the half-hour is over, two men are dead (not counting the one Dillon shot in the opening credits every week), Dillon has been wounded in a shoot-out, and the talk between gunplay deals with mayhem and the possibility of more. The action fan is getting what he wants, while the antiviolence crusaders are kept at bay by the pieties about trying to avoid all the things that still, somehow, come to pass.

Although television did not abandon other action genres, the Westerns satisfied a lot of viewer appetites and came to dominate the ratings. But they, along with the brief explosion in prime-time quiz shows, had to take time from somewhere, and the main victim was the live dramatic anthology. In a 1961 discussion of the state of television, CBS programming head Mike Dann said, "We have put too much emphasis on the film form, with the result that we have had too much repetition and too little experimentation." But he did not stop there.

> I am perfectly willing to say, though, that there *was* a time when we had too much original drama on the air—twelve, fifteen original drama shows. I suppose that's a terrible thing to say . . . but there were many of the series that went on all year long that didn't produce a single important drama out of 52 telecasts.

As if dramatic anthologies were somehow undeserving of the prime-time slots CBS was at that moment giving to *The Alvin Show* (an animated series about those singing chipmunks), *Candid Camera,* and the ever popular *Frontier Circus.*

The trouble with Dann's assessment is twofold. First, he admitted that television had overreacted against the live dramas, sweeping them off the schedule to such an extent that it was all but impossible to develop a new generation of playwrights to replace the Horton Footes and Paddy Chayefskys as they tried other ventures. "As the original-drama field declined," Dann said, "the number of writers who were coming along declined." Gone were the days when, as John Crosby said in the same discussion for *Playboy,* "television was a marvelous training ground for playwrights." He elaborated:

> Under an ideal situation these young fellows would have been followed by other young fellows. But all of the shows that these guys wrote for are gone. . . . Today, it's a boiler factory. Warner Brothers, Desilu, Ziv—they're just turning out comic strips now and this doesn't take writers.

To be fair, some series have had marvelous writers, including veterans of the live TV days; Reginald Rose went on to create *The Defenders,* an acclaimed lawyers' series in the sixties. But even at its best series writing is different from playwriting, since the idea of a series is creating and nourishing a few characters from one week to the next, where in TV plays one has to create a different set of characters each time out, then put them through a significant moment in their lives. While coming up with a compelling new character and story each week is exceedingly difficult, and pretty much impossible for one writer to do, it accordingly opens the door for many writers on a single show. The writer—along with whatever good will an anthology's title accrues— is therefore not only crucial creatively but can be a major selling point for a show that has no consistent cast, character, or situation to pitch to an audience.

But in 1955, when anthologies were still hanging on, they faced other pressures, according to historian Erik Barnouw: "In 1954, and increasingly in 1955, sponsors and their agencies began to demand drastic revisions and to take control of script problems." Representative was the long fight over Rod Serling's 1955 play *Noon on Dooms-day.* Inspired by the Mississippi lynching of teenager Emmett Till, the play was changed so much (for one, the victim became an old pawnbroker) that, in Barnouw's view, "the final show was an absurdity in a total vacuum." That, along with the creative shift to Hollywood and film, and increased pressures of blacklisting (which had not ended with the fall of McCarthy), prompted Barnouw to declare the golden age of drama over in 1955.

As has been discussed elsewhere in this book, the Du Mont network collapsed in 1955. And viewing habits in the home were changing. Between June 1954 and June 1955, 8 million television sets were sold, a new high. Although some families were simply buying sets with larger screens, *U.S. News & World Report* also discovered:

> One out of every five new TV sets being sold now is a "second" set. That's one more sign of the growth of the TV habit, since the "second" set usually is bought so the grown-ups can watch their favorite programs at the same time the children have one set turned to another channel.

The single-set, all-family viewing experience was beginning to vanish. That had implications not only for how people watched TV, but how it was made—if the viewing audience was fragmenting, then the demographic movement, targeting just part of the audience instead of the whole, was inevitable. And as some parts became more desirable to advertisers than others, the widespread disenfranchisement of some viewers—rural ones in the seventies, older ones in the eighties and nineties—also loomed.

In the complex scramble for advertisers, especially as the networks began to assume the burden of selling time in shows to several sponsors instead of just yielding the time slot to one, it became increasingly important that broadcasters give audiences what they wanted—and that, they concluded, was fantasy and escape, in which the dreams of owning a big new car or of being made attractive by a change in deodorant, did not seem so absurd. Ben Bagdikian sees therein the decline in network public-affairs shows:

> Since 1954, the power of television as a sales medium has become obvious. The problem on public affairs shows is that they are not the biggest collectors of mass audience, and even when they are, they are not good for commercials. Advertisers want people in a buying mood. . . . But when people are thinking seriously they are not in a buying mood.

One place that became evident was in the "intellectual ghetto," Sunday afternoons, where public affairs and cultural programs had had a happy home. Stan Opotowsky, in his 1961 book *TV: The Big Picture,* quotes ABC's Leonard Goldenson's contention that networks did not need much "highbrow programming." "We are a mass medium," Goldenson said. "We were created to be a mass medium and that is what we must remain." Sports, far more hospitable to advertisers, began to encroach on Sundays; Ron Powers says the omens were clear as early as 1956, when CBS began carrying National Football League games. And as the networks began to move remunerative programs into new time periods, local stations had fewer places for their own shows—and less reason to make them. The "highbrow" shows then had to turn to that new "highbrow" venue, educational television but even in 1961, Opotowsky wrote, "educational TV is subject to the same audience pressures that plague commercial TV."

We could follow various threads of disaster through the fifties and sixties and beyond, but the situation was clear by the late fifties. Live drama dying. Genre shows, in this case westerns, ruling the schedule. Scandal on the quiz shows. Scandal at the FCC. TV's most acclaimed newsman fearing for the future of his own medium. Du Mont gone. Educational TV in confusion. Whatever sense of television early observers had brought to the medium was warping into pessimism and cynicism.

The era of idealism officially ended on May 9, 1961. The new chairman of the Federal Communications Commission, Kennedy appointee Newton Minow, stood before the National Association of Broadcasters and suggested those assembled watch their own stations for a day. "I can assure you that you will observe a vast wasteland," he said,

> a procession of game shows, violence, audience participation shows, formula comedies about totally unbelievable families, blood and thunder, mayhem, violence, sadism, murder, western bad men, western good men, private eyes, gangsters, more violence, and cartoons. And, endlessly, commercials.

No longer would the battle over broadcast television be fought based on what it could do. Rather than elevate television, as critic Lawrence Laurent was assigned in 1952, the battle would be to keep it from sinking ever deeper into its own mud. Rather than urge television to greater things, its critics would find themselves railing against what it had done—and pleading that it do no more harm.

Spasms of idealism would accompany technological advances; just as broadcast TV was supposed to achieve what radio had not, so cable was meant to be what broadcast had failed to become. But cable soon was dominated by general-interest channels resembling networks, and its future holds competing game-show channels. In early 1994 Jerome Weeks of the *Dallas Morning News* brushed off cable channels such as Bravo and Arts & Entertainment because despite a culture-conscious image they "fill up large chunks of their time with old movies and reruns of *The Rockford Files*." Nor was Weeks optimistic about the information superhighway, predicting

> Rather than increased household access to the arts, the highway will provide household access to what a small group of business managers deems popular enough to risk peddling to us.

As it was ever thus. If there is one lesson to be learned from television in 1954, it is that diversity does not come when you increase the number of channels; early television showed tremendous diversity with very few. The question is instead what will be done with the channels that exist.

If I were the czar of television, I would long ago have mandated few channels, lots of live productions, big TVs, and only one set per household; I would have insisted that all children's programming be commercial free; I would have required public-affairs and cultural shows on a regular basis; I would have set aside time periods for local productions other than news, so viewers could once again have a connection and a sense of participation with television. I would have been wise and reasonable in these decisions, for example explaining that with few channels in operation, each can make enough money to justify commercial-free blocks. And then I'd wait for armies of lawyers to haul my butt into court.

When I asked people about how television might have turned out differently, they did not really have an answer. We can speculate— suppose government had been more demanding, suppose growth had been slower, suppose Du Mont had survived—but then you have to explain how those things might have happened, and we're eventually into some kind of TV rotisserie league.

"This is just off the top of a bald head," former TV reporter and critic Matt Messina said one evening in 1993,

> but it starts with the prosperity and the added power that the networks had as their audience increased, as the advertising revenues increased. Then it became more bureaucratic. The creative element was not as paramount as it had been earlier. Then things changed.
>
> But it happens all the time. You take a company that makes widgets; they all work together because they're trying to succeed. Then what happens when they succeed? They say, how much is the cost of this, and what can we get out of syndication, and why do we have to pay so much for this, and you get layers and layers of people doing what a few used to do before.

Messina suggests that we not look at television for an explanation, but to the history of great industries. That's hard, though, because we did not sit down in front of great industries morning, noon, and night, absorbing the ideas and images it brought—and losing those the people behind the box deemed no longer necessary to present. When we look at all that changed in television in the last forty years, the saddest part is not that a great industry went astray. It is that it stole some of the optimism and anticipation from that most basic of TV questions: What's on?

Acknowledgments

Mystery writer Max Allan Collins calls his acknowledgments "I owe them one." That more than applies to the many people who helped me put together this book.

While it has leaned heavily on period material to show what people thought of television from the twenties to the fifties, it also benefited from the people who shared their thoughts about what TV was and what it has become. I am immensely grateful to Ben Bagdikian, Bishop Edwin J. Broderick, Kirk Browning, Everett Greenbaum, Lawrence Laurent, Delbert Mann, Matt Messina, Del Reisman, Fred Rogers, Reginald Rose, David Shaw, and Tom Stempel. Interviews with Steve Allen, Bill Dana, and Louis Nye for an article in *The Sunday Gazette* proved very useful for this book as well.

The newspaper and magazine stories used throughout this book were obtained largely through the tireless dedication of research consultant, Rhonda Kreshover; without her ingenious efforts, I would not only have missed some things she unearthed, I would still be staring red-eyed at a microfilm reader. Andy Kulmatiski of the Schenectady County Public Library provided crucial assistance at an early point in the process. And the patient staff of the Museum of Television & Radio was unfailingly courteous, even during a winter week that proved to be one of their busiest.

Many colleagues also made notable contributions. First and foremost was Mark Dawidziak, whose friendship led to long conversations that turned into the idea for this book; he also patiently provided a sounding board for the notions in these pages, as well as listening to the whines of a first-time book writer. David Bianculli opened many doors and provided frequent encouragement. David Zurawik, Robin Bilinkoff, and Yardena Arar also helped me along my stumbling way.

At *The Daily Gazette* and Sunday Gazette, my great thanks go to arts editor Peg Churchill Wright and TV Plus editor Sherrill McGill for their patience; my thirteen years at the *Gazette,* especially time spent talking to some of the many television veterans in the Schenectady area, gave me a valuable foundation—and a place to test some of the ideas discussed in the preceding pages. At Continuum, my editor, Evander Lomke, encouraged me more than I could ask and provided guidance more than I could have hoped.

And any book like this depends on critics, journalists, historians, and memoirists who have walked the turf before, who deserve more than mere listing in the bibliography. The writings of John Crosby and Max Wylie in particular inspired and informed me. And no one would start a TV project of this sort without dipping into the program guides of Tim Brooks and Earle Marsh, Alex McNeil and Vincent Terrace.

And the list goes on: Desi Arnaz, Erik Barnouw, Leonard Goldenson, Edward Bliss, Jr., Donald Bogle, William Boddy, George Burns, Edwin Diamond, Reuven Frank, Jack Gould, Ben Gross, Michele Hilmes, Kathleen Hall Jamieson, Stefan Kanfer, Sig Mickelson, Ron Powers, Gilbert Seldes, Sally Bedell Smith, A. M. Sperber, Harriet Van Horne—all of great use, even when I disagreed with their ideas.

Thanks to their love, their good natures and Super Nintendo, my sons Brendan and Conor Heldenfels endured long weekends and evenings while Dad tapped away at the keyboard. And their goodness comes from Mary Anne Leonard, their mother and my wife, who until her death in 1989 believed in me even when I did not believe in myself. To our hearts she carries the key.

Select Bibliography

Books

Adams, Charles. *Producing and Directing for Television.* New York: Henry Holt and Co., 1953.

Allen, Craig. *Eisenhower and the Mass Media.* Chapel Hill, NC: University of North Carolina Press, 1993.

Allen, Steve. *More Funny People.* New York: Stein and Day, 1982.

———. *Hi-Ho, Steverino!* Fort Lee, NJ: Barricade Books, 1992.

———. *Mark It and Strike It.* New York: Holt, Rinehart and Winston, 1960.

Anderson, Jack, and Ronald W. May. *McCarthy: The Man, The Senator, The "Ism."* Boston: Beacon Press, 1952.

Andrews, Bart. *Lucy & Ricky & Fred & Ethel: The Story of "I Love Lucy".* New York: Popular Library, 1977.

Arnaz, Desi. *A Book.* New York: William Morrow and Co., 1976.

Bacall, Lauren. *Lauren Bacall by Myself.* New York: Ballantine Books. 1980.

Barnouw, Erik. *The Image Empire (A History of Broadcasting in the United States, Volume III—from 1953).* New York: Oxford University Press, 1970.

———. *The Sponsor.* New York: Oxford University Press, 1978.

Benjamin, Burton. *Fair Play.* New York: Harper & Row, 1988.

Benny, Jack, and Joan Benny. *Sunday Nights at Seven: The Jack Benny Story.* New York: Warner Books, 1990.

Bentley, Eric, ed. *Thirty Years of Treason.* New York: Viking Press, 1971.

Bergreen, Laurence. *Look Now, Pay Later: The Rise of Network Broadcasting.* New York: Mentor, 1981.

Berle, Milton, with Haskel Frankel. *Milton Berle.* New York: Dell, 1975.

Best Plays of 1954–1955, ed. Louis Kronenberger. New York: Dodd, Mead. 1955.

Beville, Hugh Malcolm, Jr. *Audience Ratings: Radio, Television, Cable.* Hillsdale, NJ: Lawrence Erlbaum Associates, 1988.

Bianculli, David. *Teleliteracy: Taking Television Seriously.* New York: Continuum, 1992.

Bliss, Edward, Jr. *Now the News.* New York: Columbia University Press, 1991.

Bleum, A. William, and Roger Manvell. *Television: The Creative Experience.* New York: Hastings House, 1967.

Boddy, William. *Fifties Television.* Chicago: University of Illinois Press, 1990.

Bogle, Donald. *Blacks in American Films and Television.* New York: Fireside, 1988.

———. *Toms, Coons, Mulattoes, Mammies, & Bucks.* New York: Continuum, 1992.

Brady, John. *The Craft of the Screenwriter.* New York: Touchstone, 1981.

Broderick, Edwin B. *Your Place in TV.* New York: McKay, 1954.

Brooks, Tim, and Earle Marsh. *The Complete Directory to Prime-Time Network TV Shows 1946–Present.* New York: Ballantine, 1992.

Brown, Les. *The New York Times Encyclopedia of Television.* New York: Times Books, 1977.

———. *Televi$ion.* New York: Harvest, 1971.

Bulman, David, ed. *Molders of Opinion.* Milwaukee: Bruce Publishing, 1945.

Burack, A. S., ed. *Television Plays for Writers.* Boston: The Writer, 1957.

Burns, George. *Gracie: A Love Story.* New York: G. P. Putnam's Sons, 1988.

Caesar, Sid, with Bill Davidson. *Where Have I Been?* New York: Crown Publishers, 1982.

Carnegie Commission on Educational Television. *Public Television: A Program for Action.* New York: Batam Books, 1967.

Ceplair, Larry, and Steven Englund. *The Inquisition in Hollywood.* Garden City, NY: Anchor Press, 1980.

Chayefsky, Paddy. *Television Plays.* New York: Simon and Schuster, 1955.

Coffey, Frank. *60 Minutes: 25 Years of Television's Finest Hour.* Introduction by Don Hewitt. Los Angeles: General Publishing Group, 1993.

Collins, Max Allan, and John Javna. *The Best of Crime & Detective TV.* New York: Harmony Books, 1988.

Considine, Bob. *Innocents at Home.* New York: E. P. Dutton, 1950.

———. *It's All News to Me.* New York: Meredith Press, 1967.

Cole, Barry, ed. *Television Today.* New York: Oxford University Press, 1981.

Coontz, Stephanie. *The Way We Never Were: American Families and the Nostalgia Trap.* New York: BasicBooks, 1992.

Copyright Law Symposium Number Five. Sponsored by the American Society of Composers, Authors and Publishers. New York: Columbia University Press, 1954.

Cowan, Geoffrey. *See No Evil.* New York: Touchstone, 1978.

Crosby, Bing, as told to Pete Martin. *Call Me Lucky.* New York: Simon and Schuster, 1953.

Crosby, John. *Out of the Blue.* New York: Simon and Schuster, 1952.

Diamond, Edwin. *Sign Off.* Cambridge, MA: MIT Press, 1983.

Diamond, Edwin, and Stephen Bates. *The Spot: The Rise of Political Advertising on Television.* Cambridge, MA: MIT Press, 1984.

Donovan, Charles, and Ray Scherer. *Unsilent Revolution: Television News and American Public Life.* New York: Cambridge University Press, 1992.

Einstein, Charles. *Willie's Time*. New York: Penguin, 1992.

The Faces of Five Decades: Selections from Fifty Years of the New Republic. Edited by Robert B Luce. New York: Simon and Schuster, 1964.

Fabe, Maxene. *TV Game Shows!* Garden City, NY: Dolphin, 1979.

Fates, Gil. *What's My Line?* Englewood Cliffs, NJ: Prentice-Hall, 1978.

Field, Stanley. *Television and Radio Writing*. Cambridge, MA: Riverside Press, 1958.

Fireman, Judy, ed. *TV Book*. New York: Workman, 1977.

Fontenay, Charles L. *Estes Kefauver, a Biography*. Knoxville, TN: University of Tennessee Press, 1980.

Frank, Reuven. *Out of Thin Air*. New York: Simon & Schuster, 1991.

Friendly, Fred W. *Due to Circumstances beyond Our Control*. . . . New York: Random House, 1967.

Gitlin, Todd. *The Sixties: Years of Hope, Days of Rage*. New York: Bantam Books, 1987.

———, ed. *Watching Television*. New York: Pantheon Books, 1986.

Goldenson, Leonard H., with Marvin J. Wolf. *Beating the Odds*. New York: Charles Scribner's Sons, 1991.

Gorman, Joseph Bruce. *Kefauver*. New York: Oxford University Press, 1971.

Graham, Jefferson. *Come On Down!!* New York: Abbeville Press, 1988.

Green, Abel, and Joe Laurie, Jr. *Show Biz from Vaude to Video*. New York: Henry Holt and Co., 1951.

Gross, Ben. *I Looked & I Listened*. New Rochelle, NY: Arlington House, 1970.

Gunther, Marc. *The House That Roone Built*. Boston: Little, Brown and Co., 1994.

Gunther, Marc, and Bill Carter. *Monday Night Mayhem*. New York: Beech Tree Books, 1988.

Harvey, Brett. *The Fifties: A Woman's Oral History*. New York: HarperCollins, 1993.

Hawver, Walt. *Capital Cities/ABC, The Early Years: 1954–1986*. Radnor, PA: Chilton, 1994.

Henry, William A., III. *The Great One: The Life and Legend of Jackie Gleason*. New York: Doubleday, 1992.

Hijuelos, Oscar. *The Mambo Kings Play Songs of Love*. New York: Perennial Library, 1990.

Hilmes, Michele. *Hollywood and Broadcasting*. Chicago: University of Illinois Press, 1990.

Hodapp, William. *The Television Manual*. New York: Farrar, Straus & Young, 1953.

Houseman, John. *Entertainers and the Entertained*. New York: Simon and Schuster, 1986.

Hubbell, Richard. *Television Programming and Production*. New York: J. J. Little and Ives, 1945.

Hurt, Harry, III. *Texas Rich*. New York: W. W. Norton, 1982.

Hutchinson, Thomas. *Here Is Television*. New York: Hastings House, 1946.

Israel, Lee. *Kalgallen*. New York: Delacorte Press, 1979.

James, Bill. *The Bill James Historical Baseball Abstract*. New York: Villard Books, 1986.

Jamieson, Kathleen Hall. *Dirty Politics*. New York: Oxford University Press, 1992.

———. *Packaging the Presidency*. New York: Oxford University Press, 1992.

Javna, John. *The Best of Science Fiction TV*. New York: Harmony Books, 1987.

———. *The Best of TV Sitcoms*. New York: Harmony Books, 1988.

Joels, Merrill E. *Acting Is a Business*. New York: Hastings House, 1955.

Kanfer, Stevan. *A Journal of the Plague Years*. New York: Atheneum, 1973.

Kelly, Katie. *My Prime Time*. New York: Seaview Books, 1980.

Kendrick, Alexander. *Prime Time: The Life of Edward R. Murrow*. New York: Avon Books, 1970.

King, Stephen. *Stephen King's Danse Macabre*. New York: Berkley, 1983.

Kleinfelder, Rita Lang. *When We Were Young*. New York: Prentice Hall, 1993.

Knight, Arthur. *The Liveliest Art*. New York: Macmillan, 1957.

Kuney, Jack. *Take One: Television Directors on Directing*. New York: Praeger Publishers, 1990.

Lately Thomas. *When Even Angels Wept*. New York: Morrow, 1973.

LeBow, Guy. *"Are We on the Air?"* New York: SPI Books, 1992.

Leonard, Bill. *In the Storm of the Eye*. New York: G. P. Putnam's Sons, 1987.

Lerner, Max. *America as a Civilization*. New York: Simon and Schuster, 1957.

Lewis, Marlo, and Mina Bess Lewis. *Prime Time*. Los Angeles: J. P. Tarcher, 1979.

Lewis, Tom. *Empire of the Air*. New York: Edward Burlingame, 1991.

Lief, Alfred. *"It Floats": The Story of Proctor & Gamble*. New York: Rinehart, 1958.

Manchester, William. *The Glory and the Dream: A Narrative History of America, 1932–1972*. Boston: Little, Brown, 1974.

Marx, Arthur. *Everybody Loves Somebody Sometime (Especially Himself)*. New York: Hawthorn Books, 1974.

Marx, Groucho. *The Groucho Letters—from and to Groucho Marx*. New York: Signet, 1968.

Matusow, Barbara. *The Evening Stars*. Boston: Houghton Mifflin, 1983.

Mayer, Martin. *About Television*. New York: Harper & Row, 1972.

McKeever, Porter. *Adlai Stevenson*. New York: Quill, 1989.

McNeil, Alex. *Total Television*. New York: Penguin, 1991.

Medved, Michael. *Hollywood vs. America*. New York: HarperCollins, 1992.

Metz, Robert. *CBS: Reflections in a Bloodshot Eye*. New York: Signet, 1976.

Mickelson, Sig. *From Whistle Stop to Sound Bite*. New York: Praeger, 1989.

Morgan, Al. *The Great Man*. New York: E. P. Dutton, 1955.

Mosel, Tad. *Other People's Houses*. New York: Simon and Schuster, 1956.

Moss, Nicholas. *BBC TV Presents a Fiftieth Anniversary Celebration*. London: BBC Data Publications, 1986.

Murrow, Edward R. *In Search of Light: The Broadcasts of Edward R. Murrow 1938—1961,* ed. Edward Bliss, Jr. New York: Avon Books, 1967.

Murrow, Edward R., and Fred Friendly, eds. *See It Now*. New York: Simon and Schuster, 1955.

Navasky, Victor S. *Naming Names*. New York: Viking, 1980.

Newsom, Carroll, ed. *A Television Policy for Education*. Washington, DC: American Council on Education, 1952.

Nixon, Richard. *RN: The Memoirs of Richard Nixon, Volume 1*. New York: Warner Books, 1978.

———. *Six Crises*. New York: Warner Books, 1979.

Noll, Roger G., ed. *Government and the Sports Business*. Washington, DC: The Brookings Institution, 1974.

Norden, Denis, Sybil Harper and Norma Gilbert. *Coming to You Live!* London: Methuen, 1985.

O'Brien, Pat. *The Wind at My Back*. New York: Doubleday, 1964.

O'Connor, Edwin. *The Last Hurrah*. New York: Bantam, 1957.

O'Connor, John, ed. *American History/American Television*. New York: Frederick Ungar, 1983.

Ogilvy, David. *Ogilvy on Advertising*. New York: Vintage Books, 1985.

O'Neil, Thomas. *The Emmys*. New York: Penguin, 1992.

Opotowsky, Stan. *TV: The Big Picture*. New York: E. P. Dutton, 1961.

Oshinsky, David M. *A Conspiracy So Immense*. New York: The Free Press, 1985.

Parish, James Robert. *Actors' Television Credits 1950–1972*. Metuchen, NJ: Scarecrow Press, 1973.

Patterson, James T. *Mr. Republican, a Biography of Robert A. Taft*. Boston: Houghton Mifflin, 1972.

Pearson, Drew. *Diaries 1949–1959*. Ed. by Tyler Abell. New York: Holt, Rinehart and Winston, 1974.

Persico, Joseph E. *Edward R. Murrow*. New York: McGraw-Hill, 1988.

Peterson, Robert W. *Cages to Jumpshots: Pro Basketball's Early Years*. New York: Oxford University Press, 1990.

Peyser, Joan. *Bernstein*. New York: Beech Tree Books, 1987.

Pollock, John. *Billy Graham: The Authorized Biography*. New York: McGraw-Hill, 1966.

Powers, Ron. *Supertube*. New York: Coward-McCann, 1984.

Price, Jonathan. *The Best Thing on TV: Commercials*. New York: Penguin, 1978.

Quinlan, Sterling. *Inside ABC*. New York: Hastings House, 1979.

Rader, Benjamin G. *In Its Own Image*. New York: The Free Press, 1984.

Randall, Tony, and Michael Mindlin. *Which Reminds Me*. New York: Delacorte, 1989.

Reinsch, J. Leonard. *Getting Elected*. New York: Hippocrene Books, 1988.

Rico, Diana. *Kovacsland*. New York: Harcourt Brace Jovanovich, 1990.

Rose, Reginald. *Six Television Plays*. New York: Simon and Schuster, 1956.

Rovere, Richard H. *The Eisenhower Years*. New York: Farrar, Straus and Cudahy, 1956.

——— *Senator Joe McCarthy*. New York: World Publishing, 1960.

Sander, Gordon F. *Serling*. New York: Dutton, 1992.

Sanders, Marlene, and Marcia Rock. *Waiting for Prime Time*. New York: Perennial Library, 1990.

Schickel, Richard. *The Disney Version*. New York: Avon, 1968.

Schoenbrun, David. *On and off the Air*. New York: E. P. Dutton, 1989.

Schulberg, Budd. *A Face in the Crowd.* New York: Bantam, 1957.

Seldes, Gilbert. *The Great Audience.* New York: Viking, 1950.

Selznick, David O. *Memo from David O. Selznick.* Selected and edited by Rudy Behlmer. New York: Viking Press, 1972.

Sennett, Ted. *Your Show of Shows.* New York: Da Capo Press, 1977.

Sevareid, Eric. *In One Ear.* New York: Alfred A. Knopf, 1952.

Shayon, Robert Lewis. *Open to Criticism.* Boston: Beacon Press, 1971.

Sheen, Fulton J. *Life Is Worth Living.* New York: McGraw-Hill, 1953.

Shulman, Arthur, and Roger Youman. *How Sweet It Was.* New York: Bonanza Books, 1966.

Smith, Betsy Covington. *Breakthrough: Women in Television.* New York: Walker and Co., 1981.

Smith, Sally Bedell. *In All His Glory: The Life and Times of William S. Paley.* New York: Touchstone, 1991.

Sperber, A. M. *Murrow: His Life and Times.* New York: Freundlich Books, 1986.

Sperling, Cass Werner and Cork Millner, with Jack Warner Jr. *Hollywood Be Thy Name.* Rocklin, CA: Prima Publishing, 1994.

Spigel, Lynn. *Make Room for TV.* Chicago: University of Chicago Press, 1992.

Steinberg, Cobbett S. *TV Facts.* New York: Facts on File, 1980.

Stempel, Tom. *Storytellers to the Nation: A History of Writing for American Television.* New York: Continuum, 1992.

Sterling, Christopher H., and John M. Kittross. *Stay Tuned: A Concise History of American Broadcasting.* Belmont, CA: Wadsworth, 1990.

Storm, Gale, with Bill Libby. *I Ain't Down Yet.* New York: Bobbs-Merrill, 1981.

Sturcken, Frank. *Live Television.* Jefferson, NC: McFarland, 1990.

Taubman, Howard. *The Making of the American Theatre.* New York: Coward McCann, 1965.

Taylor, Robert. *Fred Allen: His Life and Wit.* Boston: Little, Brown, 1989.

Television Interviews 1951—1955: A Catalog of Longines Chronoscope Interviews in the National Archives. Compiled by Sarah L. Shamley. Washington, DC: National Archives and Records Administration, 1991.

Terrace, Vincent. *The Complete Encyclopedia of Television Programs 1947–1976,* Volumes I and II. Cranbury, NJ: A. S. Barnes, 1976.

thirtysomething Stories. By the writers of *thirtysomething.* New York: Pocket Books, 1991.

Thomas, Lowell. *So Long until Tomorrow.* New York: William Morrow and Company, 1977.

Thomson, David. *Showman: The Life of David O. Selznick.* New York: Alfred A. Knopf, 1992.

Tichi, Cecelia. *Electronic Hearth.* New York: Oxford University Press, 1991.

Today: The First Fifteen Years. Uncredited illustrated history of the show by NBC in 1967.

Tosches, Nick. *Unsung Heroes of Rock 'n' Roll.* New York: Harmony, 1991.

Veeck, Bill, with Ed Linn. *Veeck—as in Wreck.* New York: Ballantine Books, 1976.

Vidal, Gore, ed. *Best Television Plays.* New York: Ballantine, 1956.

Voigt, David Quentin. *American Baseball, Volume II: From the Commissioners to Continental Expansion.* University Park, PA: Pennsylvania State University Press, 1992.

————. *American Baseball, Volume III: From Postwar Expansion to the Electronic Age.* University Park, PA: Pennsylvania State University Press, 1992.

Wade, Robert J. *Designing for TV.* New York: Pellegrini and Cudahy, 1952.

Watson, Mary Ann. *The Expanding Vista.* New York: Oxford University Press, 1990.

Weaver, Pat, with Thomas M. Coffey. *The Best Seat in the House.* New York: Alfred A. Knopf, 1994.

Wertham, Frederic, M.D. *A Sign for Cain.* New York: Paperback Library, 1969.

Whelan, Kenneth. *How the Golden Age of Television Turned My Hair to Silver.* New York: Walker and Co., 1973.

White, Theodore H. *The Making of the President 1960.* New York: Pocket Books, 1961.

Wilk, Max. *The Golden Age of Television.* New York: Delta, 1976.

Williams, Martin. *TV, The Casual Art.* New York: Oxford University Press, 1982.

Woolery, George W. *Children's Television: The First Thirty-Five Years, 1946–1981, Part II: Live, Film and Tape Series.* Metuchen, NJ: Scarecrow Press, 1985.

Wylie, Max. *Clear Channels.* New York: Funk & Wagnalls, 1955.

Yellin, David G. *Special.* New York: Macmillan, 1973.

Research also drew on standard references for the period including the Encyclopedia Brittanica's *Book of the Year, The Americana Annual, Current Biography, Universal Standard Encyclopedia* (1956 edition), *Popular Mechanics Do-It-Yourself Encyclopedia* (1955 edition), and *The Baseball Encyclopedia.*

Magazines, Newspapers and Short Works

Contemporary reports and analyses of television, as well as references to advertising from the period, appeared in the *Akron Beacon Journal, America, American Mercury, Broadcasting-Telecasting, Business Week, Collier's, Commentary, The Commonweal, Congressional Digest, Cosmopolitan, Library Journal, Life, The Nation, National Parent-Teacher, New Republic, New York Times, New Yorker, Newsweek, Parents, The Reporter, Saturday Evening Post, Saturday Review, Schenectady Gazette, School and Society, Senior Scholastic, Television, Time, Today's Health, TV Guide,* and *U.S. News and World Report.*

Of particular interest to people assessing the place of television in the early fifties are the *New York Times*'s series on TV and American life, June 24–30, 1951, and *U.S. News*'s package "What TV Is Doing to America," Sept. 2, 1955. For an interesting early perspective on children and TV, the Paulist Press of New York published "TV and Your Child," a pamphlet written by then-Monsignor, later Bishop Edwin J. Broderick, in early 1955.

As for more recent sources, Mel Watkins' article "Beyond the Pale," cited in chapter 3, appeared in *Channels* magazine's April–May 1981 issue. The analysis and history of *Dragnet* by Patrick Lucanio and Gary Coville appeared in a two-part article, "Behind Badge 714," in *Filmfax* magazine, August/September and

October/November 1993 issues. The *Playboy* panel, "Trouble in TV-Land," appeared in the November 1961 issue. The Museum of Broadcasting (now the Museum of Television and Radio) published "Metromedia and the Du Mont Legacy," a booklet including a history of Du Mont by Craig and Helen Fisher, in June 1984.

Dan Rather's comments about Edward R. Murrow appeared in an interview with Jane Hall for the *Los Angeles Times,* as reprinted in the *Daily Gazette* on Nov. 23, 1993; Jerome Weeks's analysis for the *Dallas Morning News* of cultural programming on the information superhighway is quoted as it appeared in the Albany *Times Union* on March 20, 1994.

Videotapes

Many of the programs and performances described in this book were viewed at the Museum of Television & Radio in New York City; others are part of our continuing television experience. *Casino Royale* was seen on a review tape from TBS SuperStation. *Color Adjustment* (written, produced and directed by Marlon T. Riggs; copyright 1991 by Signifyin' Works) was seen from a review tape for its broadcast on *P.O.V.*

Programs bought commercially include the following. ("Undated" or specific dates are what appear on the tape package. Where I have reason to question specific dates, I have noted them below. In the text I occasionally refer to undated shows by their year of original broadcast; in those cases I used time and topical references within the show to determine the date.)

Amos 'N Andy, Volume 4. Showcase Productions. Undated. Contains "The Winslow Woman" and "The Broken Clock."

Annie Oakley. Madacy Music Group, 1992. Four undated episodes: "Sharp Shooting Annie," "Annie Gets Her Man," "Annie's Desert Adventure," "Annie and the First Phone."

Caesar's Hour. Video Resources New York, 1994. Undated episode, appears to be 1955.

Captain Video and His Video Rangers. Video Resources New York Inc., 1993. Undated episode.

Colgate Comedy Hour. Madacy Music Group, 1993. Two shows, one hosted by Abbott & Costello, ca. 1951, the other by Eddie Cantor, probably August-September 1953.

Ding Dong School. Video Resources New York, 1994. Undated.

Dragnet, Volume 1. Hollywood Select Video, 1986. Two undated episodes: "The Big Girl" and "The Big Boys."

Dragnet. Madacy Music Group, 1992. Four undated episodes: "Big Deal," "Big Net," "Big Crime," "Big Lift."

"First Draw": The Premiere Episode of Gunsmoke. Fox Video, 1992. Contains 1955 premiere, "Matt Gets It," and the series pilot, "Hack Prine."

The Edward R. Murrow Television Collection. Fox Video, 1992. Four tapes: *The Best of Person to Person, The Best of See It Now, The McCarthy Years,* and *Harvest of Shame.*

The Fabulous Fifties, Volume 1. NFL Films Video, 1987.

The George Burns and Gracie Allen Show. Madacy Music Group, 1992. Four undated episodes: "The Klebob Card Game," "Beverly Hills Uplift Society," "Teenage Girl Spends a Weekend," "Space Patrol Girls."

The Jack Benny Program. Madacy Music Group, 1992. Four undated episodes.

Mama. Video Yesteryear, 1991. "Madame Zodiac" episode, ca. 1950.

The Milton Berle Show. Madacy Music Group, 1992. Two undated shows, one apparently the 1954 season premiere.

Roberta Peters in Opera and Song. Video Artists International, 1990. Selections from *Voice of Firestone* appearances, 1952–1957.

Time Warp: 1954. MPI Home Video, 1990.

TV Classics, Volume 1. MPI Home Video, 1986. *Hollywood Half Hour* play called "Dream Job," dated 1955, but more likely premiered on *Summer Theatre* in 1953; *Public Defender* episode dated 1954.

TV Classics, Volume 4. MPI Home Video, 1986. Contains *Arthur Godfrey's Talent Scouts,* dated 1953 but based on content somewhat later and *The Ed Wynn Show,* dated 1950.

TV Classics, Volume 9. MPI Home Video, 1987. Undated episodes of *The Cisco Kid* and *The Roy Rogers Show.*

TV's Best Adventures of Superman, Volume 2. Warner Home Video, 1987. Contains episodes "Crime Wave" (1953) and "The Perils of Superman" (1957), and 1941 cartoon "Mechanical Monsters."

TV Turkeys. Rhino Video, 1987. Scenes from terrible TV shows.

Index